Don Yaeger and
Douglas S. Looney

SIMON & SCHUSTER

NEW YORK   LONDON   TORONTO   SYDNEY   TOKYO   SINGAPORE

HOW
NOTRE DAME BETRAYED
ITS IDEALS FOR
FOOTBALL
GLORY

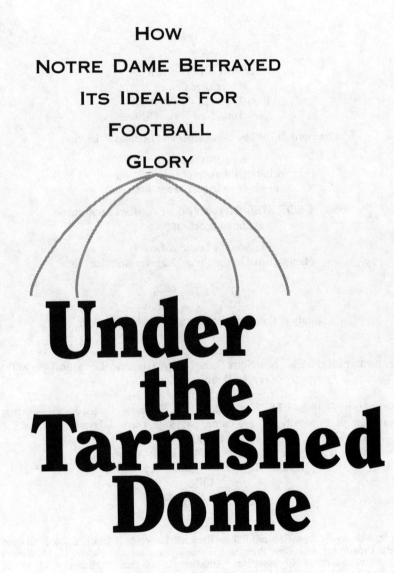

Under the Tarnished Dome

SIMON & SCHUSTER
Rockefeller Center
1230 Avenue of the Americas
New York, New York 10020

Designed by Levavi & Levavi
Manufactured in the United States of America

7   9   10   8   6

Library of Congress Cataloging-in-Publication Data

Yeager, Don.
Under the tarnished dome : how Notre Dame betrayed its ideals for football glory / Don Yeager, Douglas S. Looney.
p.   cm.
1. Notre Dame Fighting Irish (Football team)   2. Football—United States—Corrupt practices.   3. University of Notre Dame.   4. Holtz, Lou.   I. Looney, Douglas S. II. Title.
GV958.N6Y43   1993
796.332′63′0977289—dc20   93-26991
CIP
ISBN: 0-671-86950-7

PHOTO CREDITS

Kent State University Photo Services: 1; Steve Keesee: 2; University of Arkansas: 3, 4, 5; Arkansas Athletic Department: 6, 7; Gene Prescott: 8; Chicago Bears: 9; Sheri Walker: 10, 11; Wendell Vandersluis/University of Minnesota Men's Athletics: 12; University of Minnesota: 13, 14, 15; Minnesota Daily: 16; Rich Clarkson: 19, 22, 27, 32; Bob Wilkey: 20; Courtesy of the University of Missouri: 21; David Walberg: 25; University of Wisconsin: 26; New York Jets: 28; Ed Mahan: 29; Kansas City Chiefs: 30; Brian Bower: 34; Hans Scott: 35

To the towering Colorado Rocky Mountains outside my window and all around me that put on dazzling, snow-covered shows by day, then retreat reluctantly into mysterious silhouettes by night.

DSL

To Mother and Father, who worked harder than I ever knew to provide the foundation that has allowed me to weather life's peaks and, more significantly, its valleys. I love you both.

DY

Acknowledgments

Writers tend to say there is no way to thank all the people who helped them on a book.

That's wrong.

There is and here's how you do it: Thank you.

We have read, to the best of our knowledge, everything that has been written about Lou Holtz, and about Notre Dame as it relates to Holtz. Computer searches are wonderful because they don't allow you to miss much; they are awful because they find too much. For that we have to thank Sherrie Petell and Jan Thompson of Mead Data Central, who were of immense help in running these searches. We have read endless books about and by Holtz, by former Notre Dame president Theodore Hesburgh, by Bill Bilinski, and on and on. We have looked at miles of videotape, much of it of Holtz speaking. We have read the material going back for years on Holtz in *The New York Times,* the *Los Angeles Times,* and scores of others. Thanks especially to Mick Normington of the *Arkansas Democrat* and Wendy Tai of the *Minneapolis Star-Tribune* for the time and effort they gave us in the libraries of their respective newspapers. Thanks, too, to ABC's Armen Keteyian and *Sports Illustrated*'s Lester Munson and Rick Telander for picking up things along the way and sending them in our direction. The sort-of-official Notre

Dame publication, *Blue & Gold Illustrated*, edited by Tim Prister, was first-rate help.

We have interviewed—in exhaustive travels crisscrossing the nation and beyond, from Nassau to Sacramento and San Diego to Toronto—154 people, most in depth, most on tape. Their candor, in many cases, is impressive. The 84 former Notre Dame players who agreed to talk openly and on the record—in the face of the intimidating power of their alma mater—are what made this book possible, for it is not the authors but the players who have drawn the conclusions in this book.

Nobody was paid for his interview. And, significantly, only three sources asked that their names not be attached to their quotes.

We did not interview Lou Holtz, who declined after receiving our letters. Holtz also made an all-out effort to keep friends and acquaintances from talking to us. In a few cases, he succeeded; in most, he did not. We thank those people who talked with us on the record and whom Holtz will likely never forgive. They—notably former Notre Dame coaches Dan Devine and Gerry Faust—are perfect examples of men walking tall instead of walking small. We also thank those people who publicly stated that they in no way, shape, or form would help on the book—and then poured themselves into helping us privately. Late-night phone calls from homes and pay phones across the land were a godsend. Holtz rules by fear and intimidation, and most of those who declined to be interviewed did so with sadness, reluctance, and embarrassment. We understand. It must be tough to be so scared. We hope there will be better days ahead for these guys.

John Heisler, the sports information director at Notre Dame, puts out the best college-football media guide in the business and deserves high marks. We thank him for his help.

Longtime New York editor Ed Breslin was a source of early confidence and encouragement. And then, for us to get the opportunity to deal with the editor on this book, Simon & Schuster's Jeff Neuman, has been our privilege. We didn't always agree on everything, and at times we didn't agree on anything. But the undeniable fact is that Jeff made the book better. Our literary agent, Basil Kane in San Diego, is not only the best in the business, but he is unfailingly in good humor —unlike us.

—The Authors

. . .

I regret that Holtz was unwilling—or unable—to defend himself. I offered to meet with him anytime, anywhere in the world, seven days a week, twenty-four hours a day, over a four-month period. At one point, Holtz said there was no way he could squeeze in several hours of interview time—and then he left on a golfing vacation. He did have time, for example, to make a speech in Denver in February, but no time to address the serious issues raised about him in this book. Lou has, for years, been a good friend, but he became furious over an article I wrote in *Sports Illustrated* about a 1989 pregame fight in Notre Dame Stadium between the Irish and the University of Southern California team. The truth is, it was Notre Dame's fault. But sometimes truth causes Holtz problems, and he reacts to it badly. Several years ago, I asked Holtz if he would like to collaborate on a book on a year in his life as Notre Dame coach. He accepted enthusiastically. A few days later, Holtz called back. He was extremely disappointed, he said, because it had occurred to him he should run the book project past the powers at Notre Dame for what he thought would be pro forma approval; they told him no. Any book would have to be done, Holtz says he was told, by someone from Notre Dame or with Notre Dame connections. Holtz, however, said that he planned to do his definitive book whenever he left Notre Dame and he would like for me to write it. I said, "Fine," and we parted amicably. Surely he won't renege.

I am indebted to my spouse, Mary Ann, for keeping the blaze in the fireplace going, the hot tub hot, gas in the Jeep, the driveway shoveled, and food on the table up here in the Rocky Mountains. When we met in a freshman English class at the University of Colorado, she had no idea what life with a writer would be like. At the least, she—from southern California—never anticipated it included shoveling. Mary Ann understands nothing about football, doesn't know the difference between a third down and a three-putt green and long ago concluded it's not important, doesn't know Lou Holtz from Donald Duck, is under the impression she sees the real Notre Dame when she is in Paris, and is certain this football business is not important but it sure is noisy. Thanks, too, to my father, Bob Looney, for forty-two years a terrific newspaperman with *The Boulder Daily Camera*. He read the manuscript, liked parts and didn't like others, and mostly was appalled by my spelling, which he corrected while mumbling about declining public education.

In some ways, friends endure the most, since writing a book is all-consuming, which therefore makes it all-boring. Anyway, around Boulder, people who put up with more than they should have include Jo and John Kearney, Jack and Cirrelda Mills, Ami Lauer, Wick Rowland, Barrie Hartman, Dan Creedon—and all of the students at the University of Colorado who enrolled in my sportswriting class. John Timpe was one of those students, and in quest of being an honors graduate (which he achieved) he contributed a fine effort by interviewing numerous players.

Nobody was more supportive than Travis Rusheon Vardell—we go back to our days together on *The Owl* student newspaper at Boulder High School—and her husband, Ken, in El Cajon, California. They feigned interest in the many parts of this project that were, by any measure, not interesting. Any errors in this book are the Vardells' responsibility. Call them. I've written their unlisted home phone number on rest-room walls at airports around the country.

Douglas S. Looney
Boulder, Colorado

I also want to acknowledge the contributions of Pete Dunbar and Lester Abberger, talented writers both, who have read and made suggestions on this as well as both of my previous books.

Don Yaeger
Tallahassee, Florida

Contents

PART IV
A SOUL IS SOLD

NOTRE DAME PLAYERS IN
UNDER THE TARNISHED DOME

Player	Position	Years*	Hometown
Steve Alaniz	WR	1986–88	Edinburg, TX
Terry Andrysiak	QB	1984–87	Allen Park, MI
Arnold Ale	LB	1988	Carson, CA
Joe Allen	OL	1988–90	Chicago, IL
Jeff Alm	DL	1986–89	Orland Park, IL
John Askin	OL	1983–86	Louisville, KY
Norm Balentine	L	1988–89	Florissant, MO
Huntley Bakich	DE	1991	Carrollton, TX
Jim Baugus	C	1986	Dunwoody, GA
Steve Belles	QB	1986–89	Phoenix, AZ
Jerome Bettis	FB	1990–92	Detroit, MI
James Bobb	FS	1984–86	Port Arthur, TX
Ned Bolcar	LB	1986–89	Philipsburg, PA
Mike Brennan	OL	1986–89	Severna Park, MD
Tony Brooks	RB	1987–91	Tulsa, OK
Dean Brown	DL	1986–89	Canton, OH
Derek Brown	TE	1988–91	Merritt Island, FL
Tim Brown	WR	1984–87	Dallas, TX
Tom Byrne	TE	1985–87	Pacifica, CA
John Carney	K	1983–86	Centerville, OH
Bobby Carpenter	WR	1986	Amityville, NY

* The years listed are those in which they earned a varsity letter. Years in which a player was redshirted, or did not play enough to letter, are not included.

Jason Cegielski	OL	———	Chicago, IL
Linc Coleman	RB	1987	Dallas, TX
Mike Crounse	DT	1986–89	Endicott, NY
Rodney Culver	RB	1988–91	Detroit, MI
Jim Dadiotis	LB	1986–87	Littleton, CO
Bob Dahl	DT	1988–90	Chagrin Falls, OH
Greg Davis	SS	1988–91	Hollywood, FL
Matt Dingens	DT	1985–86	Bloomfield Hills, MI
Marc Dobbins	SS	1987–89	Chicago, IL
Demetrius DuBose	LB	1989–92	Seattle, WA
Tony Eason	WR	1985–86	Snohomish, WA
Pat Eilers	SE	1987–89	St. Paul, MN
Cedric Figaro	LB	1984–87	Lafayette, LA
Ted FitzGerald	DT	1985–88	Wayne, NJ
Bryan Flannery	DL	1986–89	Lakewood, OH
John Foley	LB	1987	Chicago, IL
Tom Freeman	OL	1984–87	Shawnee Mission, KS
Tom Galloway	LB	1985–86	Loudonville, NY
Mike Golic	DL	1981–84	Cleveland, OH
Tom Gorman	OL	1986–89	Evergreen Park, IL
Ted Gradel	K	1986–87	Sylvania, OH
Mark Green	RB	1985–86	Riverside, CA
Tim Grunhard	OL	1986–89	Chicago, IL
Mike Harazin	OL	———	Burbank, IL
Andy Heck	OL	1985–88	Annadale, VA
Shawn Heffern	OL	1983–86	Carmel, IN
Skip Holtz	ST	1986	Fayetteville, AR
Greg Hudson	LB	1986–87	Cincinnati, OH
Steve Huffman	OL	1986	Dallas, TX
Raghib Ismail	WR	1988–90	Wilkes Barre, PA
Alonzo Jefferson	RB	1983–87	West Palm Beach, FL
Anthony Johnson	FB	1986–89	South Bend, IN
Joe Johnson	WR	1981–84	Washington, DC
Lance Johnson	C	1990–92	Charlotte, NC
Andre Jones	LB	1987–90	Hyattsville, MD
Mirko Jurkovic	DL	1988–91	Calumet City, IL
Wally Kleine	DT	1983–86	Midland, TX
Mike Kovaleski	LB	1983–86	New Castle, IN
Scott Kowalkowski	DE	1987–90	Farmington Hills, MI
Jeff Kunz	DT	1984–87	Palm Beach Gardens, FL

Chris Kvochak	DB	1985–87	Vancouver, WA
Chet Lacheta	OL	1990–91	Chicago Heights, IL
Chuck Lanza	OL	1984–87	Germantown, TN
Marty Lippincott	OL	1986–88	Philadelphia, PA
Todd Lyght	CB	1989–90	Flint, MI
Tom McHugh	C	1984–86	Philadelphia, PA
Kevin McShane	DE	1986–89	Joliet, IL
George Marshall	DT	1988–90	Somerset, NJ
Pierre Martin	WR	———	Pensacola, FL
Rick Mirer	QB	1989–92	Goshen, IN
Tom Monahan	FB	1984–86	Arcola, IL
Mark Nigro	DT	1986	Lombard, IL
Todd Norman	DT	1990–92	Ocean View, CA
Jeff Pearson	OL	1986–87	Chicago, IL
Mike Perrino	OL	1982–85	Chicago, IL
Vince Phelan	P	1986–87	Racine, WI
George Poorman	DB	1987–91	Palatine, IL
Wes Pritchett	LB	1985–88	Atlanta, GA
Dan Quinn	LB	1986–87	Encinitas, CA
Tom Rehder	OL	1984–87	Santa Maria, CA
Tony Rice	QB	1987–89	Woodruff, SC
Troy Ridgely	DT	1988–92	Baden, PA
Tom Riley	OT	1984–86	Pasadena, CA
Aaron Robb	DB	1985–88	Coeur d'Alene, ID
David Rosenberg	LB	———	Sarasota, FL
Tim Ruddy	C	1990–92	Dunmore, PA
Brian Shannon	OL	1988–90	New Wilmington, PA
Erik Simien	LB	1989–90	Los Angeles, CA
Stan Smagala	CB	1986–89	Burbank, IL
Chris Smith	FB	1981–84	Cincinnati, OH
Shawn Smith	LB	1989–90	Minotola, NJ
Tony Smith	WR	1988–91	Gary, IN
Frank Stams	DE	1984–88	Akron, OH
Michael Stonebreaker	LB	1986–90	River Ridge, LA
Dan Tanczos	TE	1983–86	Bethlehem, PA
Pernell Taylor	FB	1985–87	La Puente, CA
Pat Terrell	WR/FS	1986–89	St. Petersburg, FL
Tom Thayer	OL	1979–82	Joliet, IL
Reggie Ward	F	1984–87	Long Beach, CA
Ricky Watters	TB/WR	1987–90	Harrisburg, PA

Ron Weissenhofer	LB	1983–86	Oak Lawn, IL
Brandy Wells	DB	1984–87	Montclair, NJ
George "Boo" Williams	DT	1987–90	Willingboro, NJ
Kurt Zackrison	DE	1987–88	Elmhurst, IL
John Zaleski	OL	1986	Chicago, IL
Mark Zataveski	OL	1991–92	Roslyn, PA
Chris Zorich	DL	1988–90	Chicago, IL

PART

I

Unnecessary
Roughness

CHAPTER 1

The Golden Rule

Treat other people as you like to be treated.
—Lou Holtz, repeatedly

Lou Holtz would never stand for people to treat him like he treats others. Nobody in their right mind would. They couldn't unless they were a slave. Does that make him a hypocrite? What it really makes Holtz is kind of worse than that because a hypocrite will say something to one person and will turn around and do something else. But when a person says it to millions of people that read about it and turns around and does something else, that is, in my opinion, worse than being a hypocrite.

—John Askin,
former Notre Dame offensive lineman

Notre Dame football practice on that spring day in 1987 was proceeding routinely. Then, suddenly, it wasn't.

What set everything in chaotic motion was a play called by Coach Lou Holtz. In football parlance, it was a run read. To make it work, quarterback Tony Rice was supposed to run the ball up the middle, his route being determined by reading the position of the defensive tackle. If the tackle is in one place, Rice runs one route; if the tackle is lined up in another spot, Rice runs another route.

Holtz had discussed it, and rediscussed it, with Rice at length and in depth. The coach had shown it to Rice on film, he had diagramed it for Rice on a chalkboard, he had demonstrated it on the practice field.

Still, Rice did it wrong. He read the position not of the defensive tackle but of the nose guard.

The result of the error, however, wasn't that the defensive tackle tackled Rice. Nor was it the nose guard. It was a screaming, mad, cursing, Lou Holtz, who came flying out of nowhere, throwing an elbow to the head of his star quarterback.

"I messed up," recalls Rice, from Woodruff, South Carolina. "I never saw Coach Holtz coming. Next thing I knew, he had tackled me. It wasn't a football hit, but, for him, it was a nice little hit. He got me down. Of course, he also got me when I wasn't looking. Just as I was going down, I remember thinking, 'Who is this?' I'll tell you, he was serious. He was screaming and swearing and kept saying, 'Who did you read? Who did you read?' And I kept saying, 'I guess the wrong person.' He got madder and madder."

George Marshall, defensive tackle from Somerset, New Jersey, says when he looked over to see what all the commotion was about, "Holtz was freaking out."

The surreal nature of the situation didn't escape linebacker Dan Quinn, from Encinitas, California, who says one of the things that made it seem so wacko was that "Tony's strong as an ox. He was taken by surprise and he's laying there in shock and everyone's looking around, and Coach Holtz is losing his mind telling him whatever he was telling him, and then Holtz kind of catches himself. He never wants to look like an idiot. He gets up and shakes himself off and pulls Tony up. It was really embarrassing because we're like, 'Is this guy crazy?' People were lookin' at each other like, 'This is unbelievable.'" New York Jets wide receiver Rob Carpenter, who was redshirted in 1987 at Notre Dame (which precipitated his transfer to Syracuse), says, "I remember him tackling Tony and holding him down on the ground and screaming in his face."

Later, Holtz tried to explain away the assault as a joke, but when that explanation failed to gain credence with the players who saw the bizarre event, he called it a motivational ploy. Says Dan Quinn, "He just lost his fucking mind." Joe Allen, an offensive lineman from Chicago, says of the Holtz vs. Rice incident, "It was dead serious. He tried to make a joke out of it, but he was serious."

There is some difference in recollection of how the episode ended. But offensive lineman Jeff Pearson from Chicago is sure he remembers correctly: "I remember pulling Holtz off."

Jim Dadiotis, a linebacker from Littleton, Colorado, heard Holtz tell Rice after their wrestling match, "Do you know why I did that?"

Rice: "No."

Holtz: "Because I want you to be a good player."

Mike Crounse, defensive tackle from Endicott, New York, doesn't feel any confusion over what happened to Rice that day. "Obviously Coach Holtz was angry," he says. "He blew up. If something pissed him off, you knew about it."

And his language was pretty colorful?

"Yeah."

Even in the violent and outrageous world of football, this was outlandish behavior. It was the type of outburst that got Woody Hayes fired at Ohio State and did the same at Colorado State for Earle Bruce. Not so at Notre Dame. To Holtz's credit, he can routinely squirm out of untoward situations like this by using his storied sense of humor. He will joke of August practice—or even this Tony Rice episode—as being "no worse than your ordinary death march."

Linc Coleman, a running back from Dallas, witnessed the event and says the moment was charged with high-voltage volatility. "I was thinking," recalls Coleman, "that, 'Oh, my Lord, he's losing his mind. Coach just lost it.' It made me nervous because he's a little man, and then he jumped on Tony's back as if to choke him and he just brought him down really hard and Tony didn't see him coming. Anything could have happened." Defensive tackle George "Boo" Williams, from Willingboro, New Jersey, had a similar reaction: "Oh, my God, this little man has lost his mind." Williams stares off, thinks back on that odd day in South Bend, then says thoughtfully of Holtz, "He's crazy."

But even in something as indefensible as the Rice attack, Holtz does have his defenders. Tim Grunhard, an offensive lineman from Chicago, who plays in the NFL for Kansas City, shrugs and says, "That was just kind of the way he was."

What did the players think about him when he did that?

"We were so in awe that we never really felt much about it. He never could get away with it at a professional level. But at the college level, you just almost look at the guy like a god."

Holtz's acts of abuse always come unexpectedly, erupting out of blue sky like a Rocky Mountain thundershower. For example, in one USC game, Tony Rice got hit in the chin, opening a gash that required fifteen stitches to close. Naturally, this made the helmet strap very uncomfortable. Three days later in practice, a furious Holtz grabbed Rice's face mask and, according to Rice, swung it back and forth, rubbing it across the player's chin. Finally, Rice screamed in pain. Holtz apologized, but to Rice the larger point is that Holtz knew about the stitches, but got so absorbed in his thoughts, and had so little concern for his player's welfare, that he forgot. To understand Holtz, never forget that if your concern is not his concern, it's not a concern.

Another of Holtz's darkest moments—at least in the minds of the players who were there—came during a spring practice a couple of years ago. Chet Lacheta, an offensive lineman from Chicago Heights, Illinois, describes it as "humiliating."

Says Lacheta, "It happened during one of our open practices, and there were about a thousand people in the stadium watching. It was my freshman year and I had had knee surgery right before I came in. I came in at about 240 pounds, not fully recovered from my operation, and then I got mono and I went down to 220. I was trying to play offensive line with no weight."

Unfortunately for Lacheta, the two players ahead of him were not able to practice, "so I had to run with the first team and I really wasn't ready for it. I made a lot of mistakes."

Those mistakes turned out to be the least of his problems. "At the end of practice," continues Lacheta, "we'd always huddle up in a group and Coach Holtz would talk to us about how practice had gone. He had just called me to come up there, and I thought he was going to say something good about my trying to come back and giving it my all in practice. Then he started yelling at me. He said that I was a coward. He said that I should find a different sport to play and that I shouldn't come back in the fall. He was pretty rough. I had just gotten to Notre Dame. It was my freshman year and I was trying to get adjusted to college football.

"First he grabbed me by my face mask and shook it.

"Then he just spit on me."

Holtz often says that the lowest thing you can do to someone is spit on him.

"That's what he says," agrees Lacheta. "I really got ticked off about it. I got out of practice and went straight back to my room and I called my dad. I was crying. It was like I was trying to do what I could and [I was] having some hard times, and your coach is supposed to give you support. Then this happened.

"Afterward, some of the varsity players, the older guys, fifth-year seniors, called my room and talked to me. They knew that it was wrong. One in particular who called me up was Brian Shannon [an offensive lineman from New Wilmington, Pennsylvania]. He said, 'Hey, Chet, we know that was wrong. Just blow it off. Don't let it disturb you.' But it's kind of hard to do when someone spits on you, because it happened. It made me feel like I'm nothing. I was out there trying to do the best at the time with what I had."

Holtz called Lacheta into his office the next day and gave him what Lacheta calls a lukewarm apology. "But," says Lacheta, "he didn't make an apology to me in front of the team, which was where he wanted to embarrass me. As far as I was concerned, it just didn't cut it. How Holtz treats players is one of the things the alumni and fans of Notre Dame never know about."

And if they did?

"It might change some people's views. But the other thing about that, too, is that they've got a really, really good way of covering things up there. There's a lot of stuff that goes on there that isn't right and that no one ever finds out about. Stuff like spitting at his own players. Everybody looks at Notre Dame through rose-colored glasses."

Erik Simien, a linebacker from Los Angeles, recalling the spitting incident, says, "I prayed he'd do something like that to me. I'd have taken off all my shit and left the field." Shawn Smith, a linebacker from Minotola, New Jersey, still shakes his head in bewilderment at the scene. "He just picked out Chet, grabbed his face mask, and says, 'You ain't worth this and you ain't worth that. You don't have no balls, no heart,' and just spit on him. Then Chet just walked away."

A devastated Lacheta never realized the potential Notre Dame recruiters had seen in him. After two years under Holtz, the player said he decided he was, as Holtz had announced, not cut out for Fighting Irish football. He dropped out of school and has never returned.

. . .

Robert Farrell, a wide receiver from Little Rock who played for Arkansas when Holtz coached there in the late seventies, vividly remembers the ways Holtz demonstrated his lack of respect for his players. One day during a hot August practice in Fayetteville, Holtz suddenly turned, reached up to the face mask worn by the 6-6 Farrell, and started shaking him back and forth. The coach punctuated his address by whacking Farrell in the face mask with a manila folder. When Farrell started to say, "But I thought . . . ," Holtz erupted anew: "Goddamn it, I didn't bring you here to think. I brought you here to play football." Farrell remembers it to this day, but he is charitable: "He probably did it to get my attention. After all, I was a high-strung, hardheaded twenty-year-old. He figured out that was a good way to make me look directly in his eyes. I think he wanted to make a point." Afterward, when Holtz was asked by a visiting writer what that sort of encounter with Farrell established, he fumed, "I tell you what that established. It established who's gonna coach this goddamn football team."

Leave it to former offensive lineman and free spirit Marty Lippincott, 6-5, 284 pounds, from Philadelphia, to have a colorful analysis of Holtz's treatment of the players: "He would get mad and grab my face mask and twist it around. I'm thinking, after I graduated, 'Marty Lippincott, why didn't you just punch him or push him away?' "

How many times did he do that to you?

"All the time."

He grabbed your face mask all the time?

"Sure. He grabbed everyone's face mask. If it wasn't for the spirit of me knowing that I needed him in order to play someday . . . If some person came to me on the street today and got in my face like that, I'd kill them. I wish I had had enough balls to grab his arm and say, 'Hey, you don't have to do that.' But when he does something like that to you, you just go, 'I'm wrong.' You can't do anything."

Scott Kowalkowski, a defensive end from Farmington Hills, Michigan, who played at Notre Dame before being drafted by the Eagles, is apoplectic over the physical abuse Holtz inflicts—jerking face masks, smacking players in the helmet with his hand or his ever-present manila folder, and so on—and he says, "It's ridiculous. You don't do that —even to a player."

When Michael Stonebreaker, a linebacker from River Ridge, Lousiana, who was drafted by the Bears in 1991, is asked about Holtz's abusive behavior on the field, he says, "I think it's terrible. I would never let somebody do that to me. Nobody should treat you that way. I don't agree with it. I don't know why somebody would act like that."

Rob Carpenter says of the Holtz treatment, "I've seen it on television. I think it was 1991 when he grabbed a kid [Huntley Bakich, a defensive end from Carrollton, Texas (1991)] by the face mask and dragged him all the way off the field, because Coach Holtz was way out on the field. I wouldn't expect that from a coach at Notre Dame because of the aura that Notre Dame has. You see that religious background that they have, all those priests."

Are you surprised that Notre Dame allows Holtz to get away with some of the stuff that he does?

"Actually I am. But then again, I'm not, because they give him total control of the football program. You can't really downplay a coach that's been winning. He's doing things that he wants to do. He brought the program back, so you really can't beat the coach down." Indeed, in the five-year tenure (1981–85) of Holtz's predecessor, Gerry Faust, the Irish record was an un-Irish-like 30-26-1. In Holtz's seven years so far (starting in 1986), the record is 66-18-1. Can Holtz coach or what?

And because he absolutely can coach—and win—his abusive behavior is tolerated. In fact, the episode with Huntley Bakich was mild in comparison to what goes on on the practice fields daily. The only reason Notre Dame officials asked Holtz to make a public apology, which he did, was that it was on national television instead of being hidden from view on a practice field in South Bend.

Dr. Rob Hunter was the University of Minnesota team orthopedist for part of the time when Holtz was coaching at Minnesota in 1984–85. He says Holtz grabbed players at Minnesota "twenty times a week, at least. He'd grab 'em by the face mask and pull them close to him and scream. It didn't hurt them, of course. It was just demeaning. Very demeaning. But the players—at least the ones who were students and thinkers—could see right through it. And they didn't enjoy playing the game. It wasn't fun. I don't know a single player who liked him. Absolutely nobody liked playing for him. I was always thinking, 'When are these people going to realize he's like the emperor? When are they going to realize he has no clothes?' "

Hunter, who moved to Aspen following his stormy tenure with Holtz (Hunter is currently the team physician for the U.S. Men's Alpine Ski

Team), says, "Lou is a repellent. Nobody can stay around him for too terribly long. He either moves or others move away. That is his personality."

Holtz can thank his lucky stars that he wasn't around to take his Let's-Get-Physical act into Mike Golic's face. Says Golic, a defensive lineman who played for Notre Dame before going on to the National Football League with Houston and Philadelphia, "I know I would have had a tough time not popping him if he grabbed my face mask like that. My father coached me at a young age and always taught me to respect my elders and my coaches. But it comes to a point in college [where] you start to become a man about the game, and that grabbing-the-face-mask stuff is a little outdated. I don't believe I could have taken that. Dragging them off the field is not very cool."

Linc Coleman is a cousin of legendary Oklahoma and Detroit running back Billy Sims. He is asked if Holtz could be described as "violent."

"Yeah, he is," responds Coleman. "Mainly he'd get mad at the offense a lot. He would curse. He would jack you up. He took an offensive lineman in practice one time and grabbed him by his pads. I'm looking at him jerking this huge 275-pound man around." Coleman shakes his head at the memory, not in admiration for what Holtz did but for what the player didn't do.

It's always a problem to determine when discipline becomes harassment, when harassment becomes abuse, when abuse becomes brutality, and when brutality becomes outright violence. One of Holtz's favorite homilies goes: "Discipline breeds success. Harassment breeds contempt. Everybody needs discipline, but he needs an equal amount of love and attention."

Erik Simien, who was figured to be the twenty-first best high school player in America in 1988 by the *Atlanta Journal-Constitution,* says, "The only time he ever grabbed me was when I was a freshman. It was in the Pitt game and I got knocked out of bounds. I slammed the guy on the ground and got a flag. It was on ESPN and Holtz grabbed me by my face mask when I came to the sideline. It was humiliating. God would have to be with him if he grabbed me now." Simien transferred to UNLV.

Yet, there are players who consider Holtz's treatment of them no big deal. Mirko Jurkovic, offensive lineman from Calumet City, Illinois, is one.

Did he ever embarrass you?

"Oh, sure."

For example?

" 'Bad ass this, you can't run, you can't do this. That's a shitty block,' grab me by the face mask."

In practice?

"Sure."

Do you think that is coaching in the eighties and nineties, or is that coaching in the sixties?

"To me, coaching is coaching. If a kid can't take good verbal abuse, or criticism, he can't play football."

Defensive end Kurt Zackrison from Elmhurst, Illinois, says his first experience with such behavior came when "my Pop Warner coach would pop me upside the head for not making a tackle. My thought was, I hope you hurt your hand because I've got a helmet on. Is Coach Holtz violent? I can't see him as an intimidating, physical, violent person to me. He's a little guy. Walking down the street, I'm not gonna be intimidated by Lou Holtz. If Lou Holtz said he's gonna knock the hell out of me, I'd say, 'Obviously you're on drugs, because you're kidding yourself.' "

Tom Byrne, a tight end from Pacifica, California, also takes a benevolent position on Holtz and his face-mask grabbing, saying, "For me, I thought . . . it wasn't out of line. If he physically abused me . . . the guy screams and hollers at you. So what? It's no big deal. He's a little guy so he's not gonna hurt you."

The justification coaches use for physical confrontations is that they'll do whatever they have to do to make a player pay attention. But when Holtz's players talk of being grabbed, pushed, poked, shoved, generally abused and sworn at by Holtz, many have no recollection of the point that Holtz was trying to make amid all the chaos. Mike Crounse's experience in practice when he was a freshman is typical. He dove at the quarterback, Terry Andrysiak, from Allen Park, Michigan (1984–87), "and ended up hitting him in the leg and giving him a bruise. Coach blew up. Grabbed me. I don't remember what he said. He just ran around screaming at me. I wasn't really listening to what he said. He was cursing. He grabbed my face mask. There was spit coming out of his mouth. I thought I made a good play."

Is this appropriate behavior for a coach at this level at this university?

"No," concedes Norm Balentine, an offensive tackle from Florissant, Missouri, and a Holtz supporter. "It's not appropriate behavior. But when you think about it, the guy is under a lot of pressure. He's the head coach at Notre Dame." Even Balentine admits suffering at Holtz's hand is a humiliating experience, and he wonders if it isn't an extreme reaction. "It kind of shakes you up a little bit," he concedes, "because this guy I know expects perfection, but sometimes every play isn't going to be able to meet perfection."

It's a dangerous catch-22 for players: their coach demands perfection and believes in putting pressure on them, but his own lapses are supposed to be forgiven because of the pressure he's under.

Possibly even more damaging to the psyche of young people is the emotional abuse. After all, you can make the case that football is such a physical, violent game that getting knocked around by the coach—in some minds—isn't much different from being knocked around by an opposing player.

But even if someone wants to try to make the case that grabbing and twisting a face mask—an act that is a penalty in a game because of the potential for injury—isn't physically abusive, it unquestionably is emotionally abusive. Every player interviewed who had had it done to him by Holtz says it humiliated him.

"There is something about him that is real intimidating," says Tony Smith, a split end from Gary, Indiana, now a wide receiver for the Kansas City Chiefs. "I remember a scrimmage during my freshman year which was right before the Fiesta Bowl. I was helping the offense run some of West Virginia's plays. Andre Jones [outside linebacker from Hyattsville, Maryland] wasn't looking at me. He was looking at the quarterback, but he was running straight at me. I stopped and turned back and hit him, and he didn't see it coming. It was a perfectly legal block, but he flipped over because it was a real hard hit and everybody thought he was hurt. He was a starting outside linebacker, but I'm just playing off of instinct. It was a scrimmage, so my adrenaline was pumping and Andre was on the ground and Holtz ran up to me and said, 'What the hell are you doing? He's a starter. Don't do that to him.' He was shaking my face mask and I was just looking at him, this guy who is about five inches shorter than me and he's shaking me like this. But at the time I was like, 'Sorry, I apologize,' and 'yes, sir' and 'no, sir.'

"But after it was over, I was sitting at my locker and I was like, 'I can't believe that.' Because it had never happened to me. Coaches in the past had never done that to me. But he did and he was shaking me and that was really something. I was real bothered but I understood he was the coach. I had tremendous respect for him as a coach and as a person, but this was one of the things I didn't feel was necessary. I felt [when he shook my face mask] more like an animal or like someone he was trying to train instead of a human being."

They don't do that in the NFL, do they?

"No, I've never seen that. I don't think it ever will happen at this level. I mean, it's just a respect thing. You treat someone with respect and they respect you back. When you violate that respect, then problems can arise."

Holtz, however, didn't become this way when he arrived in South Bend and started drinking the water. He exhibited his blatant disregard for his players' feelings when he was coaching at Arkansas. One prominent example involved one of Holtz's best all-time players, defensive lineman Dan Hampton (1975–77), who went on to become an all-pro for the Bears in the NFL. Hampton says Holtz reacted to a loss in Holtz's second season at Arkansas by placing blame on his players in general and Hampton in particular. (Hampton had been flagged for a penalty during a crucial series during the game.) It was especially galling to Hampton, he said, because Holtz always preached that teams win *and* lose together.

Hampton loves Holtz; he's reluctant to talk about it: "Now let me preface this by saying that I thought Coach Holtz was the greatest thing in the world. If I had a kid today, I'd send him to whatever school he was coaching at because he's good for young people. The only problem I've got with him—I don't know if it's just a basic character flaw of not being able to own up to a shortcoming—but I think it's really hard on a football team when you preach that 'we're all in this together, we're all in this together,' and as soon as something bad happens, he points the finger back at the players. I'm not going to get into psychoanalysis of him, but I think that was the beginning of the end for him at Arkansas."

Kurt Zackrison at Notre Dame got a fierce dose of Holtz's use of discipline without the necessary accompanying love or attention. Zackrison says that Holtz "had us fill out this questionnaire of what was going on in our lives, what classes we were taking, our family background, just a player profile. On it I put that my mother had recently deceased. So at the end of the spring, every player has a discussion with him. He basically told me he wasn't happy with my aggression and what was going on. I said I'd had a difficult first year at college, especially in the second semester. He asked why mine was any different from anybody else's. I said, 'Along with just being a freshman, I just lost my mother a few months ago.' He said, 'I'm sorry. I wasn't aware of that.' And I said, 'You said you read everybody's player profile. I put it down in the profile.' He said he must have missed it. That got me a little heated. I was mad because he hadn't noticed it.

"I was eighteen years old, I was upset and mad. I was crying. He said, 'Look, get yourself together, have your shoulder surgery, and come back in the fall in the right frame of mind.' That's all that was ever brought up."

Did you feel as if he were kind of saying, "Get out of here"?

"Yeah, at the time. He had his agenda, and at that point I wasn't fitting into it."

Stan Smagala, a cornerback from Burbank, Illinois had his own experience with the coldhearted side of Lou Holtz. Smagala was lightly regarded coming out of high school, but Gerry Faust had taken a liking to him and offered him a scholarship. When Holtz replaced Faust in the middle of Smagala's senior year of high school, the atmosphere changed dramatically. "On my recruiting visit there," Smagala recalls, "first Holtz tried to take my scholarship away. He didn't want me to go to Notre Dame. He didn't think I was good enough to play there. So he told my parents, 'I don't think it's good for your son to come here because he's not gonna get the opportunity to play. I don't think he's a good player.' He actually had my mother crying in the office. He never even watched film on me. I think it was kind of ignorant of him to do that during the recruiting visit with my parents—and then to get my mother crying. I just got real aggravated. I disliked Holtz just because of that."

Several years earlier, Roscoe Word had been on the receiving end of a similar blast of Holtz's insensitivity. Word, a former all-rookie corner-back with the New York Jets, was in his third NFL season when Holtz arrived as coach. "Although I had been a starter the previous year (at cornerback), I was used mostly as a substitute throughout the preseason of Holtz's year [with the Jets]. I played enough to make the forty-five-man roster. But in the first game, all I did was run back punts. Then in the second game, against Denver, I played the entire second half. I wanted to move my wife from Jackson, Mississippi, to New York to be with me, but I wasn't sure where I stood. I was still living in the dorms at Hofstra [University, where the Jets train]. So I decided to ask Holtz.

"I did it in a team meeting where we were all in the room. As the meeting ended, I raised my hand and I said, 'Coach, when can we find a place to stay?' He asked who asked the question, and someone else said, 'Roscoe did.' Holtz kind of laughed and said, 'Roscoe, you can find a place to stay.' Everyone started patting me on the back because that meant I made it.

"I went right to a pay phone and called my wife, and she quit her job with the city of Jackson and caught the first flight to New York. That was on Monday. On Tuesday, we rented an apartment and got a phone and all that stuff. Then I went to practice on Wednesday and Holtz cut me. It was the cruelest day of my life."

Holtz, as we are seeing—and will see—is a man of many contradictions. How can he behave so abominably toward the players, so brutally, and then at the next moment be spouting religious platitudes and talking of the importance of treating others as you would like to be treated? Says former player Mike Crounse, "I really think he believes what he says. You gotta understand. It's a professional relationship that he has with us as players. It's not like JV football or high school football. I've never seen him outside of football. Football is his life. Who's to say what he truly believes?"

Holtz's actions should never be mistaken for coaching standard operating procedure. In the book *Gerry Faust, Notre Dame's Man in Motion* by Denny Dressman, Faust says, "You can destroy [the players'] confidence in five minutes, just by harping on them a certain way and getting on them. And you don't solve anything by that." Holtz definitely has a certain way of getting on his players; his way is all the time. In that respect, he reflects the influence of Woody Hayes; Holtz coached defensive backs as a graduate assistant under Hayes at Ohio State in 1968.

All-American linebacker Stonebreaker says, "We didn't have that kind of relationship where he would ever grab me. He yelled at me one time because my hair was too long and he said he'd kick me off the team if I didn't get it cut. He did it just to shock everybody back to his world and the way things are going to be done around him and to let the younger underclassmen know. Then they think, 'If coach is gonna yell at Michael Stonebreaker like that, I better shut up so he won't kill me.' And the things he does, people don't understand why he's doing them. He did that to me another time, kicked me off the field like three times in one practice for not having my feet lined up right in the huddle."

Cornerback Stan Smagala fumes at the memories: "I think Holtz does all this because he's a small guy. You'd just like to grab the guy and beat the shit out of him. You know what I mean? That's what all the players said—'I'd just like to grab him and kill him.' Not literally kill him but just show him that 'you don't have this much power.' But he does."

In one TV game, Holtz grabbed Smagala by the face mask. "I think he thought I punched somebody," says Smagala. "There's a lot of things that happened at Notre Dame that I just block out of my mind. There was no call for that. You should treat players right, respect them.

Holtz to player: "Get your ass in there."

Hunter: "Lou, he can't go."

Holtz to player: "Aw, fuck, get in there."

Hunter: "Nope, his arm is paralyzed."

Says Hunter, "Holtz stomped away like a spoiled child. His attitude was, 'What the hell? He's got two arms. Get out there and hit with the other one.'"

Marty Lippincott tells of a time when Tom Gorman, offensive lineman from Evergreen Park, Illinois (1986–89), sprained his ankle while executing a crushing block in practice. Holtz came up to Gorman, who was writhing in pain on the ground, and said, according to Lippincott, "'You're nothing but a coward. You got your ankle sprained because you weren't in goddamn football position.' See, he thinks the reason people get hurt is because they're not in a good football position. You want to just grab the little coach, throw him against a wall, pile on him, break all his legs and arms, make him to where he can't move, and then say, 'Hey, Coach, you got hurt because you weren't in a football position.'"

Kurt Zackrison, a friend of Gorman's, was also there. He recalls how after Holtz made his statement to Gorman, he instructed the rest of the players to start running plays facing the other direction. "Turn it around and go the other way," hollered Holtz. "Trainers can do whatever to get him off the field.

"It was pretty rough," admits Zackrison. "But you got used to it. You got numb to it. It bothered me when it happened to a close personal friend like Tommy. Holtz has no use for the injured. They're useless to him."

Zackrison and others say Holtz's attitude toward the injured quickly spreads to assistants. "Assistant coaches used to come into the training room," says Zackrison, "and if you were hurt and getting treatment, they'd say, 'What's your name?' See, they'd pretend they had forgotten your name. You didn't have a name if you were hurt. [Assistant] Jim Strong would walk in and say, 'What's your name? Who are you? I don't know your name.'"

The players aren't making this up, according to Rob Hunter, who says, "If they wore that red jersey [signifying injury], he wouldn't talk to them." That's too bad on a lot of fronts, says Hunter, because "an injury is a learning process." Not for Lou, who is resolute in his disdain, as he told Rob Hunter: "If they're hurt, I don't want to know

You Gotta Play Real Hurt

*"The coaches we hire know that Notre Dame does not put winning above
. . . the health of a player.*

—Father Theodore M. Hesburgh,
former Notre Dame president, in his
book *God, Country, Notre Dame*

*When I was hurt, I wasn't included. I was nonexistent. It's kind of like
Rudolph. I wasn't included in any of the reindeer games anymore.*

—Tom Byrne,
former player

Nothing brings out the worst in Lou Holtz like injuries.

Dr. Rob Hunter, the former University of Minnesota orthopedist, says
Holtz has written the book on callousness. One time, a Minnesota
defensive back made a hit and got a stinger, which temporarily paralyzed his right arm. Moments later, the player went back in, and the
same thing happened. Holtz called for the player to go back in a third
time.

Hunter intervened: "Lou, he can't move his arm."

their fuckin' names." Responded Hunter, "Gee, Lou, that's pretty harsh."

The pattern never varies: a player gets hurt, then he is hammered by Holtz with the final insult of silence.

Offensive lineman John Askin from Louisville, who now operates an insurance agency in Kentucky, talks of tearing up his right knee in a game against Navy. But he kept on playing because "if you were hurt under him, it was like you committed a mortal sin. You felt embarrassed because you were injured. I mean, you felt really embarrassed. So what you would do is come back before you were ready. I did, and to this day, anytime the weather gets cold, I know that I came back before I was ready because I ache like crazy. You will see a lot of guys that are just beat up, but I really believe that if you were cared for the right way, you wouldn't have any problems later. There was a time I was playing and hurting like crazy, and I played in the Michigan State game and every time I hit, it was like a rip. It hurt like crazy, but you didn't want to go out of the game because you didn't want to feel like you weren't a team member and that you were a loser."

While some of this is natural football bravado, much of it is the direct result of Holtz's well-known attitude toward the injured. Not all coaches, by a long shot, are this way.

"Faust came in," continues Askin, "saw who was injured, who was not going to play, and that was it. Under Holtz, I remember him saying something to me about being 'a fifth-year senior injured, that's pitiful.' It makes you feel like you don't want to tell anybody about it because they are going to think you're feeling sorry for yourself."

As a junior, defensive tackle Mark Nigro from Lombard, Illinois, abruptly felt an arctic cold wave sweep over his career when, while lifting weights, "my shoulder blew up. I was given three options: quit, play as is, or have surgery and miss a year. I took surgery because I figured I'd come this far and I really wanted to be part of the team. During that season, it became obvious that the coaches looked at me and said, 'You're hurt and of no use to me as a football player so you're of no use to me at all.' I had put forth all the effort to be part of the team, done everything they'd asked, and in the course of that got injured. Then they made me feel like I wasn't a part of the team. That wasn't the way it was under Faust. There was a lot more concern."

One time, says Erik Simien, "we were in the training room. Lou Holtz walked in and didn't say anything to any of us who were in there.

That's just the way he felt. It is kind of cold, but I got used to it after a while. The players talked about his attitude a lot. Most people said it made them feel thrown to the side. It was like being a horse. If you were injured, you might as well get shot."

Jason Cegielski, an offensive lineman from Chicago who flunked out of Notre Dame and then transferred to Purdue where he became all–Big Ten, says when coaches would come into the training room, "they used to have a cold-shoulder attitude that it was not good that you were injured." Tom Byrne says this is hard on a player's psyche: "Christ, you're talking about eighteen-, nineteen-, twenty-year-old kids. People just want to feel like they're important, be patted on the back. It's tough."

Similar feelings are held by Tom Riley, an offensive tackle from Pasadena, who says being injured somehow meant that "you were bad luck. It was like if he ignored you, you'd heal quicker. The truth is you'll just play when you shouldn't. Holtz and his coaches were cold, unsympathetic, and put off if you were hurt." Riley quit the team.

Linebacker David Rosenberg from Sarasota, Florida, says, "After I broke my leg, the only coach I ever talked to was Coach [George] Kelly. He came by the hospital room and he brought me two McDLTs and a bag of fries. I never got a call from anyone else."

Orthopedist Rob Hunter describes working for Holtz as "awful. Lou's style created such a level of anxiety among every member of the staff that it was unbelievable—unbelievable." Hunter's opinions get heavy weight because he wasn't dependent on Holtz for income and he is not a football junkie; he has no reason to pretty up the ugly truth.

"People think being a team doctor is glamorous," Hunter says. "In reality, it's an enormous time commitment. For twelve weeks, seven days a week, you are dealing with eighteen- to twenty-one-year-olds who don't know up from down. And with Lou, every moment is an anxiety-provoking moment. When I was around with trainers and others, we'd say, 'Where's he gonna be so we can be somewhere else?' If he was gonna walk down a hall, we'd say, 'Let's go another way.' Everywhere he was, it was confrontational. It would have been much easier to go along with him. If he wanted something done, just do it. Want somebody to be healed, fine, he's healed. Bone broken, want it well, okay, done. All I would have had to do is defy the laws of medicine. I would have been much more comfortable all day and I wouldn't have been able to sleep at night. I thought Holtz was sick. He needed medication, something.

"The trainers were so anxious about telling him anything that he perceived as negative that they couldn't and wouldn't. It had a major and adverse impact on health-care delivery.

"He was always saying, 'If you're tough enough, it won't hurt.' So his view was that an injury wouldn't impact on you. He is always trying to raise the skill level—by anxiety. When he was around, everybody would get so tense that the adrenal gland was in spasm. That's uncomfortable. What he does is sacrifice a young man's physical well-being on the altar of football success."

Conversely, Hunter says Holtz's predecessor, Joe Salem, "was a wonderful man, but not a good coach and a terrible recruiter. What we had were a bunch of second-class athletes. They were not the right strength, the right speed, or the right skills. Against teams like Iowa, Michigan, Ohio State, they were really getting hurt. It was high school kids playing against college kids. When you told Salem somebody was hurt, he would say, 'Oh, shit. How long?' I'd tell him and he'd say, 'Okay.' " So Hunter had plenty of experience with college football injuries before Holtz showed up in Minneapolis.

To say Holtz didn't take bad news—which is to say, the injury report —well is a gross understatement. Hunter would start talking about the various injuries and Holtz "would stand there, and then all of a sudden he would be kind of dry-spitting on the floor. The more I told him about injuries, the more he was spitting."

Holtz, in Hunter's view, considers himself an expert on everything. Hunter says Holtz approached him during the preseason—the first meeting between the two—and said, "Now I'm just a football coach. I'm not a smart man like you. It just comes to my mind—and I'm sure it's because I don't understand—that when I was at Arkansas, I never remember an athlete missing a game because of an ACL [anterior cruciate ligament, the critical knee ligament]. Here, it's like a goddamn epidemic." When Hunter just shrugged and offered no explanation, Holtz said, "You've got to call my guy in Arkansas. I think he can help. Do you read about doing these things better?"

Said Hunter evenly, "We're on the cutting edge of orthopedics here, Lou. These things take time to heal. If it happens, a player definitely will miss the season, maybe more."

"I've got to have him this Saturday."

"No, Lou. This is how we do things."

"Goddamn it, I just don't want you to be doing it this way."

"This is the way we do it, Lou."

Says Hunter, "He was enraged. It was our first meeting and he was looking for people he could dictate to. I understand. He has complete and total control of everything."

Hunter was doing ACL surgery inside the joint, which at that point, he says, was "heresy." Hunter's technique involved rebuilding the ligament and correcting the problem—and a recovery time of around a year. According to Hunter, the Arkansas method at the time involved doing the surgery outside the joint, not doing any rebuilding or corrective work, but simply tightening up the damaged area in order to allow the athlete to play sooner, usually within three months or less. But, says Hunter, "the problem was, what was being done at Arkansas wasn't being done" in state-of-the-art surgery. "It worked, in Lou's mind, because it got the player back. The problem was, you got a player back with an unstable knee. How fast you can get a player back on the field isn't the ultimate result. He came back with a very loose knee. In medicine, slower is better. The way it was being done [at Arkansas], you end up with a forty-year-old who has arthritis, joint damage, everything. What he is, is forty and crippled.

"So that's why Lou would see an injured player and say to me, 'Well, he sure as hell can't do me any good like that, so fuck him.' This is what is so strange. He was always wanting to act like a fatherly figure, but what it really was, was Lou hyping Lou. If a person would advance him, good. If not, that person was history."

The Holtz-Hunter viewpoints just kept hurtling down the tracks, head-on, no lights, on a collision course:

Holtz: "Do these surgeries really need to be done? I mean, are you checking with anyone else?"

Hunter: "Lou, are you suggesting that we are doing operations that don't need to be done?"

Holtz: "I'm no smart guy. I'm just saying that, goddamn it, even I make mistakes on the football field. But I've got other coaches around to help me." Hunter, one of the nation's preeminent orthopedists, was outraged that a coach would question his medical opinions. Worse, in Hunter's view, Holtz was putting his own short-term interest over the long-term good of the player-patient.

Former Minnesota AD Paul Giel confirms that Holtz "did have a difference very early in the game back in 1984" with Hunter. Giel says Hunter's problems with Holtz were because of the "procedure that this orthopedist used in treating a severe knee injury, a relatively new procedure. The philosophy was it may take longer to rehabilitate but the young man would be better off in the long range, far after his days were over with, than the old way, which got you back sooner. As I told Dr. Hunter at the time, 'Look, I'm not gonna argue with you about procedures, because I don't know. I just know that this is a concern of Coach Holtz.' "

Another time, a lineman suffered a stress fracture in his foot, in the fifth metacarpal. Hunter recalls the conversation:

Holtz: "I need him this weekend."

Hunter: "Nope. He's on crutches. Six weeks."

Holtz: "Nope, he's playing. If he's tough enough, he can play. Injury doesn't matter."

Hunter: "Nope, he's not playing."

Holtz: "I want a second opinion, a third opinion."

Hunter: "Fine. But he's not playing."

The doctor prevailed, but it was bruising. "The players knew I was their advocate," he says.

Then Hunter, tired of Holtz's attempts to override his medical advice, tried to appeal to Holtz in terms he could understand: "Lou, I've had some great ideas about what you should do on third and seven. I think they'll work. I'd love to make the sideline calls. I mean, I don't have just some good ideas but some great ideas."

Holtz was silent, glared, and said nothing.

"There is an inherent and healthy conflict of interest between a coach and the medical people," Hunter told Holtz. "Your focus is on winning. My focus is on the patient. I don't care about the team. I don't care if we win. So if the star is hurt, that makes no difference. It's gonna take a week, a month, a season, whatever. I'm gonna hurt the team and that's good."

Holtz seethed: "If you're not for me, you're against me."

Hunter shrugs in reflection and says, "Medicine isn't part of the problem; Holtz is. A coach can't possibly know about a player's condition. As a physician, if I'm not sure, I hold a player out. If Lou isn't sure, he plays him."

The attitude toward injuries that Holtz holds is not in any way universal among coaches. A good example occurred during the 1992–93 college basketball season, when Florida State's star guard—and starting football quarterback—Charlie Ward dislocated his shoulder. The injury improved rapidly and Ward was ready to resume play, but Coach Pat Kennedy held him out for several additional games, saying, "When coaches get overly anxious to play them [injured athletes], that's the lowest level of win-at-all-costs."

Hunter realized from the get-go that Holtz would be a difficult personality to get along with: "It was after the Wisconsin game, and Holtz stood up in front of the team and talked about me. He said, 'This is a man who stood up to me and I admire him for it,' and he gave me a game ball." Says Hunter, "I knew I was history. When I got back to my office, I told somebody there, 'Search this ball for a pink slip.' "

Bingo. Hunter was fired as orthopedic consultant to the football team after the 1984 season. He explains, "I never compromised the care of the players for that man. That's why I got fired." He did, however, continue as orthopedic consultant to the rest of the men's athletic department until December 1989.

Additionally, Hunter says Holtz would insist on a major effort to get players to quit the team, for medical reasons. Hunter heard him tell one, "I want you out of here. You're not gonna help the team. I need your scholarship." Hunter shakes his head a lot when he talks of Holtz, who he says "belittles, intimidates, makes people feel terrible about their situation—and he thinks that will make them change their situation. He just feels you can will yourself well. Sorry, Lou."

Hunter says that the Lou Holtz philosophy was " 'kill the messenger.' All he ever wanted to do was apply a bandage to a cancer. I had a great relationship with ten coaches [in other sports] and a terrible one with one. That says something."

Doug Woog coaches the hockey team at Minnesota, which has gone to the NCAA's Final Eight for eight straight years. Says Woog, "You could sense [Hunter's] real desire to work with the hockey player. He treated our guys with respect. I treated him with respect. Our relationship always was, 'I'll coach. You tell me when they're ready.' He was the god of medicine in our program. He got it down perfectly. He knows exactly how long a player needed to be out. He told me, and that's what I did. The long-range benefit for the kid was his top concern, and I respected that."

Minnesota basketball coach Clem Haskins says, "I knew Dr. Hunter well and I was always very impressed with him both as a person and as a physician. I was so impressed, in fact, that I let him do surgery on my own knee."

Hunter says he invited Holtz to play golf, so they could work out their differences. Holtz refused.

. . .

With Holtz not wanting to accept that anybody—any body—was hurt, and that feeling permeating his staffs, the players faced devastating hardship.

Tony Smith, the Notre Dame wide receiver, is a prime example:

"I hurt my wrist in a game against Air Force in 1991. At halftime, I told the trainers in the locker room that my wrist was sore and they said, 'Okay, we'll retape it.' So they retaped it, and after the game it was still hurting. It was hurting real bad and I told the trainers and they x-rayed it in the locker room and said that 'it doesn't look like anything is wrong with it, so you probably just have a bad sprain.' So that night —I recall that night perfectly clear because it was pulsating, swelling, and it was hurting so bad that I dipped it in a bucket of ice—I couldn't go to sleep. I called the trainer at home and asked him the results of the X ray. I said, 'My wrist is really hurting.' He said, 'It's not broke or anything. It's just badly sprained.' So the next morning I went to the training room and got treatment. They just iced it down and kept telling me the whole time it was just sprained, so I played against Tennessee and I played against Penn State."

And it was still bothering you?

"It was bothering me in practice to the point I didn't even want to catch the ball, 'cause when it was coming, I felt myself kind of backing away from it. I told Skip [Mayer, an assistant trainer] that I don't know why I'm doing this. He said, 'I don't know, either, but we're trying to figure it out.' I told the trainer again that it was still bothering me.

"Finally I went and took more X rays and drove back over to the stadium and saw [associate trainer] John Whitmer. He said, 'Where does it hurt?' I showed him. He pushed down on the spot and my whole arm just got numb. It sent so much pain through my arm. John said, 'I bet you broke something. I don't know why they said it was a sprain. I don't know why they couldn't detect it. You make sure when you get the results of the X rays, you let me see them, too.'

"So when the X rays came back, I saw them and the doctor finally told me right then, 'It looks like you got a crack in your navicular, and these are real hard to detect and we didn't detect it the first time.' This is three games later and he says, 'It's not anything serious. You're gonna have surgery, put a pin in it, and you'll need to be in a cast for two weeks and you can still play. But why don't you wait until after the Hawaii game and we can do it as soon as you get back?'

"I was young. I was thinking, keep playing, keep doing good, so I played the next game in Hawaii. They taped it and I played that game with it broke. I caught something like six passes for a hundred and something yards. I had a great game."

But next thing Smith knew, it was being suggested that since he had played three games with his wrist broken, why didn't he play a fourth —a bowl game—and then have the surgery? Says Smith, "I told them no. I'm not playing with it broke anymore. It's bothering me. They were like, 'Well, you know, it's one of those things. You played with it broke for three games and there's just one more game.' I was talking with the trainers and they were saying that Coach Holtz's opinion was that I played in three games with it broke, so I could just wait until one more game and have it fixed after the season.

"I didn't want to do that because I wanted to go to the combine [the NFL scouting combine, in which potential pro players are measured, weighed, tested, and evaluated prior to the draft] in February. They told me that in six weeks it would be healed, and I figured that by December or January I would be ready. I was thinking of my career and they were thinking about winning the bowl game, and to me it seemed like they didn't really care, so I had the surgery done in December and two weeks later they took the cast off and had me back out there practicing.

"I played on the first of January and they never told me it was still broken. I went to the combine and had X rays done. They saw that it was broken, and I had to go back in April for a recheck. The whole time, the Notre Dame doctors and the team doctor was telling me, 'It looks fine, it's coming right along. You'll be able to get your range of motion back and everything will be fine.'

"I went to the recheck in April and it was still broken. I was ranked the third-best receiver coming out of college last year, so that means I could have went anywhere from the first to the third round depending on which way the draft went. But my wrist was still broken, so it was considered a medical risk to draft me. Therefore, I wasn't drafted until the sixth round [by Kansas City] and that cost me."

How much did it cost you?

"I think about it every day and it cost a lot. I ran a 4.38 [in the 40-yard run, which is fast] when the teams came and worked me out. I was 6-1, 195 pounds, so they expressed that they liked me and said to me and my agent one thing to worry about was my wrist because it was still broke and I had the surgery in December. And the whole time they were still telling me at Notre Dame that my wrist was fine, it would be okay. They could have at least told me that there was still something wrong with it, it might need new surgery, whatever. Every doctor I went to told me it was still broke, and after I got drafted in the sixth round, I was upset and I couldn't figure out what was going on with my wrist.

"The pros called me on draft day and said, 'How is your wrist?' I said, 'It's fine, I guess, it's not bothering me.' And they said, 'Well, on the X ray, it's still broken and you had the surgery in December, so you're a medical risk. We still want you to play for us, but we can't risk a higher draft, paying you all that money, and your wrist is still broke.'

"So after I heard that, I went to three different doctors and got opinions and evaluations. Every last doctor I went to told me it was crazy for me to be hurt and back out there practicing after only being in a cast for two weeks."

So, for three victories and a bowl game you may have lost how much money?

"I could have lost a million dollars. What I start off making now is what I'll make. I'll have to wait until my next contract to make more, where I could have started off making double, three times, or quadruple what I started off. This was all real selfish of Notre Dame. It's a real sore spot. If I had known that it was still broke, I wouldn't even have been in the draft. I would have stayed in school [one more] year and still been playing. If I had known more surgery was needed, I could have had it. If I could take it back, I never would have even played in a game with it broke. I would have had the surgery done, would not have played in the game, would have stayed in school my fifth year. They had me thinking at Notre Dame that it was fine, just real minor. Now my wrist will never be the same, it'll never be close to one hundred percent. The doctor says there is a good chance I'm gonna also have arthritis when I get older, and I'll never have a full range of motion."

After finally being selected by the Chiefs, he was placed on injured reserve his entire rookie year.

There is, in fact, a pattern of questionable health care at Notre Dame. Defensive tackle Mark Nigro was, and is, a big Holtz supporter. In 1987, his third year—after being redshirted his first—he was showing enormous potential. He had advanced to second team and was clearly a young man on the upswing. That was when he blew out his shoulder. Because of his admiration for Holtz, he tries to say things softly: "There wasn't much contact after I got hurt. I didn't feel so great. I could have used a pat on the back."

Nigro, who doesn't want to talk about it, is quietly furious about the medical attention he received at Notre Dame. The original surgery was not done properly, he says. "By messing it up, they took something away from me." It required major reconstruction.

When offensive lineman Jeff Pearson hurt his knee, he got two opinions from doctors, one saying he needed surgery: "When I went in to tell Holtz, he got kind of pissed off about it. I needed surgery. He was like, I was pulling a fast one on him or something like I was trying to get out of winter running. I don't know what it was. I played every game as a freshman. Started as a freshman, started as a sophomore. My sophomore year, I made sophomore all-American in *The Sporting News*. I don't know what the hell his problem was.

"He blew up. I said either I do it now and miss spring ball or I have to do it after and I may miss some games. He didn't see I needed it at all. When I came to Notre Dame, he kept telling me I was a great football player, and now he started saying he didn't know if I was good enough to start. He said, 'You used to be all-American caliber here; you had a great career in front of you,' and the whole nine yards. I walked out of his office thinking, 'I can't play football no more.' I thought I was a bad football player. It was all because he didn't think I needed the surgery."

Pearson thinks it is possible that while the doctors were telling him he needed the surgery, they were telling Holtz the opposite. Why? "They were afraid of Lou Holtz." Subsequently, Pearson was kicked out of Notre Dame for disciplinary reasons and transferred to Michigan State. When he arrived in East Lansing, they "couldn't believe how bad my knee was. Right away they scoped my knee and they didn't let me practice that whole year."

At Notre Dame, Pearson says that Holtz "would give [trainer] Jim Russ all hell when players were hurt. Holtz would just get on him. The psychological bullshit you're wrapped up in when you're a player there is a difference between pain and injury. You gotta play through it. Holtz really made you feel guilty on that. He just mentally mind-fucked you. It was all a mind game with Lou just trying to get more out of you. Lou's just really good at making you feel worse. It's a psychological thing. If you're hurt, there's a lot of guilt."

Holtz writes in his book, *The Fighting Spirit,* "We don't expect anyone to play with injuries, but you must play with pain." Of course, therein lies the rub. What's injury? What's pain? How do you tell the difference when you are eighteen?

Holtz likes to talk endlessly of the first baseman for the New York Yankees named Wally Pipp. Pipp got hurt and was replaced by another player, one Lou Gehrig. Writes Holtz, "They never got Gehrig out of the lineup again. I think a lot of our players are starting to understand that it's not a wise move to get hurt." Running back Tony Brooks from Tulsa, Oklahoma, got the Wally Pipp message. Brooks says he was hurt his entire senior year, but "I chose to play because Coach Holtz is the type that will go without you." Arnold Ale, a linebacker from Carson, California, who transferred to UCLA, keeps it simple. "Everyone," he says, "knows Holtz disliked people that were injured."

Fullback Anthony Johnson from South Bend didn't like the idea at Notre Dame of an injured player's being an outcast, of not being able to join in the reindeer games. "I don't think it should be that way in any team sport. I think you should still be part of the team. I guess here in the NFL [Johnson plays for Indianapolis], it's a business thing, but I still don't see why it's like that. Maybe it's dependent on the head coach and how they do it. I know that's the way it works at Notre Dame."

For all of Holtz's ill will toward those dumb enough to let themselves be injured, some players actually approve of his attitude.

John Foley, a linebacker from Chicago who played in 1987 before injury put him down, notes, "I'm ruined. I can't play softball, I can't play baseball, I can't play basketball, I can't play catch with my son. I can't do any of that. I couldn't use my right arm for two years." He is twenty-six years old.

Foley has heard the criticism of Holtz not tolerating the injured well, but he's not buying it. "A lot of these guys [who] get injured," says Foley, "they don't go to rehab, they don't go to class, they expect just because they got injured playing football that their university should take care of everything. Excuse my language, but that's bullshit. One thing Lou Holtz did, he was always behind me one hundred percent. I gave Lou Holtz my life, everything. I never missed a rehab, I was in the weight room, I always tried my best to get back. That's all Lou Holtz asked of me."

Yet even for those who agree with the "lesson" of Wally Pipp, there can be devasting consequences.

Asked about Holtz's sympathy for injured players, center Jim Baugus from Dunwoody, Georgia, sees it different from Foley: "He didn't have any at all. Holtz's whole philosophy was, if you make being injured so unpleasant that no one wants to be injured, guys will play with pain. If you had a sprained wrist or sprained ankle or something like that, under Faust, a lot of guys would just go to the trainer and get out of practice because they just didn't want to go through it because the purpose wasn't there. Holtz made it to the point where if you weren't at practice, you were kind of off the team for that day or that week. It really wasn't off the team, but the coaches wouldn't talk to you as much. They wouldn't treat you as a full team player. I kind of think that philosophy works, just because for minor things that you really can play through, a sprained ankle or something like that, you should go ahead and play. What I don't think Holtz understood was that when you have a major injury and you can't play, that's already unpleasant enough without being ostracized from the team."

Baugus recalls hurting his back during his junior year and having to sit out the Navy game. "It was obvious," he says, "that they wouldn't speak to you. You were on the sidelines and you weren't really spoken to. I tried to go ahead and play through it, because you could feel that environment. You really didn't want to be injured. And Holtz made it perfectly clear that if you're injured, you can't help the team. As a result, everyone tried to play even when they were injured."

Continues Baugus, "I pushed it a little bit, just because I didn't want to get the feeling of being left out. You really wanted to be a part of the team because Holtz made it kind of special. You really wanted to be a part of what he was doing because you really knew he had a flight plan. Faust may have had a great plan, but he didn't have a flight plan."

Baugus's back problems, in his midtwenties, are "really bothering me." Asked if he will think it was worth it in five years when he can't bend over, Baugus laughs and says, "I'm hoping medical science catches up to me by then. I'm still kind of in the immortality stage. When you're young, you don't think anything can hurt you. It's been keeping me out of a lot of things I really have wanted to do. Right now, I'm finally realizing that this is something that's going to be with me the rest of my life. When I'm thirty-five, there will probably be a lot of things I won't be able to do. In a couple of years, I'm sure I'm going to look at his whole philosophy a lot different. I was always taught through high school, play with pain, don't play with injury. But with the back, I didn't know where the line was. It was painful, but I didn't know if I was injuring it more by playing."

There are those who insist Holtz was sympathetic about their injuries, although they are in the distinct minority. Kevin McShane, a defensive end from Joliet, Illinois, says that in the spring of 1989, prior to his senior year, "I had a good shot at playing special teams, maybe first string, but I pulled my hamstring doing the forty. Typical slow, white Catholic Leaguer–style move." McShane couldn't answer the spring practice bell.

One day, Holtz walked over to him on the sidelines and said, "Kevin, when are you gonna get back on the field?"

"Coach, I can't make it because I'm still struggling with this hamstring."

"Take your time," said Holtz. "You know spring's important, but just take your time and just keep seeing the doctor and get that healed because I want to you to play next year." However, as McShane points out, he was an insignificant player, one who might play some on special teams, nothing more.

Stan Smagala, who certainly had his ups and downs with Holtz, takes the philosophical high road: "The coach is there to coach you. When you're hurt, he can't coach you, so he don't want to talk to you. There's no need to talk to you." That's certainly true if the coach's only concern is what a player does on the field, if he has no interest in his players as people. But Holtz and Notre Dame like to pretend otherwise.

When it comes to injuries, Holtz sometimes resorts to psychology if outright ridicule fails. Ted FitzGerald, a defensive tackle from Wayne, New Jersey, hurt his arm in a Cotton Bowl game, and subsequently, arm in sling, he ran into Holtz in a hallway at the Athletic and Convocation Center on the Notre Dame campus. Recounts FitzGerald, "He said to me, 'That's all right. I didn't think you'd be able to make it anyway,' or, 'I didn't think you're tough enough to make it.' Something like that. He said that 'we didn't have high hopes for you anyway.' Meanwhile, the year before, he told me he thought I could be a phenomenal player. He left, I walked twenty more feet and I said to myself, 'That son of a bitch.' I was so pissed off."

Former player George Williams thinks the promising career of Ted FitzGerald was ruined by the pervasive attitude of Holtz and staff concerning injuries. "He was a hell of a player," says Williams. "I mean, he was good. The first scrimmage, he sprained his ankle and he never came back from that. One thing led to another, they pushed him back too fast, he hurt his knee, and he was just never the same player, never the same." Williams shakes his head sadly at the memory.

Still, Smegala had his finger on the problem that confronts coaches like Holtz: if players don't practice, they don't get better, they don't win games, and the coach gets fired. At its core, the life of a football coach is simple: be good or be gone. Mirko Jurkovic, while not a supporter of Holtz's views on injury, had the rare maturity to figure his body out for himself. After his freshman year, he had knee surgery. Subsequently, Jurkovic would miss practice occasionally, "because my knee was hurting me. I don't know if that bothered Coach Holtz or not, but it's my leg and if I don't feel like practicing, that's my decision and I'm not gonna practice. If he don't like it, he's not supposed to like it, that's part of the coaching job. A lot of coaches try to make the players practice hurt. That's part of the job description of how to be a coach. You got to make the players play hurt or you're not gonna win the game.

"I think as a coach, he might have pushed people. He said things that would offend people. I can't answer for other people. I can only answer for myself. I never listened to him as far as when to practice hurt or not. If I felt like I could practice, I would practice. But if I felt like I couldn't, I wouldn't. If the trainer said two more weeks, I wouldn't listen to him, either. I would practice when I felt like it. It was my decision."

Alas, players with the maturity and self-possession of a Jurkovic are too rare. More common are the FitzGeralds, the Tony Smiths, the Foleys, the Bauguses, who will be living forever with the consequences of having a coach who put winning ahead of their health and well-being.

CHAPTER
3

Bodies by Steroids

Here at Notre Dame we test for steroids and we will not tolerate them.
—Lou Holtz,
in his book

First Lou Holtz arrived at Notre Dame. Then a lot of steroids did.

The connection is inescapable. It also has been devastating. The football team quickly became awash in anabolic steroids, starting in 1986.

Steroids generate superhuman gains in weight and strength. What makes them so deadly is that they work. In few cases can even slavish addiction to physical conditioning, primarily weight lifting, produce the kinds of gains that steroids can in a fraction of the time.

Sometimes steroids are taken in capsule form, other times by needle. They have many bad side effects—excessive aggressiveness off the field, hair loss, they may be carcinogenic—and they are illegal. But steroids help win football games. Notre Dame brought in Lou Holtz to win football games. Holtz brought in a new emphasis on weight and strength. The players, who also want to win games, got the message.

. . .

Little noticed by outsiders, but noticed with great concern by insiders, was Holtz's selection of Scott Raridon to be Notre Dame's strength and conditioning coordinator in 1986. His assistant, Jerry Schmidt, joined the Irish staff a year later.

Both went to school at the University of Nebraska. No school has a bigger reputation for clandestine steroid involvement than Nebraska. Raridon was starting offensive guard for the Cornhuskers in 1983, the height of steroid use at Nebraska, and was all–Big Eight. He played on the same line with Dean Steinkuhler, the nation's top lineman, winner of both the Outland and Lombardi awards. Steinkuhler, who has admitted in *Sports Illustrated* to steroid use, told the magazine that at the time he was playing, steroid use at Nebraska "kinda took off." Schmidt, who graduated in 1986 from Nebraska, worked under Nebraska strength-program director Boyd Epley.

One of the most comprehensive police investigations into steroid trafficking in the country touched Lincoln, Nebraska. According to the U.S. Attorney's Office in San Diego, where the case was prosecuted, the investigation led to the conviction of Tony Fitton, whom the feds considered the "kingpin" of steroids in the 1980s. Fitton admitted supplying Nebraska players with steroids. Further evidence of rampant use at Nebraska appeared on the pages of the *Lincoln* (Neb.) *Journal,* which reported that four of the Cornhuskers' best linemen—Dave Remington, Danny Noonan, Neil Smith, and Lawrence Pete—have admitted using steroids while at Nebraska.

Hiring anybody from Nebraska for your weight room is not a good indicator of the hiring program's intention to go clean and straight. Hiring two is double cause for concern.

So what was Scott Raridon like?

Says John Askin, "That guy was a different bird. He didn't belong there."

Why do you think Holtz brought him from Nebraska to Notre Dame?

"He brought somebody in there so he could do the same thing there that he [Raridon] did with that program."

Which was?

"It was to do whatever you needed to do. He brought him in there to do what he had to do to get done. He wanted to get the guy that was strong and that never talks."

John Foley says of Raridon, "He was a loose cracker. He needed to be let go." Asked if Raridon knew about steroids at Notre Dame, Mike Harazin, an offensive lineman from Burbank, Illinois, says, "I would imagine he would have had to know."

Still, you have to hand it to Holtz. Raridon served well the purpose for which he was hired. He was a constant reminder of steroids. He came from Nebraska. Nobody had to say anything. This was the ultimate in body language.

The problem, however, was not all Raridon. Many of the high school recruits Holtz brought in were steroid users. Time will tell whether this is past tense or not.

The best—or worst—example of life with Scott Raridon came in 1986 after that brilliant come-from-behind 38–37 Irish win over Southern Cal. Askin, Shawn Heffern, Wally Kleine, and Steve Huffman were among a group of players who went to various L.A. bars to celebrate. They were climbing into a truck to go back to the hotel. Along came Raridon.

Relates Askin, "We didn't have enough room for Raridon. So the guy whips out a knife on me, and it was bizarre. He had it up against me. Shawn was shocked. Everybody was shocked. I mean, this guy here [was] representing Notre Dame. I mean, it was just shocking that he even had a knife. I had a lot of beers in me, and I remember looking down and seeing the street lights shining off that knife, and I remember looking at Raridon and thinking, 'Oh shit, what is the matter with you?' "

And what did he say?

"He just threatened, he said something threatening, but I can't remember what it was. It was really bizarre. Several of the other players stayed right with me in case this guy went nuts."

How can a guy like that survive in a system as structured as Notre Dame's?

"Nobody told. Here is what happened. It was my last game, and I didn't care anymore. I was going to go on to my better life as if it never happened, and it made no sense wasting my time on it. I think everybody else felt this way, too. Holtz would have just covered it up anyway, just like everything else was covered up with that guy. So there was no point in me wasting any of my energy on it—or anyone else wasting theirs."

So you don't think Holtz knew or ever found out?

"I don't know. There were so many people that knew of the story, and he knew everything. He probably knew, but it was the end of the season and he probably wanted it to blow over."

In separate interviews, Heffern and Huffman supported Askin's version of the knife incident.

For his part, Raridon adamantly denies the knife incident, insisting he was out to dinner with Barry Alvarez, now the head coach at Wisconsin, "a twenty-year friend" of Alvarez's, and another coach, John Palermo.

So what the players say is totally made up?

"It has to be," says Raridon. "I don't know why kids like that would say that. I know exactly where I was at and exactly what I was doing. I wouldn't do that."

Whatever, Raridon's track record is spotty.

He was hired as a graduate assistant at Notre Dame in 1986, by Holtz. When Raridon arrived from Nebraska, he found there was really no Irish weight program. "All the coaches said we needed a better strength program," says Raridon. "Coach Holtz knew I could probably motivate the players, plus he knew I was from Nebraska." After just five months in South Bend, Holtz was so impressed he promoted Raridon, then twenty-four, to strength and conditioning coordinator.

After the 1988 national championship season, Raridon left, saying vaguely that "being a strength coach really wasn't my lifelong ambition." He worked briefly for the YMCA in Des Moines, then shortly thereafter went to Wisconsin as strength coach, working for his buddy Barry Alvarez. There, his career continued in a downward spiral.

In August 1992, he was charged with misconduct in public office and forgery. This was after the university pressed charges, alleging that Raridon hired his girlfriend, Traci A. Ferren, in May 1990, then filled out her time cards, along with forging her signature. The police investigation disclosed that the university paid Ferren, a former shot-putter on the women's track team, for 381.5 hours. However, Ferren admitted she worked only ten hours—if that—during that time. Raridon's story was that he inflated her hours to recover $2,000 he had loaned the woman to buy a car. That, of course, doesn't explain much, but it's Raridon's explanation.

Ultimately, Raridon pleaded no contest to the felony charges. He was fined $1,880 and given eighteen months probation.

These days, he is an artificial-joints salesman in Omaha, which is also probably not his lifelong ambition.

Steve Huffman, who exposed the tip of the steroid iceberg in an article in *Sports Illustrated,* is asked if Raridon ever helped players find steroids.

"He knew who was holding what brand."

How did he know?

"He'd just find out. I don't think he was dealing them. People talk to him all the time and he'd talk to them."

About using them?

"Um-hum. He came up to me a couple of times and said, 'Your workouts are going all right, you're looking pretty good, you're improving, but a few of us feel you could do even better.' I was like, 'What are you talking about, Scott?' "

What did he say?

"He said that 'a few of the coaches feel you could be improving and feel that you could go on this or that brand.' "

He would name a brand of steroids?

"The big one was Winstrol. That's what a lot of linemen got, because it put on poundage and it put on the strength. People just beefed up incredibly huge very quickly. Somebody had some connection somewhere where they could get to it really quickly, because it was always up there."

Where'd he tell you to get it from?

"Um, [offensive lineman Chuck] Lanza always had a lot of Winstrol. I always talked to Jeff Pearson, because I even thought about doing it a couple of times, so I talked to him because he knew people who were dealing. I'd talk to them about what this or that would do. After listening to Raridon and his b.s., it kind of piqued my interest. So I approached Pearson a couple of times."

Pearson didn't have that brand?

"No, but he knew who had it. Once I was talking to Pearson, just walking back to [defensive end] Frank's [Stams's] one day, and I asked Jeff if he did anything and what was helping him. He said Winstrol was really good for him."

But Raridon told you to talk to whom?

"In the brief amount of time I talked to Raridon about it, he said Pearson would help and 'go talk to him because he's really getting strong on his weights.' So just out of my own curious nature I went up to him and started talking to him. He was like, 'yeah,' and very casual about it. It's like if you started asking me questions about this blue-and-gold ashtray right here, I could start answering questions about it."

Very factual?

"Yeah, yeah. If he didn't know, it was like, maybe ask this person or that person. I thought, 'Jesus, am I this naive or what?' I could never go through with it. Besides, it was always too expensive for me."

How much was it?

"I think a six-week cycle of Winstrol was $120 or $130. I was more concerned with stashing up enough pennies to buy a case of beer that week."

Huffman says that in one room occupied by two Notre Dame star players, there "was one section in particular looking like a Mary Kay outfit. This guy just had stands for things, different brands, different bottles, and different types ready for use. Whenever I'd go over and visit one of the guys who lived there, two or three times a week, at least twice a week there'd be somebody in there dealing."

Raridon disputes the steroid accusations at Notre Dame, yet unwittingly supports the same charges against Nebraska. He says the Irish had only six to eight players who could bench press 400 pounds, and had Notre Dame players been on steroids, more would have been able to.

How many could bench 400 pounds at Nebraska?

"We'd have fifteen, twenty. It was very rare an offensive lineman didn't bench 400." Although bench-pressing 400 pounds is considered extremely good—Raridon says he could do 405—he says that "if a guy starts hitting 550, 575, then you're talking about an oddity."

If Raridon is correct, Notre Dame is a lot closer to Nebraska now than it was when he arrived in South Bend. Notre Dame's 1993 team—when tested just before spring practice—included fourteen players who bench-pressed more than 400 pounds. According to *Blue & Gold Illustrated*, starting center Tim Ruddy increased his bench from 430 pounds in January to 505 pounds in March.

Raridon is asked if Holtz's first group of freshmen came in as steroid users.

"I wouldn't have known that."

So you never saw any steroids at Notre Dame?

"No."

And if any of the players said you might have encouraged their use . . . ?

"I'd challenge them to a lie detector test. I mean, there's no way that would be, because as a strength coach, that's the quickest way to get fired, the quickest way to hurt people. It would be stupid. You don't need to do that at Notre Dame with the kind of kids you're bringing in. You're bringing in athletes who are the best in the country. The difference between what Faust brought in and what Holtz brought in was there was a huge difference in speed—Rocket, Brooks, guys like that. We were more interested in speed at Notre Dame than strength. That's kind of Lou's philosophy. I felt more pressure to get the players faster than I ever did stronger."

So all the stories about steroid use at Notre Dame are just talk?

"I think this: Anytime you get 120 athletes on any campus, and you've got 120 factory workers, you're going to have some drug problems with the factory workers and you're going to have some drug problems with the athletes. It's just the percentages."

Raridon denies having ever used steroids at Nebraska.

Chuck Lanza says, "Steroids is an issue that's going to be around as long as football. I certainly didn't have any knowledge and never saw any steroids while I was there. The people I hung with, that wasn't their thing."

So did you ever use them?

"Absolutely not."

Would it surprise you if people said you did and you were in the middle of the steroid problem at Notre Dame?

"Naw, that's what people say about linemen," says Lanza.

Holtz likes big players. In football, especially along the offensive and defensive lines, big is good. Bigger is better. A big guy will usually handle a smaller guy, so it's not as if Holtz is crazy in his thinking. The question is, does the end, which is winning football games, justify the means, which is often steroids?

Dr. Rob Hunter, the former University of Minnesota orthopedist, says that when it came to drugs of any kind—including steroids—Holtz "clearly was soft." To this end, when members of the medical staff, including Hunter, urged drug testing, Holtz finally agreed—but he insisted it be announced well in advance. Hunter shakes his head in disbelief. Says Hunter, "All I know is some of these guys got real big real fast, and they weren't spending any more time in the weight room."

Clearly, there was no reason to think that Holtz would shift his opinion on steroids just because he moved from Minnesota to Notre Dame. And he didn't.

Tom Riley says steroids were not an issue at all when Faust was the coach, and they became a huge issue when Holtz arrived. Says Riley, "It doesn't take a brain surgeon to know what was going on. One of the things that spurred it on was [when] Lou Holtz had a conversation with me and others that 'when you're playing O-line at Notre Dame football, you need to bench 400 pounds.' My max was 340 to 360 pounds. There aren't many guys who can lift 400 naturally. There was never a strong message that you *shouldn't* use steroids. What was made a priority was that you needed to bench 400 pounds if you wanted to be an offensive lineman at Notre Dame. That was the message I got. The pressure from hearing that was so intense that I was so close to taking them, you can't believe it. But I got scared off. All I knew about steroids was shrinking testicles.

"But other guys started making great strength jumps, and it just doesn't come that naturally. If those guys [who used them] outlive me, I'll be pissed off. I could have taken them and played. I want the last laugh out of this. If Holtz didn't know, then he's a fool. You can't be in the business for all those years and not know the symptoms."

Telling that a player is using steroids isn't very tricky. Jim Baugus says that when you see a football player gain forty pounds in the off-season, maybe more, "you've got to question something. I guess the coaches' point of view was, 'We tested him for steroids, he didn't test positive, therefore he's not on it.' Maybe the coaches don't know as much about steroids as they need to. That may be selective knowledge. They choose to learn about what they want to learn about." That's a strong point. Coaches want players bigger and stronger, and experience has taught them not to pursue questions like who, what, when, where, why, and especially how.

Tom Freeman, an offensive lineman from Shawnee Mission, Kansas, is one of those who doesn't think Holtz should take the total fall for the vastly increased steroid use at Notre Dame. Freeman admits that "it's a little less clean than when Gerry Faust was there, but I just think that you can't blame it on Lou Holtz. It may have evolved that way anyway; I mean, most of these guys that were doing it came from high school doing it. If I had come in as a freshman and was competing with a bunch of guys that were using steroids, it would have been a lot tougher not to do them. It's the only way to compete. When you're a freshman, all you want to do is play, and if that's what your peer group is doing and everybody who is competing with you is doing, well . . . I mean, I was fortunate enough by the time I knew what was going on, I was mature enough to make the decision not to do it."

But George Marshall wants no part of providing Holtz with cover. He, for example, was not impressed when Holtz held a press conference in the wake of the *Sports Illustrated* article to deny there was steroid use at Notre Dame. "I just think," says Marshall, "that it was more political bullshit. Of course he's gonna say that. I mean, what is he supposed to say?"

Is there a way that he could not have known?

"He knew about it, but it was just that no one knocked on his door, came into his office, and said, 'Coach, I'm using steroids. I need help.' Or, 'Coach, I'm using steroids. What do you think?' Because it was like, if it wasn't actually formally addressed to him, like his name wasn't on a letter, he didn't have to open the mail. He didn't have to deal with it. So he didn't."

You say pretty unequivocally that he knew about it. Why do you feel that way?

"Because he is a control freak. He has to have his finger on everything and anything that goes on. If you think about it, his job as head coach isn't necessarily to tell how to run an offense or run a defense or actually getting into drills to show a back how to run or actually running up to tackle somebody. But he does this. That makes him a great coach, because he's very hands-on, he gets in there and he does it. But by the same token, I just can't believe that somebody that is that involved with his football team doesn't even know about the vitamins that you are taking, what goes into the guy, what goes into their bodies. I mean, he knows that, I honestly believe that he knew that."

The temptation to do steroids was everywhere. "When I first got there," says Marshall, who arrived in Holtz's second year, "they were widespread. They could be taken. There were a few guys I know that did it even up until the year before I left [in 1991]. I mean, it was there even though Holtz was saying it wasn't."

Did you ever see kids getting punished for it?

"No, I never did."

What kind of message did that send out to the other players?

"That it's okay, it's fine. In fact, when I first got there, I was walking back from the dining hall and one of the older guys says, 'George, you got a nice frame on you. All you need is a little beef, a little something extra.' That's when he went down the whole line and let me know that I can come to him or others on the team to get what steroids or whatever it was that I might want or need. And it was there. There was an easy way to get it."

So it was well known where to go to get the stuff?

"Oh, everyone definitely knew where to get it. It was just not spoken. I mean, it wasn't like you were gonna tell the guy next door in your dorm that somebody is using steroids or selling them. It was just that you knew where to go to take care of your end of the bargain, and it wasn't like we had to go out and advertise it. I mean, that is something we definitely wanted to be quiet."

Former player Chet Lacheta says that "there were people who I know for a fact that I was friends with and played with who were doing it." Use grew, he says, because the tests were so easily flummoxed: "There were a lot of ways around the test, and everybody knew them. They've got the herbal tea stuff [goldenseal] out now that you can drink three to five hours before a test and it will let anybody test clean of almost any kind of drug—any kind of steroid, marijuana, heroin, or cocaine. It wipes everything clean in your system. Even when the NCAA comes in to test, they'd give the list of people who need to be tested the night before. They'd say, 'These are the people who have to report to the stadium tomorrow morning at eight to be tested.' "

John Askin denies that he took steroids, denies ever buying any, but admits having them "in my possession. I mean, that kind of stuff, I don't take it lightly."

What brought you to actually want them in your possession? You obviously were on the verge of thinking you needed to do this?

"Seeing these freshmen and sophomores coming in every year and benching over 400 pounds, and I was four years older and was thinking, 'Look at this guy.' It was bizarre."

Why were you tempted?

"You were tempted because Holtz always said, 'If you can't bench over 400 pounds, I don't want you playing for me."

Is there any way Lou Holtz could not have known players were using steroids?

"I don't think so. I mean, you're around athletes long enough and you see a guy jump from benching 350 to 420 in a few months. There is just no way. I mean, you have been around enough athletes so you can tell. If I use steroids, my arms feel like steel. You can tell a guy that uses."

How well known was it on the team that steroids were being used?

"Everybody knew."

In Holtz's first year, you actually saw vials. Where were they?

"They were in trash cans, used, in people's dorm rooms. It shocked me so bad that I remember calling up Mike Perrino, who was my roommate, up in Chicago. He got drafted by the San Diego Chargers, and I said, 'Mike, you won't believe what is going on down here.' I'd never seen this stuff before and I didn't want to see it. I remember a lot of these young, new players of Holtz's, and you'd go into their room and the stuff was all over. Anyone could see it. I was afraid, I swear I was so nervous, I was afraid somebody was going to die."

If the steroids had been available under Faust, would you have done them?

"Yeah. But Faust would have gone bananas. He would have had a heart attack and screamed and went to church and just went to see a priest and everything else."

What was the message you got from Holtz about not doing it? Do you remember Holtz saying don't do that?

"No, see, Holtz was smarter than that. Holtz separated himself from any way he could get caught. He would never put himself in that situation. But the message he always said was, 'If you don't bench 400 pounds, you don't play for me.' "

Thinking about doing steroids was as far as Ted FitzGerald says he ever got. He says, "To be honest with you, I thought about it because when I was a sophomore and I was playing against those guys [Holtz recruits], I knew I had to get stronger. One thing with me is I never had powerful benching. I said to myself, 'If I'm gonna make it, I'm gonna have to do steroids.' I ended up getting hurt and not doing it because I talked to somebody and they said if you're hurt, there is no sense doing it. . . . Fortunately I got lucky and didn't do it."

Mirko Jurkovic takes a cavalier attitude toward steroids, saying, "In college football there are steroid stories everywhere, whether people admit it, people don't admit it. In football, there are going to be steroids."

One of Notre Dame's bigger stars, Michael Stonebreaker, understands steroids and is candid about them: "Of course people took steroids. It's a problem [at schools all over the country]."

Have you ever tried them?

"No."

Were you ever tempted?

"Well, sure, you would have to be tempted. But I've never needed to take them. I've always been physically very strong and fast. People take steroids to make up for a handicap they think they have or to try to improve. It could be something they think will help them improve their game, and it's also that people aren't confident enough in themselves to think they can do it on their own, so they need that, they need something to help them."

Mike Kovaleski, a linebacker and team captain from New Castle, Indiana, says, "I seriously contemplated taking them to help my physical structure. There is just a lot of pressure to compete and to be as big and to be as strong as you can, because physical appearance is a large part of what makes up the mental psyche of playing. If you're a hundred pounds lighter than somebody standing across from you, if you had to take a bet on who's gonna win, you're gonna say the bigger guy is gonna win. That gets transposed into the attitude of steroids. It's unfortunate.

"I know guys who were doing them, and I had guys come to me and tell me to use them. They said, 'Hey, it's easy. Just take these and it'll get you where you want to get a lot quicker.' "

The situation was clear to Shawn Smith, who says, "There was a lot of steroids, you could see steroid use." Smith says he didn't use at Notre Dame, but he did in high school, quitting because "I didn't feel nothing so I was like, 'Forget this.' " Once at Notre Dame, he says some of the players talked to him about using. Says Smith, "They'd say that over the summer 'maybe you should take a cycle of some, come back and destroy.' It was like that. They would do it for football. There was such a demand on the sport to be the best, to start for Notre Dame, which is such a big school. People would do anything to start. Notre Dame football is such a big business that it didn't surprise me that people would do anything they could to be a part of it."

Pat Terrell, originally a wide receiver from St. Petersburg, Florida, says of the players from Chicago, "I hate to say it, but they were big-city guys and they knew how to get the stuff and how to use it. I think if you wanted it, it was there to get for you, through certain individuals."

Do you think the players were using it because it was so competitive at that stage?

"It was very competitive. Maybe at a smaller school, it wouldn't be as competitive, because you get this great high school recruit and he's gonna come in and play. Here, everybody is an all-American. Everyone was the player of the state, the player of the year. So there was so much competition, I guess they did do that to get ahead."

Notre Dame describes its current steroids policy as follows: The University conducts random drug testing of its football players approximately every two to three weeks during the season, and roughly every six weeks off-season. The entire squad is tested in August and during winter conditioning; the rest of the time approximately twenty players are tested at a time. School policy requires "continuous supervision during specimen acquisitions" and no prior notification is given to the players. One positive test—including presence of a masking agent in a player's urine—results in drug counseling and suspension from games or practice while a steroid is present in the body. A second positive test, and the athlete is permanently barred from varsity competition at Notre Dame. The school says it has found no positive steroid test since 1990 and has never ignored a positive test.

When the August 1990 *Sports Illustrated* article appeared in which Steve Huffman said there was heavy steroid use at Notre Dame—but didn't name names—Holtz vigorously denied the article's accuracy. A university physician said at a press conference that since 1987 only five out of 466 had tested positive. If true, then the testing in South Bend clearly failed to cast nearly a big enough net.

Eight examples:

—Jeff Pearson, among Holtz's first recruits, walked that walk, and he gives a blazingly direct analysis of steroids at Notre Dame and his part in the scheme: "Sure I sold steroids. If I hadn't, someone else would have. It was pretty well known what kind of stuff I had. You have to remember, it was just a part of college football. Hell, it was just a part of high school football where I played, too. [He played at St. Laurence High in the Chicago suburb of Burbank and was considered among the top one hundred prep players in 1986.] Players at other schools were doing it. That's why I thought it was okay. We needed to compete. When I got there, the Faust guys were pathetic. They just weren't very strong. A bunch of the guys that came in [as freshmen] with me, guys who were doing steroids, were stronger than the seniors. By my second year, I'd say almost all of the linemen—especially those who were starters—were doing them. And everybody knew about it. It was really kind of, I guess, an open secret."

The problem, as Pearson sees it, is that the Irish "don't want that image tarnished. They don't want to admit Notre Dame did it by using steroids or Notre Dame did it by letting kids in who were not up to par. The first time I tested positive for steroids, Holtz came up to me on the practice field and said, 'We don't need to do that here at Notre Dame. We're not like Michigan.' But he had this smile on his face. It was the week of the Michigan game and he let me go ahead and play. What kind of message do you think that sent? Once, I remember he was real pissed because a bunch of players had gotten caught the winter after my freshman year. It was something like ten got caught for either marijuana or steroids."

Asked about Pearson, who had a short-lived career with the Washington Redskins (he was placed on injured reserve before his only season), Mike Crounse said Pearson "looked like a bodybuilder. He always stood out as somebody that could possibly take steroids. He is one person I can confirm because he told me." Pearson today owns a Gold's Gym in a Chicago suburb.

—Marty Lippincott, who received a bachelor's degree in management from Notre Dame, wonders if he didn't miss a great NFL opportunity by not making better use of steroids. "I'm not saying I couldn't have juiced up and tried out somewhere," says Lippincott. "I think I was good enough. I'm taking a Philadelphia police test. If that don't work out and I don't pass, I'm gonna juice up so big and give it one shot [in the NFL]. So in case my kids say, 'Dad, did you ever try to play in the NFL?' I can say yes. I say this even though I'm twenty-six years old. I don't lift now, I don't work out, and I'm 315 pounds. I'll bet my body fat's not over fifteen to eighteen percent. That's just me. I have two big bodybuilder friends now that say they'll train me, give me a six-months' training program, and if it don't work, then I'll just quit. What's it gonna cost me? Eight hundred dollars for some juice for six months."

Did you ever try steroids or anything?

"Yeah."

But you didn't test positive?

"No."

How did you get around it?

"There's a certain time period in between that if you take a water base, you only need one to two weeks to get out of it and that's how they did it."

You were probably always tested because of your size?

"Not that, but they knew I was a partyer. I grew up in this environment. I'm an inner-city kid. I've been in a bar since I've been fifteen. I'm still in a bar, I still work in a nightclub, I want to own a nightclub. You're always around it."

Lippincott points to 1986 recruits like Pearson and Jason Cegielski and says, "When you have freshmen coming in benching 400 pounds, you're like, 'What the fuck is that?' " He has a point. Often in life, when something seems too good to be believed, it's because it is.

At one time, at least three members of the starting defense were on steroids, according to Lippincott. He knows, he says, because "I did it with them."

Additionally, Lippincott recalls that "we used to have to say to [one lineman that he named], 'When you come into the gym, put on a sweatshirt so they don't see how big you're getting.' The shit worked good for him. He just got big as hell. You don't want to attract any more attention when you're getting stronger or bigger. The weight coaches knew who was on them. How can you look at a weight chart, and in January he's benching 330 and in May it's 370. Okay, maybe that's your freshman year. Let's just say that's your freshman year because you're not used to a good training program, but from your junior year to your senior year or just during your senior year? No. I think the most ever benched was about 345 to 350 because I never lifted. I still don't lift. I hate it. My senior year I was almost getting 400. Come on. Everybody knows everything at Notre Dame. The question is what they tell."

—Jason Cegielski, another player who came in with Holtz, says, "I can only say what I saw there. God, I remember in winter conditioning my freshman year there must have been at least twenty-five guys I knew about."

That were doing steroids?

"Yeah."

You knew about it because you all talked about it?

"Yeah."

Did you ever get caught?

"Yeah, I got caught. Actually, when I first came in there, I wasn't taking much. I stopped, too, right before practice started. It was a couple of weeks into doubles (two-a-day practice sessions in August and September before classes start). I get a call to go see Holtz. I come in and he's kind of smiling. He goes, 'You know, Jason, you tested positive.' I go, 'Really?' He goes, 'Yeah. That's positive for steroids.' I went, 'Yeah.' He took my hand and gave me a light slap on the hand. Honest to God. I laughed. I thought, 'Maybe he's not a bad guy.' He obviously knew what it was about and he wasn't shocked by it at all."

Some players said the key was after being tested, they would jump on a cycle, hoping to complete it and not get caught. Is that true?

"Yeah. You don't even know who they're testing because they might not pick your specimen for an actual test. There were guys who thought they were gonna get busted that didn't."

Pearson said he tested positive, but Holtz never did anything to him despite all this stuff about how players are suspended.

"No. Jeff was second team, offensive line. He got caught with me."

That made a difference?

"It does seem that way. He got a slap on the hand."

Notre Dame says that only five players ever tested positive for steroid abuse. Do you think that's a lie?

"That's ridiculous."

Do you know more than five that tested positive?

"I can think of five people that tested positive in my freshman year that I talked to. And I know there's twenty to twenty-five other people."

Did any of those guys get suspended?

"No."

Despite all their talk, they didn't suspend the players?

"No, no."

Could it have been possible that those things were going on and Holtz didn't know?

"I find it very hard to believe. He's the kind of coach that wants to know everything. He wants his hand in everything. I don't think it's possible. It's just the law of averages, he'd have to know."

—Jim Baugus, who quit the team in the spring of '87, admits there were Irish players on steroids. "I actually did them for a while, for six weeks or whatever a cycle was," says Baugus. "We had a drug test and I was caught. . . . There was myself and a few other people. I thought it would be a good idea just because I knew how small I was, and for a lineman, I knew there was no way in the world it was going to work. I thought I'd go ahead and give them a shot. They do work. Towards the end of the cycle, I realized it really wasn't worth it. But I went ahead and finished it out. Then I got caught. I was getting them from another player who was getting them from a source he had."

Baugus says after he was caught, Holtz said, " 'If you're ever caught again, you're off the team. We've written a letter to you, we've written a letter to your parents.' Thank God my brother got the letter out of the mail before they ever saw it. I've never told them. I've kind of hinted around because the steroid issue keeps coming up and my mom is a nurse and so she hears about it a lot.

"I got up to 265. I went from 245 to 265 in six weeks. I trimmed down a lot and got a lot stronger and a lot faster. But I also got the side effects, a little bit aggressive, stuff like that. If I had kept playing and not gotten caught, I don't know if I would have done it again or not. That's partly because I got a pretty good view after being injured that football really isn't life. I just couldn't do it. It wasn't right. I couldn't sleep at night. It was a problem."

—Kurt Zackrison says, "Some guys, I'm not gonna say names because I don't think it's my place to bring up names, there were guys that did steroids. Would I have done it? I had a serious scare. After my surgery [for a shoulder injury] I didn't think I was gonna be ready to play. I had a friend that was into powerlifting and he said, 'Listen, I've got some stuff for you.' "

Did this guy play with Notre Dame?

"No. He was a powerlifter in my hometown. I ended up getting it from him and then went to summer school. I was seriously concerned about injuring myself in the fall. I took it for two days and decided I couldn't do this. This wasn't right for me. I didn't touch the stuff again. Then we went into camp and we had a test. Coach Holtz pulled me aside one day and said, 'You tested positive.' I said, 'Coach, there's no way.' He said, 'I just wanted to let you know that we don't do this. This is not the way we do things at Notre Dame.' I told him, 'Coach, I tried them for two days and I had a moral problem with them.' Football was not that important that I was gonna risk ten years of my life. I'll tell people now that, 'No, I didn't mess around with them.' As soon as you say to someone, 'I played with steroids,' they think, 'Oh, man, this guy was on a death cycle.' Even some of my close friends don't even know about it. For me it was a moral issue.

"I'm ashamed that I did it. I don't regret many things that I've done. There's not many things I would change. Those two days I would change. I've never told my dad that."

. . .

—Ron Weissenhofer, a linebacker from Oak Lawn, Illinois, who went to the same Chicago-area high school as Pearson, takes the position that steroids are everywhere, and he says, "Everyone has tried them sometime. I've tried them. I took them for three weeks or something. I only took them to see what they were like. It's just like smoking pot or something. Hey, try it, whatever. But I hated them. I didn't like the way I was feeling, so I never took them again. I can't see why people would take them for two, three, four years." He says he never tested positive for steroids.

—In Sacramento, Joan Quinn, mother of the former player Dan Quinn, is forthright: "Dan took steroids the summer after his freshman year. He got them and learned about them through Notre Dame, from other players there. He came home and took them and he got them in San Diego. People on steroids are more aggressive and they do strange things."

Did Dan tell you he was taking steroids?

"He told me. I was real upset. He was living with me and there's no illegal substances in my house."

For his part, Dan Quinn says steroids "became a big deal after that first Holtz freshman class came in with all those guys who were, A, doing them and, B, selling them because they were different kinds of persons."

What encouraged you to use them?

"Doing steroids was one of the worst things I ever did. It did make me marginally stronger, it made me bench 400 to 410 pounds, and all I could bench before was 385 to 390. There was kind of this attitude because Coach Holtz came in and he would harp on us that the team 'isn't strong enough, we're getting pushed around in the trenches.' Subliminal steroids, steroids all through his speeches."

Did everyone know that that was the subliminal message?

"I think so."

Is that how you took it?

"Yeah. Before Holtz came in, I never thought about doing it. I know guys that under Faust did it, but not very many. You had a running back benching about 410 pounds. I don't want to say who it is because he's a good guy. He's little and benching 410 and at first people were like, 'Oh, man, he's strong.' And then when Holtz came in with all these people, we're looking at each other going, 'Man, were we fucking gullible or what?' We just thought that so and so was strong—but he was on steroids."

What percentage of the players, according to your knowledge of the team, were using steroids after Holtz got in there?

"Huge. I say huge. Steroids is kind of like a thing where you didn't tell everybody. You tell your friends that you're doing them, but . . ."

—When Jeff Kunz, a defensive tackle from Palm Beach Gardens, Florida, tried steroids, he was not impressed. "All these people were doing them and I needed to compete," he says. "I started doing them and I started feeling bad. It just wasn't worth it. It was my summer before my senior year and I went up there for summer school. I can't even remember when I took them because it wasn't even a month that I took them. It was like two weeks. I finally said, 'Screw it, it ain't worth it. If they want to do them, they can do them.' I knew guys that were doing the needles and stuff. Giving themselves shots and I was like, 'No way.' After a while they were everywhere. I don't remember them as much in the summer as I do after the season was over. I remember guys talking about doing cycles, eight-week cycles and get off, and if you take water-based, they're better and you won't get caught."

So you had all the advice one could ask for?

"It was all around. It got pretty bad there for a while."

Do you think coaches knew?

"It would be pretty bad if they didn't know to a certain extent. Because a lot of guys just got huge all of the sudden. From small to huge. Basically that's all it was. I think they would have had to have known."

What prompted you to try them?

"Just thinking they would get me stronger and better. It wasn't worth it. Luckily, I didn't get into doing the shots and I didn't do them for a month or two months or whatever. It was stupid."

How did you find them?

"They were there. If you wanted them, they were there. The only thing that I ever heard about Holtz with steroids was bringing players in who tested positive or who did something and just slapping them on the wrist. Other than that, as far as seeing people go from 210 to 270 over a summer, some people did it naturally, but there's not a whole lot of people who can do that natural. Supposedly those things don't happen at Notre Dame."

. . .

George Williams, who was twice kicked off the team for nonsteroid drug use, says that "most of the offensive line were doing steroids. I mean, they were all doing it." Williams says he never tried them but "I was approached by a couple of guys about using them." He says that one star player said to him, "Why don't you get on cycle? It'll help you and buff you out nice and strong for next year."

But Williams says that one reason "I didn't want to use steroids was because I heard they made your dick shrink. I have a small enough one as it is, and I didn't have time to deal with that shit. I mean, you used to think a lot of black guys on the team just weren't gonna do it, because we had this thing, you know, with black people being stronger and bigger. But then you come to find out that's not true. A lot of guys who said they weren't doing it, were doing it."

How many football players were doing steroids while you were there?

"I'd say at least forty to fifty, half the guys. Maybe more."

Further, says Williams, the guys who were selling "had connections to Chicago and they were selling big time."

Williams's knowledge is intimate. Because he wasn't using steroids, he was asked to help his teammates pass drug tests: "I remember the times when we would have tests my freshman year, and these guys would be like, 'Piss in this bottle for me.' They would get alcohol bottles and get us to piss in them. So I would always piss in the bottle."

You would piss in the bottles for these guys from Chicago?

"For a lot of guys."

How did that work?

"I don't know how they did it, but they got away with it, so I knew it went on."

Desperation always sets in with athletes—some athletes—when they are suddenly confronted with a drug test. Often, a player would prefer that the urine specimen with his name on it actually be somebody else's urine. Says George Marshall, "It was easy for them to say, 'George, why don't you help me out?' "

Were you solicited to do this by another player?

"Yeah, by another player."

To help him out?

"Yeah, to help him out."

Was it successful? Were you able to help him out?

"I didn't get a chance. We went in at different times to be tested, so the combination didn't click."

Very quickly, how to avoid being caught in the drug tests became topic A for conversation around Notre Dame. Shawn Smith says, "They used to tell you while you were pissing, take one of your hairs and drop it in there because it would contaminate the thing so they would have to come back and do another test. You know, it was perfectly innocent when a few hairs fell in there. Or dip your hand in some bleach and while you piss, stick your hand in front of it, a whole bunch of stuff."

Linc Coleman says he heard the rumor that some of the players "had someone else taking the test, using someone else's urine."

Do you think it was true?

"Yeah. Of course."

Asked how the players managed not to get caught, Mike Harazin says that "Notre Dame would use tests that were kind of obsolete, and there are ways of getting around tests, like masking."

What kind of masking?

"Different drugs or diuretics that people take. People would use non-oil-based natural hormones so you couldn't even detect it."

When George Williams is asked how he felt when he watched the press conference about steroids at Notre Dame and Irish officials and others were saying it just doesn't happen, he says, "It was funny because we knew it happened. It was all funny. We were sitting there going, 'I can't believe this,' but they couldn't really come out and say that we knew it all along, so I guess they had to protect themselves."

Everybody says that Holtz is a control freak and he knows everything.

"That's what I'm saying. He had to know. I mean, he is a smart person. He knew what the effects would be and what they would do to you. He saw players that were small one year and large the next. Something had to be going on."

Erik Simien isn't inclined to take a bullet on behalf of Notre Dame. "There were a lot of damn steroids being done," he says. "It's like everywhere else. They were being used up until the time I left. I know that. When that story [in *SI*] came out, we all knew the truth. We knew it was true. But we were told to say it's not true."

Jim Baugus, like most of the players who were around under both Gerry Faust and Lou Holtz, says he didn't know of any steroid use during Faust's watch. Says Baugus, "No one was strong. You'd go in the weight room and no one could do anything. With Holtz, I think everyone wanted to be good. It was kind of a sacrifice and you'd sacrifice anything for it. Holtz recruited a different kind of character than Faust did, and I'd never seen a steroid until Holtz's first class came in. And a lot of those guys were huge coming in. All us upperclassmen started saying, 'We'd better start working out to keep up with the freshmen.'

"But when all these huge kids came in, that was when I realized that football wasn't for me any longer. There was no way I could keep up. I think some of the freshmen that came in were on steroids because that's how we got the steroids. That was pretty obvious that they were using them. And in my two years before that, no one was really that strong."

Kurt Zackrison says the difficulties occurred because while "under Faust it didn't matter if you could bench-press 400 pounds," it mattered a lot with Holtz. When the Holtz recruits started appearing, Zackrison says that some of them "brought their steroids and steroids they were selling. A different kind of guy came, and he brought with him something Notre Dame hadn't really experienced before. It's true."

He says that when talk surfaces of steroids, it causes attention because "it's Notre Dame and you're supposed to be above reproach. It's not realistic at all. But it is the Notre Dame mystique."

Says Mark Nigro, "With Faust, we only had four or five guys who could bench over 400 pounds. Under Holtz, that number went up a lot."

The truth is there was a relatively small amount of steroid usage going on under Faust. The truth is there has been a relatively large amount of steroid usage going on under Holtz.

Plenty of players didn't do steroids, of course. One, John Foley, says that "the reason I didn't even consider it was I honestly thought the way I was that if I ever took them I'd kill somebody."

Joe Allen insists that the offensive line didn't care enough about football to hit the junk. "We would go golfing every chance," says Allen. "I mean, we worked out, but I don't think it was important enough to us to juice just to make that 400 pounds."

Mark Green, a running back from Riverside, California, says, "Of course there were steroids. But I think they [school officials] had to say there weren't because of all the people who look at Notre Dame as pure and everything. It was what they had to say."

Tom Freeman, whose last year was 1986, which enabled him to see the changes that Lou Holtz brought to Notre Dame, says, "I didn't take a lot of pride in the 1988 national championship. I thought they were great athletes. I wish I had been there. But I would have loved to have seen them do the same thing by doing it naturally. I guess that's what I'm trying to say."

PART
II

Good
Intentions

CHAPTER
4

Image

Image is so big at Notre Dame that the school has spent endless
decades, millions of words, and countless dollars cultivating it. Notre
Dame presents itself as all that is good and great about college football.
It is an image of winning without breaking—or even bending—the
rules, as everyone else does. It is an image of winning without becoming
a football factory, without forfeiting its academic soul. But even more
than symbolizing all that is wonderful about football, Notre Dame
stands for the very best in American higher education.

So what, really, is Notre Dame?

In so many ways, it is a state of mind—and, historically, a perfect
state of mind. That's what makes trying to quantify it so difficult.

It's located ninety miles east of Chicago in South Bend, Indiana; it costs around $18,000 a year to attend; only 9,700 students are enrolled, which includes 2,200 graduate students. People who see the campus for the first time almost always find it far smaller than they imagined. It is dominated by the gloriously uplifting Golden Dome, atop the administration building. It has ninety-eight buildings on 1,250 acres. It is one of our most national universities, and one of our best.

The formula for synthetic rubber was discovered at Notre Dame. The school says that the nation's preeminent expert on mosquitoes is working on new ways to control the spread of disease, while at the National Accelerator Laboratory, people are looking for clues to the origins of the universe. The school's Center for Bioengineering and Pollution Control has pioneered, according to the university, "technologies using specially bred microorganisms to remove contaminants from soil, municipal sewage, and industrial wastewater."

Notre Dame attracts money like beaches do sunshine. One school publication says, "The University's quest for excellence is underpinned by extraordinary financial strength. From 1980–90, endowment grew from $150 million to almost $600 million. Now, the University is committed to increasing student aid endowment by $100 million before the year 2000, enabling more outstanding students to attend Notre Dame regardless of their ability to pay." Notre Dame's 85,000 alums contributed $22.6 million in fiscal 1989. They are, make no mistake, a generous and a grateful lot.

Says Father Edmund P. Joyce, for thirty-five years the executive vice president at Notre Dame under Pres. Theodore Hesburgh until both retired in 1987, "We see ourselves as an exceptionally fine university, always improving, with a high level of integrity and a stellar reputation."

Oh, yes, the school also has a football stadium. It was designed by Knute Rockne, was built during 1929, and has more than 2 million bricks and a seating capacity of 59,075. In it, the Irish once beat Haskell 73–0 and once lost to Oklahoma 40–0. Overall, the Irish win nearly eight of every ten games in Notre Dame Stadium.

Irish football history is bedecked in glory. The 1909 team was unbeaten. The 1924 team had the Four Horsemen and the Seven Mules. The 1930 team was terrific, the best Knute Rockne ever had, with a record of 10-0; it outscored its opponents 265–74. The teams from 1946 through 1949 compiled a record of 36-0-2. Since the Associated Press began selecting a national champion in 1936, the Irish have won eight titles—1943, '46, '47, '49, '66, '73, '77, and '88. Next best in the nation is Oklahoma with six.

Notre Dame football has a spectacularly successful history replete with classic anecdotes. For example, in 1930, the apparently over-matched Irish went to Los Angeles to play powerful Southern California. The Irish problems were exacerbated when all-American fullback Joe Savoldi was booted off the team for getting married. The day before the game, according to Dave Anderson's research, which appeared in *The New York Times,* Notre Dame coach Rockne visited with the USC team and said, "When that game is over tomorrow, and I know you'll do everything possible to hold down the score, I'd like to ask you fine young men of Troy to come over and congratulate my boys on a fine game. It will mean so much to them to have a firm handshake and a kind word from a team like yours." Notre Dame won, 27–0.

Everything in football in South Bend traces quickly back to Rockne —as well it should. He is a monument to what is good and great in college football. In fact, if you had to select one person to represent the ideals of the game, it would have to be Knute Rockne. And while cynics may scoff and those who don't understand may laugh, the spirit of Rockne lives in Notre Dame Stadium. No person who comprehends— yea who feels—can walk through those old portals and not be overcome by the spirit of Rockne.

The stadium cost about $750,000 to build, it's a half mile in circum-ference, it stands forty-five feet high, and it required four hundred tons of steel and fifteen thousand cubic yards of concrete. Those are the numbers, the facts. But the price didn't include the spirit of Rockne, and that is Notre Dame Stadium's single most precious and priceless ingredient. For twenty-six seasons, every home game has been a sellout —save one, a Thanksgiving Day contest against Air Force in 1973.

Sadly, Rockne got to coach just one season in the new stadium before dying on March 31, 1931 when a commercial plane in which he was a passenger crashed in a Kansas wheat field. But, predictably, in that one season in which he got to coach in the new facility, the Irish were 5-0 at home.

Knute Rockne. The name trips gloriously off the tongue. In our hearts we remember Rockne as an all-American in 1913. In truth, he was only a third-team all-American, as an end. But while football has defined Rockne in history, football doesn't define Rockne at all. He was a Norwegian immigrant who, after graduating from high school in Chicago, worked four years in the post office to earn enough money to go to Notre Dame. Once there, he was the quintessential Notre Dame man, a student for all seasons. Rockne wrote for the student newspaper and yearbook, played a major role in every school play, played flute in the orchestra, and reached the finals of the Notre Dame marbles tournament. He worked his way through school, as a janitor and later as a chemistry research assistant. Above all, Rockne considered himself a student. He graduated magna cum laude with an average of 90.52.

If all this doesn't draw a picture of the perfect Notre Dame student, the perfect Notre Dame man, then such a person has never existed.

So it seemed simply an exclamation point when Rockne succeeded mightily as coach. In thirteen years, he had five unbeaten and untied seasons. His lifetime record was 102-12-5, a winning percentage of .881. That remains the best record ever in the history of either college or professional football.

And talk about knowing how to make an exit: Rockne won the last nineteen games he coached.

There has been only one Rockne and Notre Dame got him. In view of this, it almost seems unfair that his legend should be joined to that of yet another towering giant—one George Gipp. All Gipp was, was the best college football player ever.

While Gipp played in the backfield for Notre Dame—he could run, pass, and punt—the Irish were 27-2-3; in 1919 and 1920, Notre Dame went undefeated.

At age twenty-five, on December 14, 1920, Gipp died, of strep throat. Dying young is a tragedy; dying young nobly is the stuff of legend. On his deathbed, Gipp made one of the most emotional statements in the history of sport, to his coach, Rockne: "I've got to go, Rock. It's all right. I'm not afraid. Sometime, Rock, when the team is up against it, when things are wrong and the breaks are beating the boys—tell them to go in there with all they've got and win just one for the Gipper. I don't know where I'll be then, Rock. But I'll know about it, and I'll be happy."

Eight years later, Rockne trotted out Gipp's words, just as his underdog Irish were getting ready to play unbeaten Army. Said Rockne to his team, "The day before he died, George Gipp asked me to wait until the situation seemed hopeless, then ask a Notre Dame team to go out and beat Army for him. This is the day and you are the team." Never mind that Gipp hadn't specified Army; the Irish won 12–6 in a starry demonstration of inspired football. "Win one for the Gipper" has become a basic part of the American lexicon.

Then, in 1940, an actor named Ronald Reagan played Gipp in the movie *Knute Rockne, All-American.* Reagan's own subsequent achievements only added to the luster of the image and the size of the legend.

Then there were the Four Horsemen, the most famous backfield in college football history.

They—quarterback Harry Stuhldreher, left halfback Jim Crowley, right halfback Don Miller, and fullback Elmer Layden—were fine players, but it was their good fortune to be immortalized by *New York Herald-Tribune* sportswriter Grantland Rice.

Rice wrote the most memorable start ever to a sports story: "Outlined against a blue, gray October sky the Four Horsemen rode again.

"In dramatic lore they are known as famine, pestilence, destruction and death. These are only aliases. Their real names are: Stuhldreher, Miller, Crowley and Layden. They formed the crest of the South Bend cyclone before which another fighting Army team was swept over the precipice at the Polo Grounds this afternoon as 55,000 spectators peered down upon the bewildering panorama spread out upon the green plain below."

Purists have observed that for the players to have been outlined against a blue, gray sky, Rice would have had to have been lying on his back on the field, looking straight up at them. Well, maybe he was.

Naturally, the Irish went on to a perfect 10-0 season. In the thirty games the Four Horsemen played together, they lost only twice, both times to Nebraska. Other teams have done as well; none have combined accomplishments with such a memorable nickname. Of such luck are legends born.

Rockne, Gipp, the Four Horsemen. These six are the bedrock on which Notre Dame football is based.

Yet, incredibly there is more—much more. Seven times Notre Dame players have won the Heisman, college football's top award, which goes to the season's best player: quarterback Angelo Bertelli in 1943, QB John Lujack in 1947, end Leon Hart in 1949, halfback John Lattner in 1953, QB Paul Hornung in 1956, QB John Huarte in 1964, and flanker Tim Brown in 1987.

And name after great name is etched indelibly in Irish memory: Joe Theismann, Bob Crable, Joe Montana, Ken MacAfee, Nick Eddy . . .

It all gives chills to those who know and care.

Great, great games over the eons have produced those chills in abundance. Again, it is the purists—God love purists—who get teary over Notre Dame's 0–0 tie with Army in 1946, simply a brilliant display of football. In 1957, a very average Irish team stopped Oklahoma, in Norman, 7–0, to end the Sooners' 47-game winning streak, still a collegiate record. Notre Damers still aren't certain how they feel about the 1966 10–10 tie the then No. 1 Irish played with No. 2 Michigan State; coach Ara Parseghian played safe to preserve the tie, but again, it was terrific, guts-and-glory football. In 1980, Harry Oliver booted a 51-yard field goal as time ran out for a 29–27 Irish win over Michigan—and grown men insist it happened because God calmed the wind briefly to make possible the feat.

Notre Dame, over 104 years, has the highest winning percentage (.760) of all college football teams.

Chills?

To stand in Notre Dame Stadium as the Irish drive for yet another come-from-behind win, everybody screaming, chaos everywhere—and the band playing the Notre Dame "Victory March"—is almost more than a body can stand. It just may be the most exhilarating experience in sports. Or in life.

All of this history and achievement and legend and image thrills millions, notably the Subway Alumni. That's the name given to that huge group of people, many of whom have never even been to Notre Dame and certainly didn't attend school there, who hold her indescribably close to their collective breasts. Their devotion is, well, legendary. They are so fanatical that they can't separate themselves from the Irish. They are, simply, one.

Domers see themselves as special. They point to their football team's record and rest their case. But Notre Dame fans see the achievements on the field as a collective achievement—all of us. Not just the team and the coaches. All of us.

Central to understanding Notre Dame's infatuation with its own image is understanding Theodore Hesburgh, president for thirty-five years until 1987. He was, no question, a tower of strength and a towering personality. Like all priests, he attempted to create a fatherly air about himself, to be a loving presence everywhere he went.

Arrogance, however, does sometimes seem to come too easily to Notre Damers. Hesburgh, in his book *God, Country, Notre Dame,* describes himself as "college teacher, theologian, president of a great university, counselor to four popes and six presidents." Then he adds, "Excuse the list, but once called to public service, I have held fourteen presidential appointments." He wants us to know he has 122 honorary degrees. His widespread interests meant frequent and long absences from his desk under the Golden Dome. That led to a favorite joke in South Bend:

Question: Do you know the difference between God and Hesburgh?

Answer: God is everywhere and Hesburgh is everywhere except Notre Dame.

When Hesburgh became president, he wrote, "I envisioned Notre Dame as a great Catholic university, the greatest in the world!"

To sit at Hesburgh's knee and listen was a rare treat and a distinct privilege. He was articulate and thoughtful. On one occasion, a writer for *Sports Illustrated* wandered by his office; Hesburgh saw him, invited him in, and went on to discuss eloquently the athletics vs. academics situation at Notre Dame. He discoursed for more than an hour against a backdrop of light snow falling and soft classical music playing on the campus radio station. It was one of those unscheduled pleasures that travels with a person for a lifetime. Asked what it would mean to the school if it never won another football game, Hesburgh smiled and said, "It would mean that we wouldn't be known for football anymore."

Yet Hesburgh found some value in sports and once wrote that they are "a fine training ground for developing character and responsibility in youngsters, which often derives from the character and integrity of the coach and the college or university behind them."

The numbers Hesburgh hung up at Notre Dame are impressive by any measure. While he was boss, Notre Dame clearly was not an institution marching in place, humming softly. Between the time he became president in 1952 and when he left in 1987, the operating budget grew from $9.7 million to $176.6 million; the endowment from $9 million to $350 million; research funding from $735,000 to $15 million; enrollment increased from 4,979 to 9,600; faculty from 389 to 950. Hesburgh was chairman of the U.S. Commission on Civil Rights from 1969 to 1972. He led the charge in 1972 to admit women as Notre Dame undergraduates.

Hesburgh was, and is, a popular figure, in South Bend and everywhere. He declined to be interviewed for this book, citing his concern there would be "negative" aspects about Notre Dame in it.

It was important to Hesburgh, as primary keeper of the Notre Dame image, that it appear that sports were being kept in their place. For example, when the Athletic and Convocation Center was being contemplated in the sixties, Hesburgh said he wouldn't raise any money for it and it had to cost less than the library, which is named after Hesburgh. As it turned out, the Convocation Center cost $8.7 million; the library cost $12.5 million. Hesburgh clearly believed that if he could send a message and portray an image to the public that academics mattered most to Notre Dame and athletics least, then he was successful.

Hesburgh found his most comfortable stance in saying that Notre Dame pursued excellence in all things, and football was one of those things. "We don't want to be third-rate in anything," he told *SI*. And make no mistake that excellence to Hesburgh meant real excellent. He points out in his book that Dan Devine, coach from 1975 through 1980, won three bowls and one national title: "His overall record of fifty-three wins and sixteen losses is not great by Notre Dame standards, but it's not all that bad, either." Five years, three bowl wins—two Cotton, one Gator, and a narrow loss to Georgia in a fourth bowl, the Sugar—and a national title? Not all that bad?

When Father Edward A. Malloy—who played varsity basketball for the Irish 1961–63—took over for Hesburgh in 1987, he said he wanted to continue Notre Dame's emphasis on "top-caliber intercollegiate athletics" while still having its "criteria of proper academic credentials, a high graduation rate, and high standards of personal conduct of the athletes." There's nothing in those thoughts that Hesburgh disagrees with.

However, there are many differences between the two. Former player Kevin McShane considers the two and says, "Father Hesburgh is world renowned. He was in very tight with the Vatican, with President Kennedy and Nixon, and he served on presidential commissions for civil rights. Hesburgh had the talent to be involved in national and world politics and to solve world problems. Malloy is different. He is more tuned in to the student body. He eats and sleeps at Notre Dame and very rarely leaves campus. He doesn't generate the outgoing personality that Hesburgh did. Hesburgh seemed to be bearing the weight of the Catholic institution of the country. He was serving on all these councils. Malloy is more concerned about those few acres in South Bend, Indiana."

In a pamphlet titled "Notre Dame: The Unfolding Vision," Malloy demonstrates his ability, however, to be fully attuned to the importance of image: "The vision was born when Notre Dame's founder, Holy Cross priest Father Edward Sorin, took possession of a single log cabin on a snow-covered lakeshore and dared to call it a university. It would be several decades before Notre Dame would deserve that designation, but Sorin's example—set no modest goals, but pursue greatness—would become the University's driving force."

In a letter to the authors dated December 17, 1992, Malloy expressed concern over the investigative nature of this book and criticism it might contain. He wrote, "Notre Dame is far from perfect but we do make every attempt to represent the best about intercollegiate athletics and about our academic and religious mission as a University. Lou Holtz has done a fine job as football coach and represented us well both on and off the field."

While Notre Dame spends many of its waking hours worrying about and working on its image, so, too, does Holtz. Understandably, he was pleased when a letter appeared in *Blue & Gold Illustrated*—the quasi-official publication that is itself the best example of image-making extant—from Joe Delutis II, Camp Hill, Pennsylvania: "Lou Holtz epitomizes all the good things that Notre Dame represents. He is a first class coach, but more importantly, he is a first class Christian."

Shawn Smith was stunned by the adulation the Irish football team received. "When you are with Notre Dame, you get all this respect," he says. "I mean, the aura we had. We would just step off the plane, walk through the airport, and wherever we were playing, the whole community was there just to watch us come off the plane."

In Holtz's first game ever as Irish coach, against Michigan in 1986, the Irish lost—and promptly became the first team in the history of the Associated Press poll to move from unranked status into the Top 20 on the strength of a loss.

But Jim Dadiotis, who subsequently transferred to Colorado, says, "When I would go into that stadium, I wasn't just pumped up for that game. I was pumped up for all the games that had been played on that field." Such is the power of The Mystique. In the book *Champions: Lou Holtz's Fighting Irish*, author Bill Bilinski writes of the mystique, "The minute you make up your mind to believe in it you feel it."

The mystique, the image, is palpable, and remained so even during the failed Faust years. Anthony Johnson says, "I could have gone to Michigan. They were doing well at that time. They were actually a consideration, but even still there's nothing like Notre Dame football." Derek Brown, a tight end from Merritt Island, Florida, whose hero when he was growing up was Pete Rose, agrees and says, "There was just something there that makes you want to go there. You can't put a finger on it. It makes people in awe, I guess."

Ted FitzGerald still gets emotional when he thinks back to going into the locker room before his first game. "I started looking around at all the names of players I recognized from being a Notre Dame fan," he says. "I just kept thinking to myself, 'I don't believe I'm actually here and being a part of this team.' The first time I was walking out of the tunnel and seeing the crowd, I could hear individual voices even though there were sixty thousand people. I felt like I was in a different zone. I was totally out of it. You could have come up and punched me in the face and I wouldn't have even noticed. It was like dreaming."

Chris Smith, a fullback from Cincinnati who played for Faust, is a kindred soul, and he says, "Just to wear the gold helmet and come out of the tunnel is everything that I always wanted to do, and that's what dreams are made of." Mike Crounse has also felt the fire, and he loves to rekindle the flame: "Every time you came out of a tunnel it was a euphoric feeling. I would think, 'It doesn't get any better than this.' You've got the band playing the fight song behind you, and for some reason, in the tunnel when they're pounding the drums, it's like it's going right through you. The energy there is unbelievable."

Others are not so captivated by the Notre Dame splendor. Erik Simien, for one, is candid about his two-year tenure in South Bend: "I never fit the Notre Dame image. I wasn't into the aura."

George Marshall says that "the fans at Notre Dame are very fair-weathered. It's like now they are very spoiled and if you lose or if you tie, they spit on you." Somehow that doesn't sound quite like what Rockne envisioned on a fall afternoon.

Another former player, Jeff Pearson, knows he got caught up in the glitter as a recruit and was blinded. He says that "it was a big deal coming out of Chicago Catholic League to go to Notre Dame. If I could do it all over again, I wouldn't. I went to Notre Dame for all the wrong reasons. I went there for the so-called prestige. I didn't go there necessarily for myself. I went there for my parents, who were big Notre Dame fans."

Of course, Pearson wasn't Little Lord Fauntleroy while he lived in South Bend and was ultimately kicked out. "All I know," says Pearson, "is if something hit the media, the players were fucking wrong. Period. I didn't like that about Coach Holtz. Me and Lou basically got along. I don't have any hard feelings about it. I just think you should go to bat for your players. Don't sell them out to the university. I was suspended by Lou as a freshman for having a beer in my hand when a photographer from the school newspaper took a picture of a World Series party. He made me feel like I robbed a bank. Holtz is too much into image. And the university is, too. Like when Tim Brown [wide receiver from Dallas who won the 1987 Heisman] was chosen for the *Playboy* all-American team, they wouldn't let him go and have his picture taken because they didn't want a Notre Dame player in *Playboy* magazine. Give me a break." *Blue & Gold Illustrated*'s Tim Prister says it has been Notre Dame policy not to let players pose for *Playboy.*

Nobody talks long about Notre Dame before the subject of its arrogance comes up. Sally Jenkins, then a reporter at *The Washington Post,* wrote in 1988 how the Irish "have stepped back into their former persona, the supercilious bullies of college football, the royal family that expects titles and rankings to fall to them in the normal course of a season." She quoted Holtz: "When someone pays tuition at Notre Dame, that entitles them to a national championship every four years. That's the feeling I get."

Former coach Devine is a keen observer of arrogance and sanctimony, which are close cousins. "I don't think," says Devine, "that former Notre Dame players, for example, get any better jobs than anybody else. It seems to me players who played for Ara [Parseghian] and me and so on are always looking for jobs, just like everyone else. But Lou seems to like to talk it up that they do. It's sanctimonious. And I feel that being sanctimonious is almost sinful."

Nothing reveals more about Notre Dame's image consciousness than a shooting involving Mike Crounse. In spring practice before Crounse's senior year in 1989, he was terrific and was named most-improved defensive lineman. Then came June. He was at a bar, Bridget McGuire's, where he encountered trouble—or trouble encountered him.

"It was an authentic gang, a street gang that lives in that neighborhood down there," says Crounse. "I was only in there for about five minutes just to see who was there. I walked out to the parking lot and there was a group of them around my friend Steve Huffman. He was sitting out on his motorcyle and they approached him and kicked over the motorcycle. There was at least twenty of them. They were just looking for fun. That was their thing.

"I walked right out into the middle of it. It just ended up in a big brawl with me and Steve. We didn't do too bad. They were like flies.

They were all over us. Then things started escalating and I was in fear. I didn't know what was gonna happen.

"So I saw another friend standing there. I yelled to him to open the trunk of his car and I pulled out a tire iron. If somebody was gonna stab me, I've gotta defend myself. I just stood there with the tire iron and they kind of backed up in a horseshoe. Then, the guy in the middle just started shooting."

How many times did he shoot?

"I think four."

How many bullets hit you?

"Four. One in my leg and three in my stomach. It was only a .25-caliber automatic. The doctors were amazed that the ones in my stomach didn't penetrate that far."

You'd done a lot of sit-ups, huh?

"Yeah, I was in pretty good shape at that point. A couple of shots in different places could of . . ."

But all the bullets were lodged in your body?

"Yeah."

So that basically ruined your senior year?

"Yeah, but I still played. They released me to do pretty much anything on my leg on the first day of fall practice. So I started practicing right away. After about the third practice, I couldn't even walk. The bone wasn't quite healed in my leg yet."

Then, from Notre Dame's standpoint, the worst happened: a TV crime show in South Bend wanted to air a piece on the shooting, offering a reward for information about the crime. That was fine with Crounse, but not so fine with Holtz and Notre Dame. "They were probably concerned more about the embarrassment," says Crounse. "But to me it was about something that I don't consider to be my fault." Rather than encouraging participation in the show in hopes of finding the assailant, Notre Dame was more interested in protecting its image. Over Notre Dame's objections, Crounse went ahead, and as a result of the show, a suspect was arrested in the summer of 1989.

What all this taught Crounse, he says, is "you're naive to believe you're a person. Once you're on a football field, you're a football player. It's practically a professional relationship. They don't care about you as a person other than what you can do for them on the field."

It's observations like Crounse's that open the door to charges of hypocrisy. In early January 1990, the *Boston Globe* quoted Holtz as saying, "I'm not concerned about being No. 1. My mandate is not to win a national championship. When I went to Notre Dame, I was told we wanted to have an honest program and that we wanted to educate people." Along the same line, Father Hesburgh wrote in his book that the football team normally is back in South Bend by Saturday night "in time to do some studying." But it is difficult for most people to believe Holtz is not concerned about a national championship, or that the players return to South Bend after a game and dutifully hit their books.

Further, the God-is-on-Notre Dame's-side attitude also grates on some. Best example: one year, when the Irish played the University of Miami, whose players have traditionally been beset with behavioral problems, arrogant Irish fans wore T-shirts that said, "Catholics vs. Convicts." For his part, Holtz routinely says, "God does not grade on a curve; do right at all times."

Understandably, there is plenty of defensiveness among Domers. Matt Dingens, a defensive tackle from Bloomfield Hills, Michigan, says, for example, that "Notre Dame is so much under a microscope that it gets a little unfair treatment on trivial things, growing-up type stuff. Like Michael Stonebreaker. He did some stupid things, but none of it was malicious. The auto accident, obviously, was very bad. He hurt himself and he hurt a girl, but then he gets kicked off the team the next year because he had a car on campus." Just to set the record straight, Stonebreaker wasn't merely in an auto accident; he was found guilty of DUI in the incident. He wasn't kicked off the team just for having a car on campus; he was kicked off because driving the car on campus was a violation of his probation after the earlier incident.

John Carney, the kicker from Centerville, Ohio (1983–86), who was drafted by Tampa Bay and then traded to San Diego, also has enormous affection for the Irish, but pushed up against the wall, he concedes, "Notre Dame is not as pure as we like to think or we wish it was, but compared with ninety percent of the other schools, it's as pure as the driven snow."

Jeff Kunz, now a special agent for the Bureau of Alcohol, Tobacco and Firearms, says, "I think it's still one of the best schools for academics and athletics. I don't know if Holtz has put a shadow over it or not, but things definitely changed." However, Mike Golic, who played for Faust before his long NFL career, knows for certain it's Holtz casting a long and dark shadow over what was once the shining university on the hill. "Look at Lou," says Golic. "He is one step ahead of trouble. Anytime things got tough, Lou was out of that place and coaching the next place. I think Lou was good for Notre Dame at the time he was hired because we came off of Gerry [Faust] and a lot of losing during my four years. So Lou was a good acquisition as far as bringing back the winning ways to Notre Dame. I just don't know if Lou's exactly what Notre Dame wanted to stand for it as a coach."

Experience, says Jason Cegielski, who transferred from Notre Dame to Purdue, tells him that Notre Dame's image simply doesn't match reality. "It has just as many problems as any big-time school, maybe more even," says Cegielski. "Steroids. Discipline problems. Look, whenever you take so many guys from all over the country and put them in one spot, there are bound to be problems."

Author Bill Bilinski writes: "It's not about tradition and living up to it; it's about creating it." That's nicely said, and greatly troubling these days to Notre Dame's image-conscious insiders. Clearly, the question facing the whole of Notre Dame is whether Lou Holtz is creating tradition, and if so, what kind of tradition.

Even those who are not certain that the image is deteriorating are wondering whether the school's approach to football hasn't changed. Mark Nigro says, "You'd like to think not, but it looks like it has. If you can graduate kids and get them to contribute to the community, I guess I'd have no problem with that. I would not want to see Notre Dame be used as a proving ground for professional athletes. There always used to be the Notre Dame community and the academic community there to check and balance the athletics."

Nigro says he wonders if that's still the case.

CHAPTER 5

Gerry Faust: Good Guy, Better Guy, Best Guy

He was the high school football coach with the best record in the country, and Ned [Father Joyce] and I thought it was worth taking a chance on him.

—Former Notre Dame president
Hesburgh, writing about Gerry Faust

Say hello to Gerry Faust, the coach right out of Central Casting who, as it turns out, was perfectly miscast as head football coach from 1981–85.

There is no way to overestimate Gerry Faust's role in the Notre Dame decision to hire Holtz. It is huge. If Faust hadn't been at Notre Dame, Holtz never would have been.

That Faust was selected for the most storied and honored job in collegiate sport is a decision that makes the mind reel. He was a high school coach. Period. Faust had no collegiate experience unless you count watching games on TV. He did put up incredible numbers as coach of Cincinnati's Moeller High School for twenty-one years: his record was 174-17-2; between 1975 and 1980, his record was 71-1; more than three hundred of his players received college football schol-

arships; he once had a 37-game winning streak; he posted nine undefeated seasons, five state championships, and in his own book claims
four mythical national championships.

Impressive—if you're looking for a high school coach.

One day not long ago, Faust was waving his hands and shouting in
his hoarse voice—he always waves his hands and shouts in his always
hoarse voice—in his office at the University of Akron. He became head
coach there in 1986. Behind him is a sign: "A man never stands taller
than when he is on his knees."

And that, more than anything, goes to the heart and to the core of
this eminently decent man. Faust seems always to be on his knees, if
not in prayer—one of his favorite pastimes—then having been battered
into that position by his critics. But before large amounts of the blame
are put at Faust's doorstep, as they will be because they deserve to be,
don't ever forget that Gerry Faust embodies all the qualities Notre
Dame says it wants in its football coach: decency, honesty, integrity,
piety. Every mother in America would want her son to play for Gerry
Faust. Fathers generally wouldn't, because they are more into winning.

This is no small point in Faust's favor. Among coaches who have
plied the trade, most would be hard-pressed to name a more decent
coach in the history of the game. There isn't anyone who even makes
the cut. Gerry Faust has retired the Most Decent Fella trophy.

Matt Dingens says, "Faust's first concern would probably be what's
going on other than the football life." Offensive lineman Tom Thayer,
who played at Notre Dame and is now with the Chicago Bears, says that
Faust "was just one of the best guys you could imagine. He's like the
male version of my mother—a good-hearted type who cared about all
the right things." And Mark Nigro can't help himself; he gushes like a
teenager over a first love: "As a person, Coach Faust was exceptional.
And he cared about you as a person. I remember that the day I signed,
he sat down and talked to my grandmother for fifteen minutes. He
cared about things besides football. He was head over heels the perfect
man for Notre Dame. He encompassed everything Notre Dame embod-
ied. His priorities were faith and family, and football just happened to
be what he did."

Walk-on player Tom Galloway, a linebacker from Loudonville, New
York, tells a story that describes the Faust character more than a zillion
words. There was a senior on the team, John Wakowski from Buffalo,
who had worked hard for four years but had never made a traveling
squad. For a marginal player, just getting to go with the guys on the

bus or the plane to an away game is reward enough for spending endless boiling days under the August sun in South Bend and enduring the raging wind and cold and snows of November. Recalls Galloway, "A couple of this guy's roommates went to Coach Faust and said, 'Is there any way he can maybe travel with us?' And Coach Faust paid for that trip for John to the Meadowlands out of his own pocket. Nobody knows that, but everybody knew Coach Faust was a great guy." Says David Rosenberg, "I don't know if there can be that nice of a guy as a football coach. He's a very, very nice guy."

Faust overflows with decency. It runs out of his pores. You can damn near see it, like sweat. One star player—whom Faust refuses to name for the record—had a nervous breakdown because of the pressure of Notre Dame football and was institutionalized for a time. Faust hid this information from the media and feels it was justified. "Frankly," he says, "I don't think any coach wants to deal with the press. But I do believe that life is too short to shortchange a kid, and that's what I didn't want to do in this case." Faust says the former player is fine, now.

Shame on Faust, for being deceptive with the press. Shame on the press, for being hoodwinked. Shame on Notre Dame for allowing the cover-up. But, doggone it, hooray for Gerry Faust, who did it out of decency. That doesn't make him a terrible person in a too often crummy world.

Faust's problems erupted when it came to coaching the Irish. He couldn't. Too harsh? Nope. Faust even admits to it himself, sort of: "I don't know if I will ever be considered a great college coach. What's important is that I treat people right for the right reasons." Hesburgh once mused, "I think he should have been a priest."

Possibly anything except a football coach. Once, after Michigan had thrashed and trashed Notre Dame, former Wolverine boss Bo Schembechler was finally alone in the locker room. Having praised the Irish effort, blah, blah, blah, to the hordes of reporters who had by now taken their leave, Bo was finally free to confide the truth. "That," Bo snorted in disdain, "was the worst-prepared football team I have ever played against." Bo sneered in disgust. He thought the Irish play-calling was weak, intensity lacking, fundamentals of blocking and tackling in need of a lot of work. Even Faust concedes, "There were some dumb things I did."

Often, Faust would be his worst on the sidelines—which is, of course, precisely the spot and time when a coach needs to be at his best. "Whenever a situation came and there was a close score, you could just see the pressure taking over," recalls Ted FitzGerald. "It was more panic than it was sitting back figuring what do I have to do. It looked like fifty things. I think he thought too much responsibility was on him." A prime example came against the Air Force one year "and we were behind," recalls split end Tony Eason from Snohomish, Washington. "I remember Coach Faust running up and down the sidelines yelling, 'Throw the bomb play. Do we have a bomb play? Don't we have a bomb play?' The players were just looking at each other like, 'What in the world?' He kind of lost it a little bit." But that's Gerry. He is emotional to the core. He is emotional about everything. Say hello to him and he is overcome by your salutation.

Still, by getting so worked up over everything, his thinking often was clouded. For example, former defensive back Aaron Robb from Coeur d'Alene, Idaho, says that at another Air Force game, at Colorado Springs, jets were flying in the pregame show. Screamed Faust to his players, "They're trying to intimidate us with these planes, and they're not going to do it." It made no difference that the Air Force always has flyovers before games. Always has, always will. It had nothing to do with Notre Dame and everything with its being another home game for a school that's rather proud of its intimate connection to jet aircraft, and where show biz is always the order of the day. Faust didn't quite get it.

Mike Golic remembers how it was with Faust when the Irish were in a difficult situation, say a fourth and one: "He'd yell, 'Say a Hail Mary,' and I'd be thinking to myself, 'God doesn't care if we make one yard. Let the guys on the field worry about if we make a yard.' I'm a firm believer in praying before the game that nobody gets hurt and that you're able to play to the best of your ability; but for a fourth-and-one situation, you don't say a Hail Mary. I never really agreed with that at all. He'd do that and there would be some smirks on the sidelines like, 'Oh, jeez, this is kind of off-the-wall a little bit.' "

But while Golic always disagreed with Hail Mary as a football strategy, he is gentle with Faust: "That was Gerry's way and it worked for him for twenty-one years at Moeller High. I give him credit. He brought the system that he won with at Moeller to Notre Dame and tried to implement it. He tried. I'm sure he tried. It's a shame, because the guy's passion for Notre Dame was unequaled. He loved the place. I love the place. He's a great guy, a good man."

Matt Dingens agrees that throwing up a verbal Hail Mary had "a lot of people rolling their eyes. I think it was a game against Mississippi where we were going for a fourth and inches. He turned around to all the guys that were around him and said, 'Everyone say a prayer for us, everyone say a prayer for us.' Everyone's like, 'Huh?' I was sitting next to Wes Pritchett, who is not Catholic, and he looks at me and says, 'Do Catholics always do this?' "

Faust sometimes displayed an almost comical sense of bad timing. Tom Byrne recalls one instance: "I don't remember who we were playing, but we were getting our asses kicked the first half, we really were. Ron Hudson, the offensive coordinator, came into the locker room and he just blew up. Mike Stock was there, too. He was a receiver coach and he blew up. They were ranting and raving and they just went nuts. The team was fired up. I never saw fire in everybody's eyes like that in my life. They were just screaming and yelling and hollering and people were going crazy. They were literally ready to go out and just beat the shit out of somebody. Hudson punched the chalkboard and put his fist through it. He was shaking. He was going crazy. People were looking at him. It was rubbing off on everybody. Everybody was gettin' real antsy to get out there. Faust saw that and he came running in and he stuck everyone down on one knee and made everyone say, 'Hail Mary.' Just wrecked it. It kind of shot [all that energy] out the window."

What went a long way toward doing Faust in is that the players started laughing at him. If players laugh with a coach, great. If they laugh at him, bad. Ted FitzGerald says, "I remember looking around at the team huddles and people [were] making fun of him, imitating him."

Before the team flew to Hawaii for the Aloha Bowl, says center Tom McHugh from Philadelphia, Faust was worried about the hookers they would encounter: "I characterize Coach Faust as everybody's goofy uncle that they have in their family, who comes over with his shirt untucked and shaking everybody's hand and telling jokes and patting you on the back. So he comes in and he starts talking to us about venereal disease on the island of Hawaii. There's a big naval base and there's a lot of prostitutes around, and he told us, in the way only he can, using kind of run-on sentences and kind of talking like George Bush, I guess, you know how he does it, but this whole thing. He told us to watch out about venereal disease, because [there are] certain strains of venereal disease that they don't have cures for yet, and if you get it, they send you to Guam for life."

Indeed, like the goofy uncle, sometimes Faust would blunder into things that would further dilute his standing with the players. Tom Riley says that before the Michigan game, in his next-to-last year, Faust "was giving a speech about how we'd always remember this game if we won. He said there are things he never forgets, like when Kennedy was shot in Houston. The whole team said, 'Dallas.' He just said, 'Whatever,' and went on." And then there was the time, says Riley, that Faust "brought in this guy and sat us all down in the volleyball court and worked with us on ballet moves. The next year it was a sprint specialist on how to be fast. It was like every snake-oil guy with an idea how to make a team better would come along and Faust would buy in." Trying to put a charitable twist on all this nonsense, tight end Dan Tanczos from Bethlehem, Pennsylvania, says, "I think he was trying to get it together on the run, which is an awful hard thing to do."

Also, when things start rolling downhill, both momentum and force pick up dramatically. In the mind of Jim Baugus, it was "impossible to totally commit yourself to something if you don't know if it's going to work or not. It is kind of like getting married and your partner saying, 'I really like you, but I'm no longer sure I really want this marriage thing.' You're not going to invest in it what you need to, so it's going to fail anyway. I think a lot of guys were just not willing to invest what you needed to win because they knew no one else was and it didn't seem like Faust was, because he didn't seem to be doing the job. He was a great motivator, but I just think he was in way over his head coaching at that level. I think we were outcoached a lot of times—and outplayed quite a few times, too."

Faust was outcoached often. A good example occurred in 1985, Faust's last year, against the Air Force Academy in front of the Falcons' largest crowd ever, 52,153. Notre Dame was ahead 15–13 with just over five minutes left in the game. The Irish advantage was largely because of three field goals by John Carney. Carney lined up to attempt a fourth, a 37-yarder, which was well within his range. But AFA coach Fisher DeBerry had noticed not only that his team had nearly blocked two of the earlier three kicks, but that Faust had not made a single adjustment in Notre Dame's blocking scheme in light of the close calls. Armed with this knowledge, inside linebacker Terry Maki blew in against the same suspect Irish blocking and smothered the kick attempt; the ball popped up in the air, and defensive back A. J. Scott grabbed it and raced 77 yards for the winning touchdown. Final score: Air Force 21, Notre Dame 15. Any one of a number of possible changes would almost certainly have thwarted the Falcons and preserved the Irish win.

A succinct Joe Johnson, a wide receiver from Washington, D.C., says of the Faust years, "Let's just say I knew we should have been winning and we weren't."

Nigro shakes his head sadly and says of Faust, "The will to win was there, but the know-how was not." Matt Dingens feels extremely protective of Faust—most people do—and says, "You can't say anything bad about him other than the fact he wasn't a very good collegiate coach, and that's not the worst thing in the world."

Wasn't very good?

The Irish failed to go to a major bowl, never finished in the Associated Press final Top 20, and never threatened to win a national crown. Faust's five-year 30-26-1 record was by far the worst of any Irish coach since Joe Kuharich—against whom ineptitude is always measured in South Bend—who was 17-23 over four seasons. Faust's record by season:

1981—5-6-0
1982—6-4-1
1983—7-5-0
1984—7-5-0
1985—5-6-0

It's even worse than it appears. For example, consider that Knute Rockne and Frank Leahy, Notre Dame's legendary coaches, coached a combined total of twenty-five years and had a combined 23 losses. Gene Corrigan, AD when Faust was hired, once said to a reporter, "Gerry would say he was a good coach, and I have no doubt he was. But you have to be a great coach to be successful here."

Excellent insight into Faust's problems as a coach is offered by Pernell Taylor, a fullback from La Puente, California, who says, "I don't think the players respected him as a coach. They loved him as a person. There's a fine line between being your coach and being your buddy, and Gerry was just everybody's buddy. There's a big difference. I can't really think of the best thing of playing for Gerry." Tim Brown says, "Coach Faust's biggest problem there was the players got to the point where they weren't respecting him. And whenever you have that situation, you can't get anything accomplished." Linebacker Ron Weissenhofer sees the sunset through different-colored glasses: "He was too much of a rah-rah person. I think he was an immature college coach." Yet, in fairness, dealing with one hundred or so immature college football players can definitely bring out any latent immaturity in any coach.

. . .

So how did Notre Dame end up with Gerry Faust?

Easy. The last coach the Irish administration and fans had liked was Ara Parseghian. All of his winning over those eleven years—more than eight victories out of every ten tries—contributed to the general affection he enjoyed. But, in 1975, along came Dan Devine. Devine is a quirky, maddening, flaky, enigmatic person. Devine, too, is key and central to the Notre Dame saga.

If the problem with Faust was his coaching, the problem with Devine was his personality. As one high-level Notre Dame source once said of Devine's frosty demeanor, "You can catch a cold standing next to him." Hard-line critics contend that Devine, along with former New England Patriots and University of Colorado coach Chuck Fairbanks, were the only two coaches ever to survive personality-bypass operations.

Almost from the day Devine arrived after three highly successful years at Arizona State and thirteen years as Missouri head coach (and four less-successful years as coach and general manager of the Green Bay Packers in the NFL), a lot of Domers just didn't like him. During Devine's waning days, his parking place sign—"Coach Devine"—was painted out and then over with "5 Minute Parking Only." No question, many wanted Devine to back out of that parking place and hit the road, sooner rather than later, today much preferable to tomorrow. The prevalent feeling was that the sooner he saw South Bend in his rearview mirror, the better everyone else would feel about looking forward.

It is easy for Devine haters—and there are many who could never see past his strange ways to his genius—to conveniently forget he won a national championship in 1977. These same people also overlook his six-year winning percentage of .764. But Devine had the misfortune to follow the eleven-year reign (and .836 winning rate) of Ara Parseghian, who has been lionized and elevated to equal status with Knute Rockne and Frank Leahy in Irish history. Indeed, Rockne and Leahy rank No. 1 and No. 2 in NCAA history.

Defensive tackle Mike Golic offers a straightforward appraisal of Devine: "He was very introverted, kept to himself. Maybe he was a little off-key, but who cares? I wouldn't care if my coach stood on his desk in his underwear as long as we won games and obviously didn't do bad things. Dan just didn't fit Notre Dame's mold of a coach."

Overlooked was one fact: Dan Devine was a brilliant football coach. Then-AD Corrigan, who hadn't hired Devine (the late Moose Krause did), sat in his office one cloudy, cold, late-fall afternoon, musing about

Devine; Corrigan, now commissioner of the Atlantic Coast Conference, was never a Devine fan, but he is always fair. He looked up on his wall where pictures hung of Parseghian, Frank Leahy, and Knute Rockne. "The day will come," Corrigan mused, "when Devine's picture will be up there."

Indeed, in one of the finest modern-day coaching jobs ever, Devine cajoled the Irish to a national championship in 1977, despite a horrendous 20–13 loss to lowly Mississippi in the second game of the year.

Devine was so uncertain of his future with the Irish at the end of the 1979 season that this incredible scene occurred: Notre Dame had just played, and beaten, Miami 40–15 in the season-ending game in Tokyo. That left the team with a not-so-hot 7-4-0 record. Devine was sitting in the Tokyo airport afterward next to Father Joyce. Finally Devine blurted, "I don't know where I'm going. I don't know if I should go back to South Bend, if I should go recruiting. I don't know what's going on." Joyce looked surprised and said, "I assumed you knew that you were going back to Notre Dame. You are, aren't you?"

There had been serious dump-Devine chatter at Notre Dame's highest levels, but there never was a consensus. Ultimately, a decision was made by no decision. Still, feeling that he was about to have Notre Dame's welcome mat pulled from beneath his feet—indeed, Devine felt the tugging—he told Hesburgh in June 1980 that he would leave after the '80 season. Devine vehemently denies he was pressured, but he admits he heard the rumors—which he attributes entirely to Joe Doyle, the former sports editor of the *South Bend Tribune*. Doyle and Devine were poles apart.

By the latter stages of the 1980 season, Devine was doing his usual masterful job and eventually got the Irish to a 9-1-1 record. On Wednesday night of the week of the Alabama game, Devine invited a *Sports Illustrated* writer over for steaks and conversation. He was, as much as possible three days prior to having to play the Tide in Birmingham, relaxed and affable. The next night, Devine went over to the campus to talk to Joyce. Rumors flew later that he had "begged" with Joyce to hold on to his job and for his resignation to be declared null and void. Nonsense, insists Devine; he swears that 90 percent of the conversation was about which bowl to go to—Orange, Sugar, or Cotton. (Notre Dame took the Sugar, where it lost to Georgia, 17–10.) He says 5 percent concerned his wife, Jo; Devine wanted to take her on the team plane to Los Angeles for the USC game, but Joyce turned him down, saying Notre Dame had never done that. (Jo took a commercial flight.) The other 5 percent of the conversation, says Devine, "was miscellaneous, but having nothing to do with my job."

Father Joyce supports Devine's description of the conversation and insists that while he understood Devine "was never accepted" by Domers, he would have given him a contract extension. Yet Joyce confesses that he "didn't twist his arm to stay." But the feeling had developed that Notre Dame would win no matter who the coach was, and so the school big shots decided they might as well have someone they liked as opposed to someone they didn't.

At one of the darkest points just before Joyce forced him to go over and wait next to the hangin' tree, Devine asked a friend to accompany him across the street to the stadium, and down into the locker room. There, silently, Devine stood in front of the plaque of the famous deathbed quote from Notre Dame star George Gipp. Devine, eyes glistening, then walked back to his office, solemn and silent. A few days later, it was all over.

Dan Devine loves Notre Dame. Despite being mistreated during his tenure there, and grossly underrespected, the depths of his devotion to Notre Dame are infinite. He now lives in the Phoenix suburbs, and his home—and his heart—are awash in Irish memorabilia. His front doormat celebrates the 1977 national championship. Wipe your feet on it if you must, but nobody can wipe away the memories or the pride. When he refers to the Irish, he still calls them "us."

The hard truth is that Faust was hired by Joyce as an impulse purchase. One Notre Dame insider—who loves the school and who loves Holtz but is too frightened of the power of both to attach his name to his thoughts for this book—says, "Before anybody had a chance to offer an opinion, Father Joyce just went off and hired Faust." The Notre Dame campus was shocked; the rest of the football world felt as if it had been stun-gunned. Everyone kept waiting for the correction that would say published reports of the hiring of Gerry Faust at Notre Dame were in error. Then all would be made right with the announcement that then Navy coach George Welsh would get the most coveted job in college sports; that, after all, was whom God intended to have the job.

It was at best a half-baked decision by Joyce. "He just refused to leave the job open," says the Irish insider. "He didn't want the phone calls, the alumni, the media, the pressure." A few Notre Dame players who had played for Faust at Moeller High School in Cincinnati suggested

Faust to Joyce, and Joyce had generally been impressed with the quality of the fifteen scholarship players whom Faust had sent to South Bend over the years. This constituted Joyce's research. It seemed to be enough that Faust claimed he sang the Notre Dame fight song while riding his bike to and from CYO football practice in the fifth grade.

Understandably, Joyce is defensive about his choice. "His hiring was a reasonable gamble, he was gung ho, he wanted to come," says Joyce. "I hoped he would be as good in college as he had been in high school." Regardless, Joyce says that after he hired Faust, then basketball coach Digger Phelps told Joyce that he "looks like another Rockne."

Ironically, Joyce did toy briefly at the time with the idea of hiring Holtz, whom he didn't know well at all. However, Arkansas athletic director Frank Broyles, at that point still cozy with his coach, headed Joyce off. It was Broyles who, in Devine's dying days, had originally suggested Faust to Joyce.

Faust told everyone then and since that he prayed for the Notre Dame job as soon as he heard Devine was leaving. See, a good guy wouldn't pray for somebody else's job in unseemingly haste.

On November 24, 1980, Faust became the twenty-fourth head coach at Notre Dame. Said Joyce, who was also chairman of the faculty board in control of athletics, "We feel quite strongly that Gerry Faust is the perfect individual to carry on the great tradition associated with athletics at the University of Notre Dame."

Then everyone went bonkers. Welcome to Fantasy Island. Former Navy and Cowboy great Roger Staubach told a reporter, "Gerry Faust is the man for the job." Former Irish coach Terry Brennan, whose five-year record in the fifties of 32-18 got him tarred, feathered, and fired, said, "I'm sure Gerry will do very well." The most embarrassing assessment came from Ohio newspaperman Denny Dressman, who took a deep breath and said of Faust, "He will be the greatest success since Rockne." Another reporter, former *Cincinnati Post* sportswriter Enos Pennington, said, "He is the greatest coach they've ever had. He will coach twenty years, win two hundred games, and die at Notre Dame. They will never want to drive him out." A fellow named Lou Holtz said, "Gerry's an outstanding person and an outstanding coach. I know he's going to do a great job."

Writing in *Sports Illustrated,* the late Ray Kennedy got sucked in, once writing, "If enthusiasm is what it takes to shake down the thunder, then Faust is Thor himself." Then Kennedy went completely around the bend: "Listen up, America, because if Faust's rookie season is anything like his spring debut, you should get to know him before he's canonized for succeeding in the most visible job in college sports." Finally, Kennedy lost it, concluding there is "some very solid evidence that Faust just may live up to his supercoach billing." What, pray tell, would that evidence be on the basis of spring practice? But such was the euphoria that greeted Faust. Then, when he lost four of his first six games, people made excuses for him and agonized with him.

As off-target as the comments and expectations were, it is true that the ecstasy was world-class—except in the mind of Roger Valdiserri, veteran sports-information director and more recently an associate AD. At the time rumors erupted that Faust might be selected, Valdiserri got it dead correct when he grumped, "We're not running a kindergarten program."

Former player Mike Golic, Faust's first recruit, smiles as he thinks back on that heady time: "It was like the Second Coming. Gerry was out eating pizza with the students, playing Frisbee with them. They all got a kick out of that. It started off really good. We were preseason number five, we were called the best freshman class ever to come in, and the first week of the season we whipped LSU twenty-seven to nine. It bumped us all the way to number one. So it's Gerry's first year there and [before] our second game we're the number one team in the country, and everyone thought, 'He walks on water.' We went in the next week and got shelled by Michigan, bad [25–7]. That was pretty much the beginning of the end."

Faust's 5-6 record his first season was the worst in South Bend in eighteen years. Rockne, Parseghian, Leahy, and Devine all won national championships in their third year on the job; Faust was 6-5 in his third year.

The teams were, flat out and case closed, an embarrassment to the Notre Dame football tradition. Along the way, Notre Dame lost twice to lowly Purdue; it got beat by Arizona and by South Carolina and by LSU; the Irish even managed to get tied by Oregon. The Golden Dome still glittered in the sun, but it seemed out of place, as if it were laughing at a funeral. Notre Dame has had just five losing seasons since 1933; Faust had two of them.

Near the end of Faust's days, even the extremely circumspect Joyce took to saying about his hiring of Faust, "We thought we were taking a calculated gamble. You may now underline *gamble.*" Nice line. But Notre Dame does not have to gamble on its football coach. It gets, with very few exceptions, whomever it wants. Joyce took Faust because he felt Faust was the best coach for Notre Dame. Joyce screwed up.

Mike Golic is highly critical of the Notre Dame hierarchy for selecting Faust, who was fully unprepared for the task. "He just wasn't ready, and the administration shouldn't have put Notre Dame in that situation," contends Golic. Explains Chuck Lanza, Germantown, Tennessee, who was on the Pittsburgh Steelers roster for three years, "Gerry was thrown in without a life preserver. It was a sink-or-swim situation. Unfortunately, he didn't swim for us."

A year after Faust was gone, Joyce told the *Los Angeles Times* of being "surprised by the amount of mail he received last season in support of Faust. 'A lot of our alumni thought Gerry Faust stood for all the things Notre Dame is about and that was enough,' he said. 'He did. But we also have to think of our players. They spend a lot of time at football, they take it very seriously. They deserve superb leadership there, just like in the classroom.' " Joyce pulled it off as slick as anyone could, which still left Notre Dame's intent transparent: win. Just like everywhere else.

That, Gerry Faust didn't do.

Faust—ridiculously upbeat these days as head coach at the University of Akron—sits back and reflects: "I had five wonderful years at Notre Dame. I realized that people didn't like me [just] because I was Gerry Faust but because of the position I held. The problem is, you get so idolized by so many people that you get to thinking you are better than you are. But I was so close. In my second year, we could have been 9-1-1 and in the national championship picture. It would have made such a difference. That's how close we were. But then things went so wrong. But that's the way the Good Lord works." This is a perfect example of how Faust—and, be fair, all of us—can rewrite history. Was 9-1-1 a possibility in 1982? Hardly. National championship contender? Hardly. The Irish won two of their last seven games. They were 6-4-1, and fortunate at that. But Faust is not easily deterred. "I would have liked to have done better for Notre Dame, not for Gerry Faust. We lost sixteen or seventeen games by seven points or less. [Actually, fifteen.] Doggone it, we could have been 47 and 6, something like that." True, and up could be down.

More telling is the fact that the Irish only won three games by seven points or less during Faust's five years. Notre Dame, bluntly, just didn't have a stomach for competing. Too often, when the game was on the line, they spit the bit. That is coaching, pure and simple. No coach can do too much about a player's speed, his height, or his IQ. But a coach can and must instill the will to win. Despite being such a physical sport, football is heavily mental.

Pushed, Faust will admit to some woeful performances. In 1982, Notre Dame figured a way to get itself tied by Oregon. In 1984, it narrowly beat a terrifically average Navy team in the last fourteen seconds, 18–17. Above all else, Air Force Academy whipped Notre Dame four of five times while Faust was in charge. The Air Force Academy? Notre Dame, obviously, has far more talent than the Air Force; they are bigger, faster, stronger; Notre Dame players have far, far more time to devote to sport than AFA players. It is not unusual for the Air Force not to have a single player who was recruited by any other major school. Notre Dame players want to be pro football players; AFA players want to be fighter pilots. That's a big difference.

Faust's problems, which is to say Notre Dame's problems, were everywhere. But everyone wanted him to succeed. If Faust wanted success, others wanted it for him even more.

People who should have known better—which includes everyone who understands even the rudiments of the verities in college football —expected too much. So did Faust. He talked about winning national championships. More important, so did they. Too, says Faust, "the last ten years at Moeller had been out of sight. People expected me to do the same thing right away at Notre Dame. I did, too. It was more not knowing what to do in the beginning. I had to learn everything on the run. I didn't have the solutions when things turned the wrong way. I had to make decisions without having experience making them at that level. People say it's not your fault, but it is your fault. I became very humble very fast. I learned immediately I was not invincible."

Still, he was visible everywhere, flapping around campus in his splay-footed way, his shirttail inevitably out, his trousers only generally fitting. Gerry Faust always looks like an unmade bed. That's at his best. At his worst, he looks like a spokesman for the town dump. All of this adds to his appeal. He is warm and generous and kind.

He is also real religious.

Indeed, while it is unfair—and maybe even out of line—for one to judge another on so private a matter as religion, Faust wears it on his sleeve. There is no person on the planet who has ever met Faust and escaped without being God-blessed many times. At the top of the yellow legal pages on which he is always writing, he first writes, "J.M.J." That's Jesus, Mary, Joseph.

Yet, again, Faust doesn't see Faust as Faust is. Says Faust, "I don't try to wear religion on my sleeve. It's something you keep to yourself. I don't want to be hypocritical. To be honest with you, I'd rather that nobody ever know about it." That's just wrong; he wants everyone to know. An Akron player walks in and Faust says, "It wouldn't hurt you to get back to going to church." Moments later, he's talking of a friend at Notre Dame, but can't quite get his name: "It's John, John . . . doggone it . . . John, John . . . I don't know why I can't remember his last name. Gosh, maybe I took him off my prayer list." And a moment later, he is talking of his dark days at South Bend when "I would tell the Blessed Mother, 'You've tested me enough. And I've hung in there.' " At games, he always has a rosary in his left front pocket and he says, "In tight situations, I grab it and say a little prayer."

These days, he admits that what he may miss the most about Notre Dame is being able to visit the Grotto and to have his pick of thirty-seven masses a day. Religion, clearly, is a big deal with Faust. But what he has discovered is that God may not be a Notre Dame fan, and in fact She frankly may not care who wins football games. Faust realizes he can go to extremes. One of his favorite letters came from a fan who wrote, "I'm sick and tired of you making the sign of the cross on the sidelines and not crossing the goal line." Faust should take to heart the words of Frank Leahy: "Prayers work better when the players are big."

John Askin recalls that Faust would be praying at seven A.M. daily. "That," says Askin, "is what the whole basic chore of being a devout Catholic is all about. I remember there would be snow on the ground at Notre Dame and Faust's car would be parked by the lake and he would be over there praying." Kurt Zackrison shares Askin's admiration for Faust's belief: "Gerry is very Christian. He was God-fearing. Gerry had conviction. Maybe if everyone felt the way Gerry did, we could have won a championship under him. The talent on that team, when I was a freshman, those guys were phenomenal." Chris Smith is another in a long line of players with kind words for their coach's religion. Says Smith, "He's a man of his word, true to God. I respected him because he stayed the course, no matter how bad things got."

Another troublesome area for Faust, says Matt Dingens, "was that there wasn't that fear that you could get in trouble. We used to take advantage of it. You know, you're young kids, and if we could get an inch, we were gonna try and take a foot."

Another troublesome area—if you still feel Faust was short on troublesome areas—was his staff. If ever a coach needed an extraordinary group of assistants, it was Faust; if ever a coach surrounded himself with a generally slovenly group of underachievers, it was Faust. Kurt Zackrison sensed that "there was some unrest between the coaches and Gerry. It just didn't seem like there was a whole lot of respect between some of the coaches and Gerry. They may have been a little jealous or envious of Gerry because here he comes from a high school and gets the job."

Tom Byrne agrees and says that among Faust's problems was that he had what amounted to a "mutiny on his hands with the assistant coaches, too. A lot of the assistant coaches recognized that he didn't have full control over the situation. Christ Almighty, if the leader of the pack doesn't have control over the situation, how can you expect anybody else to have control over it?"

"One of the biggest problems with Faust," says Mike Kovaleski, "was when he was up in the tower [that overlooks the practice field], the assistant coaches would say things like, 'Don't listen to him. Just do what we tell you.'" Ron Weissenhofer has a similar take on the matter: "He was always up in the tower, and that's one thing I really couldn't understand. A head coach should be coaching. He was always up there. He never coached on the field at all. Basically, he had assistants who did it for him. A lot of times he'd tell the assistants something to do and the assistants would turn around and be like, 'Fuck him.' The thing with him [was], I don't think he knew how to coach."

Then what happened, according to Chris Smith, is that when the team isn't winning, "you begin to look around and wonder, 'Are we being coached the right way?' or, 'Is this the right procedure?' You could see Gerry aging. You could look in his eyes and not see that same sparkle and fire as when he was first there on campus. That's what that job will do to you." When respect takes flight, the jig is up. By the end, Scott Kowalkowski says that older players told him "no one would even listen to his pregame talks and [no one had] any belief in him."

Smith tries to understand the Faust firing. "I know," he says, "that it's Notre Dame and there is emphasis being placed on personalities and classroom and academics, but in my mind Coach Faust was there to win ball games, and when that didn't happen, the morale of the school, the morale of the entire Notre Dame community, suffered. Notre Dame has a big, big, probably the biggest, football history, the winningest college football tradition in the entire nation. When that doesn't happen, it's just a shame that the coaches feel the brunt of that. That's life."

Good guy, Gerry Faust, with no answers.

So Faust clearly put Notre Dame in a muddle. The school tries to act as if winning is not as important as lots of other things—academics, character, religion—and Faust was making an A+ in each of those. He was everything Notre Dame always said it wanted in a coach. How to get rid of him? In one private conversation, AD Corrigan did finally tell Faust after his third season, when the Irish lost their last three in a row, that Faust might have to consider resigning if he was unable to beat Boston College in the Liberty Bowl. Faust, decent even in horrible times, said he understood and used a line he has used a hundred, no, a thousand times: "I would never want to do anything to embarrass this great university." That crisis was avoided when Notre Dame won 19–18.

These days, Gene Corrigan admits that he was considering sending Faust to Our Lady of the Guillotine—until he had a conversation with Hesburgh.

Corrigan: "Father, I'm not sure it's gonna work out [with Faust] and I'm not sure what to do."

Hesburgh: "Oh, well, let me help you. How much longer is his contract?"

Corrigan: "Two more years."

Hesburgh: "Then he will be here two more years unless he dies."

The former AD laughs and says he immediately called a staff meeting and told his workers, "Coach Faust will be here at least two more years, so let's all work our asses off so that he will be here for the next thirty years."

But from then on the nightmare that was the Faust tenure at Notre Dame grew worse. He would either be fired or he would quit. As his fifth year neared its close, he quit. And even that didn't go smoothly: Hesburgh was in Baltimore for a nuclear-disarmament conference; when Faust called to tender his resignation, he was asked to call back because Hesburgh was at mass.

There was never any question that Faust was done. "The season was a terrible failure," said Tom McHugh. "This was recognized by everybody." Faust made a few futile stabs at acting as if he weren't fired; Notre Dame, of course, was careful to point out that he had a five-year contract and both sides had fulfilled that contract. Trying to grab at any straw, Faust said if he could keep coaching at Notre Dame, he had a whole bunch of ideas for doing much better.

Faust's last team meeting was not memorable. All that Pernell Taylor can remember is that "basically, it was just that he felt that he had a wonderful time coaching for Notre Dame and he wished us all well in the future and basically that he was sad that he was leaving. That was about it." Somewhere, The Gipper was not impressed.

Faust isn't sure what he will do when he is out of coaching, except for one thing: he'll go to every home Notre Dame football game. He can hardly wait. "When I was coach, I'd walk on that campus on Thursday night, see the band marching four abreast to Washington Hall, see the Blessed Mother in lights, and they'd strike up the fight song. I'd get tears in my eyes, and goose bumps. When I'm there, I'm the happiest guy in the world. I was back one time two years after I left, and I got a standing ovation. I said to myself, 'Holy mackerel, what a place.' I mean, I didn't have the greatest record and they treat me as if I were one of their own." And he's right. Whenever a coach is fired, acrimony usually sours things forever. Not so with Notre Dame and Faust, to the enormous credit of both.

CHAPTER
6

New Sheriff
in Town

Coaching is not what you do to somebody but what you do for somebody.

—Lou Holtz

Hiring a new football coach at Notre Dame is an exercise conducted in slightly more secrecy than naming a pope. Everyone looks for puffs of smoke. The waiting is agonizing.

While no one man picks the pope, Father Ned Joyce had almost total authority with the football program—except in rare instances, such as the Parseghian hiring, when Hesburgh would step in. Normally, when it came to hiring a coach, Joyce would bounce the final name off Hesburgh, who, almost always, recited his familiar line: "Just make sure he's clean."

Former AD Corrigan says he assured Joyce that Holtz was clean. Nobody made any great effort to check it out. The feeling that Holtz was clean was based on hope, not evidence. A source at Notre Dame's highest levels says Holtz was asked specifically if there were skeletons left over from his conduct at Minnesota; Holtz swore there were not. End of investigation.

In a letter to the authors, Joyce says, "I was instrumental in [Holtz's] engagement as a Notre Dame coach, and it was based totally on my conviction that he was a man of absolute integrity, which would be the only kind of candidate that we would consider for Notre Dame. I also have evidence supporting this belief." He didn't say what the evidence was—and later admitted in an interview with the authors that he didn't raise the issue of Holtz's character and integrity with anybody prior to hiring him. Added Joyce, "Also, after six years of following Lou's career at Notre Dame with considerable interest, I have no reason to alter my opinion of him as a coach of great integrity."

Roger Valdiserri recalls being at the College Football Hall of Fame some years ago when Holtz walked up and introduced himself. Valdiserri, a Notre Dame graduate, marvels that Holtz "started naming the starting lineups of Notre Dame teams in the forties. I was flabbergasted. 'Forty-six, 'forty-seven, 'forty-eight, 'forty-nine. I thought, 'He knows more about Notre Dame than I do.' "

Somewhat oddly, it was Arkansas AD Broyles who, back in 1982, offered up his own football coach to Notre Dame. In retrospect, that should have been a clue to everyone that the Broyles-Holtz relationship was rocky. It happened when Broyles, then a college football analyst for ABC, was in South Bend to do a game. Broyles walked into Valdiserri's office, closed the door, and said, "I understand this could be Faust's last year."

Valdiserri: "That's the rumor."

Broyles: "You ought to try to get Lou Holtz."

Valdiserri: "Can we get him?"

Broyles: "Lou loves Notre Dame."

Valdiserri: "I'm not sure we can afford him."

Broyles: "Lou does very well speaking. I don't think money will be a problem. Throw his name in the hopper. He'd be good for this place."

Dan Hampton, who played for Holtz at Arkansas, says, "Lou always had his eyes on Notre Dame, even back at Arkansas. This is not a flattering comment, but he's a very driven guy like Hitler was. He wanted to be the biggest and the best, and he could tell at Arkansas he would never be able to recruit well enough to be a national contender."

Corrigan once told a *Sports Illustrated* writer that the most important thing an athletic director must do on the day he hires a football coach is make sure he has a list in his desk drawer, headed by whom he would like for his next coach. Of hiring Holtz, Corrigan says, "I thought he was the best guy to come in and get it going again."

Asked if he, in fact, selected Holtz, Corrigan says, "Yes, and here's what happened. Father Joyce told me, 'Last time I picked [Faust]. This one is yours."

In Tucson not long ago, Joyce was asked who selected Holtz. "I did," was the instant response.

Having witnessed Holtz from afar, Joyce says, "I thought that if an opening came up at Notre Dame, he would be exactly the guy I'd like to have." Holtz further enhanced himself in Joyce's eyes when Lou's son, Skip, tried to get into Notre Dame but was denied admission because of his grades. Skip went to Holy Cross Junior College in South Bend to try to correct his academic shortcomings and was subsequently admitted to Notre Dame. The key point, however, is that Skip's dad neither called nor wrote asking for favors, according to Joyce.

As Skip Holtz had to go somewhere he would rather not have en route to Notre Dame, so, too, did his dad, who had to work at the University of Minnesota for two years before he could get accepted at Notre Dame.

Here's the question, class: Did Lou Holtz have an escape clause written into his Minnesota contract that would allow him to break his deal with the Gophers if Notre Dame should want him?

No.

Never mind that some people say yes. Other people with intimate knowledge say no. Holtz, for example, says yes. He says he was free to leave Minnesota because "the only stipulation we did put in [the Minnesota contract] was if Notre Dame did ever contact me, I would be free to go. They understood that from day one."

It's Father Joyce's story that the Holtz situation evolved like this: As Faust teetered and faltered, Holtz—having just been fired at Arkansas—called Joyce and "asked me if Notre Dame was going to make a coaching change. I told him that Faust had another two years, but he could judge for himself" if the Irish would keep him. Said Joyce, "Maybe there will be an opening." It was at this point—days before Holtz signed up with Minnesota and promised he would be there forever—that the deal was essentially made that would bring Holtz to Notre Dame in two years. That's because Joyce then said to Holtz, "We're very, very interested in you." Joyce says that in this conversation he suggested to Holtz that he "make his acceptance at Minnesota conditional" by having a clause inserted that he would be free to leave early if Notre Dame rang him up.

Interesting, no? It's a done deal—totally secret—that Holtz will be in South Bend two years hence. Holtz is elated, but being a lot of things, including bright, Lou knows the only thing that could scuttle his getting college football's best job would be disgracing himself with too much losing in Minneapolis. From that point on, Holtz was determined to win with the Gophers—their losing being the only possible barrier to his moving to South Bend.

However, former Minnesota AD Paul Giel says that when Holtz signed on, "we had a five-year contract and he said he fully intended to fulfill that contract."

But Giel, forever the good sport, says Holtz did say—but nothing was written down—that if he should ever be in position to be offered the Irish job, he wanted to be in position to "accept or decline it. All we ever said was, 'Well, you've got to give us at least a couple of years.' It just so happened that Faust had about two years to go on his contract, and Notre Dame had the reputation of not really firing anybody but if the contract runs out, they just don't renew it. That's happened very seldom. There was nothing in the contract like an escape clause."

That's what the athletic director says.

Holtz wrote in his own book, *The Fighting Spirit,* "There was nothing accidental about the clause I had put in my contract at Minnesota. When I signed my contract at Minnesota, it included a clause that said I could leave if we had accepted a bowl bid at Minnesota and the Notre Dame job were offered to me."

That claim was in stark contrast, though, to statements Holtz made in a *Minneapolis Star-Tribune* interview in October 1984. Asked specifically about an escape clause in the contract that would allow him to go to Notre Dame, Holtz said, "I never wrote anything into the contract. I never really read the contract. I couldn't care less. They told me the contract was a standard contract they have, and I signed it." Most standard contracts do not contain a Notre Dame escape clause.

Then, in a *Los Angeles Times* interview published after he was at Notre Dame, the newspaper reported that Holtz "still is uncomfortable with that episode, as evidenced by the fact that four times in less than two minutes he repeats these words: 'I lived up to every commitment I made at Minnesota. Everything was aboveboard.' He stopped, realizing he was repeating himself: 'Let's just leave it at that, okay?' "

When it came time for Joyce to move his boy Lou to South Bend, it was not a crafty maneuver because the situation had been resolved two years previous and because, says Joyce, Giel "knew all about the escape clause."

Maybe the best and final word on the clause came from *Sporting News* columnist Mike Downey, who noted Holtz's quip that he told his wife, Beth, that he would never want to be married to anyone else, "but if Linda Evans calls . . ." Downey concluded, "I keep thinking that Notre Dame ought to stick a clause in Lou Holtz's contract that says that if they can ever get Don Shula . . ."

Reviewing his thinking with the *Los Angeles Times* in 1986, Corrigan said, "We wanted an experienced head coach. We wanted someone who wouldn't be intimidated by big bowls, by pressure. We wanted a winner, someone who had worked with college kids. We wanted someone who would wake up the echoes." Had these been the criteria in 1980, Faust wouldn't have qualified under a single point.

In a book compiled by *Blue & Gold Illustrated,* Corrigan talked of the requirements for a Notre Dame football coach and he said that "the most important thing is that the integrity of the man has to be unquestionable." As we will see later, Holtz's integrity was indeed being questioned: Had he been involved in paying players and breaking NCAA rules at Minnesota or not? That's called questioning integrity. Why didn't Corrigan?

Today, Corrigan says that at the time he was hiring Holtz, he was hearing no rumors about any improprieties at Minnesota or Arkansas. If that's right, Corrigan should have visited the Hearing Center. While it is true that back then most of the NCAA's investigation at Minnesota related to basketball, questions were being raised about football, too. Corrigan further admits he had no discussions with Minnesota AD Giel about Holtz—none, on any subject—but he does say defensively that he consulted with Frank Broyles. Broyles? The best piece of evidence in any employment situation is the last employer.

In fact, the Notre Dame inquiry with Minnesota into Holtz gives new dimension to the word *shallow.* It was Joyce who called originally. Says Giel, "Basically, he asked me if they could have permission to talk to Lou. He never asked me any questions about my impressions of Lou, his coaching, his personality, his idiosyncrasies, nothing. Just, would we give them permission? I've had some people criticize me, including some that were close to me, who said, 'Why didn't you just tell Notre Dame to go to hell? We've got a contract here. You can't talk to him.' I didn't go into any emotional speech, like, 'He's just starting to get us turned around. Jeez, Father Joyce, you can have anybody in the country.' I didn't go into any of that."

But Joyce didn't ask any questions about Holtz, about the turnaround, about your impressions of him as a coach?

"No."

Ultimately, the bigger point is if—*if*—Corrigan and Joyce had asked people who knew about Holtz, would they have told the truth?

Father Joyce gets bristly and edgy when it is suggested that his—and Notre Dame's—investigation into Holtz was weak at best. Among Joyce's objections, he says that to probe into such questions and/or suspicions makes for "a bad beginning."

"Isn't it ironic?" Holtz likes to say. "I wasn't smart enough to go to school at Notre Dame, but I'm smart enough to coach at Notre Dame." Further, he likes to say that "I never felt I had a chance because I always thought they hired only alumni." For a man who could name starting Notre Dame lineups back in the forties, it strains reason to think that Holtz was unaware that among the nongraduates who have been coach at Notre Dame are Parseghian, Devine, and Faust.

Oddly, Holtz got the job, as much as anything, because of two snap decisions he made along the way.

One made a big impression on Corrigan. As Corrigan retells it, Holtz was at North Carolina State, where his team had a fourth down and goal on the eight, six points behind, ten seconds to play. The dilemma, of course, was what play to call—sprint-out, option, sweep. Holtz called a fullback dive and it worked. Corrigan loved the call. However much this impressed Corrigan, it shouldn't have. If it hadn't worked, can't you just hear it? "What the hell? Fullback up the middle? Why didn't he run that flood-right pattern that had been working all afternoon? Or at least a power sweep. Anything but the goddamn fullback up the middle." Holtz made a guess—which is a large part of what play-calling is all about—and that time he got it right. This is not evidence of any particular genius; this is evidence of luck.

The other key factor was that Joyce was greatly impressed when Holtz suspended three of his best Arkansas players, including his leading rusher, shortly before the already undermanned Razorbacks were to play overtalented Oklahoma in the 1978 Orange Bowl. Holtz claimed the three violated team rules when they were found in a dorm room with a female student. (See Chapter 8.) Joyce told *Newsday* in 1988,

"When I saw that he kicked those players off his team, I said to myself, 'That's the kind of man I want at Notre Dame.' Even better than that, he won the game."

P. A. Hollingsworth, the attorney in Arkansas who represented the players, is amazed that Holtz's performance at Arkansas, and in particular his suspension of those athletes, was a plus in Joyce's and Notre Dame's eyes: "What he did with those players should have hurt him. If Notre Dame based its decision to hire him partly on what he did here, I'm ashamed for Notre Dame, because they should have looked into the complete circumstances about what happened, to see the real character of Lou Holtz." Hollingsworth was also a Supreme Court justice in Arkansas, having been appointed to the job by then-governor Bill Clinton.

Holtz's appointment was greeted with cascading euphoria. Dick Rosenthal, who became athletic director in 1987 and therefore had nothing to do with the Holtz hiring, nonetheless lost his perspective. He told a reporter, "Honest to gosh, if somebody had an assignment to mold a Knute Rockne and a Frank Leahy, they couldn't have done a better job than Lou Holtz. He is Notre Dame."

Fans generally were thrilled with the selection of Holtz simply because they wanted a new coach. The Faust years had been losers, the Devine years were dour, the Parseghian years too long ago. Lou Holtz looked like the coach from heaven. Fans thought of Holtz as a miracle worker; after all, in sixteen years as a head coach, twelve times he had gotten his team into a bowl game—and getting the likes of William and Mary, NC State, and Minnesota into bowls could be equated with pulling rabbits out of hats. The Magic Man had come to town, an incredible blend of The Music Man and The Rainmaker.

When Holtz was hired, Joyce said, "I would hope that Lou Holtz stands just as much for the right things as Gerry Faust but might also be a much better coach." For his part, Holtz said, "How many people at age forty-eight get a chance to chase their dream?" Then he, accompanied by his wife Beth, flew off to Palm Springs and seclusion in a friend's home to escape the tumult of being named the Notre Dame coach, and to gather his wits.

Faust had quit the week before Notre Dame's 1985 game in Miami against the powerful and talented Hurricanes. The Irish showed up and gave a new dimension to awful in Gerry's last game. They lost 58-7.

The players quit on Faust, they quit on Notre Dame, they quit on themselves. That made their season record 5-6, including devastating losses to Purdue, Air Force, and LSU. Player behavior deteriorated so much during Faust's last year that it was a raging joke. Morale hit an all-time low. During the final Miami game, Cedric Figaro, a linebacker from Lafayette, Louisiana, says, "on the sidelines the guys were yelling at each other. Some guys didn't even want to go in."

The Miami loss, before a crowd of only 49,236 in the Orange Bowl, put Notre Dame at its lowest football ebb since 1963, when Hugh Devore coached the Irish to a record of 2-7.

It was one of those games that was too painful to watch. Those with compassion averted their eyes. Holtz, in Palm Springs, watched the game on TV and repeatedly shook his head at the awfulness of the view. Periodically, he'd inquire as to the name of a player. He clearly didn't want to know the name so he could send a congratulatory note. Miami coach Jimmy Johnson ran up the score unmercifully. Naturally, after the game he said he didn't, but when was the last time you heard a coach admit to such a thing? A loss of this scope is a horrible defeat for any team; for Notre Dame it is unthinkable. Looking back on it, Frank Stams, from Akron, Ohio, who was drafted by the Rams in 1989 and later traded to Cleveland, shakes his head and says, "We went out and they kind of ran it up on us and embarrassed us in front of the whole country, and it really felt humiliating to the players. And we felt bad for the coach because nobody wants to go out like that."

Yet, even in the wake of this humiliation, Faust to this day refuses to point out what a lout Johnson was. "It was okay," says Faust. "He was trying to win a national championship. Would I have done to them what they did to me? Well, I'll let you answer that. I don't have anything against Jimmy Johnson. I've seen him several times since and we have visited. We haven't talked about that game." But Faust does recall that just as the game ended, one Notre Damer advised him not to shake hands with Johnson. "Baloney," shot back Faust, "that's part of being the Notre Dame coach."

That may be the ultimate definition of class. When somebody does something totally classless, respond with class. Nobody does this better than Gerry Faust.

Because of weather problems up North, the airplane scheduled to pick up the Irish in Miami and return them to South Bend was delayed. That left a bunch of badly beaten players and a coach who had just been all but fired in the Miami airport with six hours or more to kill. Mike Kovaleski admits that, almost suddenly, the wait "turned into kind of a race issue." Some of the black players started pitching coins, says Kovaleski. That prompted trouble.

Cedric Figaro quickly says whites were also pitching coins; whatever, Figaro says that Coach Rick Lantz, who is white, came over and said, " 'If you guys had put this much effort into the game, we might have done better.' The guys were kind of loud, they were getting excited, I guess. And he said that and that kind of ticked off Coach [Bishop] Harris [who is black], because Coach Harris said these guys worked hard all year."

Says Kovaleski, "Here we are, we're Notre Dame, we're a football team, and granted, the airport is practically empty, but we take up the majority of this section because there's so many of us. You have to constantly think about who you are, what you are, what you're doing, what you're trying to accomplish. Then we have these guys over there . . . yeah, it's a harmless thing, it's no big deal, it's not gonna bother anybody, but you've got to understand where we'd come from that last week. There was a lot of animosity about the program, about the coaches, about the players. You name it, it was there. We'd just gotten beat fifty-eight to seven and they [the coin pitchers] and a black assistant coach [Harris] are laughing loud. So this white coach [Lantz] goes over and stopped it, which probably should have happened, but that's a volatile action.

"When Lantz went over, it was a typical reaction. 'You coming over here to stop me? What are you gonna do about it?' It was just a bad situation. It wasn't good. It calmed down. All that was, was just a picture of what was going on. That was just one instant of one day that shouldn't have been part of our program."

Unbelievably, an athletic debacle then nearly turned into a human tragedy of the first order. The flight home from Miami turned into sheer terror.

Delays kept the plane from leaving until about two A.M. Mike Kovaleski recounts the trip: "When we tried to land in South Bend, it's a blizzard with snow everywhere and I can't believe the pilots even tried to set down. The plane is about a hundred feet above the ground. We can see the runway lights just kind of glowing in all the snow, and there was turbulence all the way like I'd never felt before. The plane would probably drop literally hundreds of feet in just a split second. It was terrible. The whole way in it was like, I don't know if we're gonna make it or not. It was a white-knuckle ride. We're trying to land and everybody can see the runway lights, and then all of the sudden we pull up and take off again and don't even hit the ground and everybody's like, 'Oh, no, no more of this.' The plane was quiet. You could hear a pin drop."

Split end Tony Eason still shudders as he recalls the flight: "I thought the plane was going to crash because it was such a bad storm. Some people were holding hands. Everybody thought this was incredible. The South Bend airport was closed, but they opened it up for the team to come in. We were bouncing. It was so turbulent for the last hour of the flight. We got so close that we could see the lights and the tops of some trees. And then the pilot starts pulling up. He overshot the runway. I was looking out, and I was almost in shock. Everybody was just scared shitless. It was incredible. Then we pulled up, and we headed into Chicago, and we landed there. I went into the john, and I had to splash water on my face when I realized I wasn't going to die. I heard the pilot say after that that he didn't know if we were going to make it back up." Then Eason laughs when he recalls hearing Faust say to assistant coach George Kelly in the midst of all this, "I've got to find another job."

Says Kovaleski, "After we landed in Chicago, we had to take buses from Chicago back to campus. That was a long ride because there was a lot of snow. The roads were terrible. That took two and a half to three hours to get back. By the time we got home, it was probably nine A.M. We'd been up all night. We had classes that started that day. This was right after Thanksgiving break. We're getting ready to get off the bus and the coaches say, 'Everybody's required to go to class today and be back at the ACC, the meeting room, by like two or three and Lou Holtz is gonna be there to address the team.' "

When Holtz made his first appearance before his new Notre Dame team, the day after the Flight From Hell, Mike Kovaleski says, "He walked up onstage and he just said, 'My name is Lou Holtz and my goal is to lead you guys to a national championship and we can do that. If it's important to you, you're gonna do exactly what I say.' It was like a parent talking to a five-year-old who is disobedient and wants to do his own thing. Sit up straight, tuck in your stomach, stick your chest out, that kind of stuff. Get their attention. It was kind of juvenile, but it hit home. Everybody listened to what the man said. From the very second that he walked onstage, everybody knew that this guy was here on business. Coach Holtz's point was, 'This is where I want to be, this is exactly what I want to do.' It was business. There was a big difference. It was day and night. He laid out his program."

At the meeting starting center Chuck Lanza was sitting in the front row. Says Tom Byrne, "Chuck was sitting down there and he kind of had his feet propped up on the stage. Holtz said, 'Son, how long have you been playing football?' And Chuck said, 'I don't know, thirteen, fourteen years.' Holtz said, 'This will be your last day if you don't get your damn feet off this stage.' It just changed the tone. That was the first thing out of his mouth when he walked in and introduced himself to the team. So people knew this isn't the guy to screw with and it's gonna be different. Simple as that. It really set the tone. It really did. That was never really set ever before."

Never mind that, later on, Lanza put his feet back on the stage again and Holtz spoke to him again: "If you want to be a part of this program, son, you get your feet off the stage."

The image of that first meeting is etched in Ted FitzGerald's heart. "All these guys were sitting in their chairs sideways," he recalls. "Everybody's lounging, hats on, hats turned backwards, faces full of beards. Holtz walks in, and in about two seconds everybody was sitting like they were in church. Sitting straight up, hats off. The discipline and respect he got in about five minutes was just phenomenal."

Offensive lineman Tom Rehder, from Santa Maria, California, who has subsequently been with the Patriots, the Jets, the Giants, and the Vikings, recalls the good feeling the players had about Holtz's arrival: "Everybody was looking forward to it because everybody knew how bad it was, and we knew he had been a winner. Everybody was excited, but we didn't know what to expect. We just knew that he was good and everybody really wanted to win. That's why, I think, he was able to turn it around as quick as he did—because everybody did want to win. That school has a lot of winners. People don't go there to be average."

Offensive lineman Tom Freeman thinks back to Holtz's first meeting with the team and it's all a blur. Says Freeman, "He comes in and introduces himself to us, and then he immediately goes through every play we're gonna run against five or six different defenses. He's up there on the chalkboard going all over the place, and I'm like, 'Holy shit, this guy knows what he is doing.' He knew how all the twenty-two positions should react to a play being run, all these different plays, every position. I just sat there and thought, 'This guy is a walking encyclopedia and he has a photographic memory.' Then he went through what the policy was if you miss a practice when you're going to play in a game, or if you're late for practice, when you're going to play. It's pretty complicated: if you play in a Monday practice, but you don't play in a Tuesday practice, you can't start but you can get in after the first series. Something like that. Miss Monday or Tuesday and you can't play until the second half. It took about twenty minutes for him to go through it and the whole injury policy, and then again it's real fast and we're all sitting there like, 'This is amazing.' I mean, this guy has got everything worked out and I know it, and I walked out and Chuck Lanza says to me, 'This guy knows his shit.' "

Freeman says the Faust-Holtz comparison was stark: "Faust didn't show that he had real control of the situation, where Lou was always in control of the situation."

Heisman winner Tim Brown says of Holtz's arrival, "It's hard not to sound corny or whatever, but it was like a breath of fresh air. Everything was just so different, and he came in with this explosive offense and this take-charge attitude. You know it's gonna be the Notre Dame way or you're gonna be out of here, and the guys really bought into it. It really turned the program around. I think just because people knew that he was confident enough to make the right decisions, or what plays to call. He called every play on offense while I was there." Faust, says Brown, was not nearly so involved.

Nobody who was there that day has forgotten. Greg Hudson, a linebacker from Cincinnati, is still awestruck: "That first speech he gave to us the day he got there was a pretty big eye-opener. He just laid it on the line. He told us the truth. He told us we weren't a very good team. He told us we just weren't playing up to our potential. He told us what was going to change. He said he was going to meet with everybody individually, and everybody could speak honestly to him then. And he was going to turn this thing around. From that point on, it was a winning program."

PART
III

Who Is
Lou Holtz?

CHAPTER
7

The Man

I would like to ask: If you had a choice, would you take a 6-5 honest team with Coach Faust or an 11-0 Holtz-coached dishonest team? . . . Yes, I hope you're all happy. One less Gerry, one more Barry Switzer. Yes, truly a blow against doing things the honorable way.

—Letter in *Blue & Gold Illustrated* from a reader

Who is Lou Holtz?

Those four words comprise one of the most difficult questions in sports.

Lou Holtz is warmhearted and he is mean; he is kind and he is vicious; he is reasonable and he is unreasonable; he is a terrific human being and he is a despicable human being; he tells the truth and he lies; he speaks with total candor and total deception; he is the textbook example of Dr. Jekyll and the textbook example of Mr. Hyde.

If you are ever given a pop quiz on this question and told to respond with one word, let it be this one: *illusionist.*

Whatever Holtz decides to be this moment has nothing to do with what he was the last moment nor with what he will be the next moment.

. . .

For openers, and never forget this, Lou Holtz can flat-out coach this game.

He had a 23-game winning streak at Notre Dame, longest in the school's history. His record in South Bend through 1992 was 66-18-1. The consecutive 12-win seasons in 1988 and 1989 marked the first time a major football school has accomplished the feat since Nebraska did it in 1982–83. Perhaps most impressive of all is that Holtz's 1989 success came against a schedule the NCAA rated toughest in the nation. In eighteen of Holtz's twenty-three seasons as a college coach, he has taken his team to a postseason bowl, and thirteen times his team has finished ranked in the AP Top 20. How do your last twenty-three years measure up to Lou Holtz's last twenty-three years? Depressing, huh?

In fact, the pattern for Holtz is carved in stone. At each of his collegiate head-coaching jobs—William and Mary, North Carolina State, Arkansas, Minnesota, and Notre Dame—he took over a losing program, and by the second year he had each in a bowl. That, by any measure, is a remarkable achievement.

There is evidence of Holtz's ability everywhere. For example, one of the key aspects of a coach's job that fans pay little attention to is putting players in the right position. It's simple in some cases: Tony Brooks came to Notre Dame as a running back and he would remain a running back unless he somehow forgot how to run. Many others are not so simple.

Holtz gets his players in the right positions. Examples:

—Tom Rehder went from being an average tight end to a third-round pro pick in 1988 as a tackle, in one year.

—Andy Heck, from Annandale, Virginia, went from tight end with only sixteen catches in three years to first-team all-American at tackle and a first-round Seattle draft pick in 1989.

—Chris Zorich went from linebacker to nose tackle and a second-round Chicago pick in 1991.

—Frank Stams was switched from fullback to defensive end; in three years, he was a first-team all-American and a 1989 second-round Rams pick.

Ara Parseghian had this same kind of ability. In Parseghian's 1966 national championship year, three of his top defensive players had been moved over by him from the offense. It is the hope of all coaches that a player will bloom where he is planted, but planting them in the right spot has a lot to do with how pretty they end up looking.

Holtz has also built a reputation for having a first-rate offensive mind —partly because he is never shy about putting that theory forward. But that's okay; if you don't point out how terrific you are, you run the serious risk of nobody else doing it, either. Former Holtz assistant Coach Kurt Schottenheimer says of Holtz, "As an offensive coach, he's got the ability to see things and I have no doubt that he is outstanding. He did things with [quarterback] Steve Beuerlein and that offense against real good football teams, always improving his passing game, and later on improving the option game. It was very impressive to me."

With Holtz, says Jim Baugus, "you knew if you went out there and did what what you were supposed to do, you had a damn good chance of winning because you were very well prepared. That was a good feeling."

Tom Freeman has a scholarly thesis on what Holtz did right: "My idea is based on working on my MBA and taking some classes on management, and Lou is a textbook manager. The number one rule that you're supposed to show when you are leading is that you're an expert at what you are doing. That's because if you're an expert, then they know that if they do what you say, they will also succeed."

Former player Bryan Flannery, a defensive lineman from Lakewood, Ohio, is another Irish player who gives Holtz high marks for ability: "One thing that I thought was great that he did was he had his beliefs on how to run a football game. He would show you after every game the things we need to do, and this is what we did, and this is what we didn't do. And the results speak for themselves. He would go over these every time. The little, basic fundamentals he would go over and over and over until people would say, 'Yeah.' Things like the basic areas for winning a game: fundamental football, the goal-line stand, don't give up the bomb, turnovers, lost-yardage plays, things like that. Mental errors, you don't know your assignment. They're very simple, yet they stress it so much. He would pound it into our heads. It goes on for four years. You can see people started listening and they started saying, 'Yeah, you're right,' and they started doing it. And then success resulted."

Father Ned Joyce covers Holtz with adulation: "I think he has a fairly brilliant football mind. He's a real hands-on coach. He's not chairman of the board. He teaches his players that they have to pay a price in order to be good." Hesburgh, in a letter to the authors, wrote that Holtz "is one of the finest christian gentleman [sic] that I have ever met. For example, the last time I heard him speak, he was raising money for the homeless here in South Bend. I also believe that Lou

Holtz is one of the best football coaches whom I have ever known. I don't mean the technique of coaching but in the relationship he maintains with his players—to improve their lives as well as their playing."

Another good insight comes from Ted FitzGerald, who says, "Looking at Lou Holtz, he was always concentrating on the next play. Gerry seemed like he was concentrating on the play before and what had just happened. Faust was always confused. I think Coach Holtz is always looking three or four plays down the road or setting something up, whereas I don't think I ever saw Gerry doing that."

Faust, with plenty of reason to be bitter, isn't. When the Irish went 12-0 in 1988 and won the national championship, the mainstays of the team were players Faust had recruited. Faust waves it off and says, "Lou's the one that taught them how to win."

Kevin McShane thinks part of Holtz's ability comes from the coach's lack of size. Says McShane, "I'm sure, going way back into Coach Holtz forty years ago and his development, he was not very athletic and he was not very good in athletics. So he had to strengthen his personality and his leadership abilities. I think that's why he's so successful today. If he was six-two and one hundred and ninety pounds, he might not be the person he is. I think if you have his kind of physical stature, you have to excel in other areas, and he has excelled in those areas." Tom Riley agrees and says that "Lou Holtz is a classic example of figures throughout history who suffered as a child—he for being small—and developed skills like public speaking to compensate. He probably doesn't realize the image he thinks he projects to people versus the image he really projects."

In Arkansas, former Board of Trustees member Raymond Miller is another in this very long line who gives Holtz raves. Miller says he "is bright. There are not too many minds that are better on the field than Lou's. But I don't know that Lou will ever be happy. I don't know that Lou would be happy having someone to answer to, wherever he is. I think that Lou is basically accustomed to being governed by what Lou thinks."

Having ability and imparting wisdom often go hand in hand, and former Arkansas player Dan Hampton thinks he benefited from both at Holtz's knee. Upon completion of his senior year, Hampton was eligible to be selected to play in the Hula Bowl, an all-star game in Honolulu. Happily, Holtz was one of the coaches. Unhappily, he didn't choose Hampton for the team. Hampton was an all-American, arguably the best defensive player in the country, and destined to be the fourth player taken overall in the NFL draft. "I told him I wanted to go," says Hampton. "Not being selected by him really bothered me for a while, and I figured if anybody earned it and deserved it, it was me. But basically what happened was he took a bunch of guys that were good college players that never had the chance to play pro. He probably felt that I would be able to go and play at the pro level, and he would give these last-year guys something instead of me. I kind of respected that."

Another contributing factor to Holtz's coaching success is that he is a full-blown perfectionist. "Our opponent," says Derek Brown, "was perfection. Holtz always talked to us about getting as close to perfection as we could." Says former linebacker John Foley from Chicago: "Let me tell you about Lou Holtz. You have a meeting at two P.M., you better be there at one fifty-five. Because if you come at one minute after two or three seconds after two, that's as good as being four hours late. You got your ass reamed."

Says Ted FitzGerald, "Holtz was in the huddle. You were so nervous. You wear Adidas shoes because that's the shoes he chose. You have to line up with the three stripes on your shoes lined up with the three stripes on the guy's shoes next to you in the huddle. If you don't do it, you run. It's one of those discipline things he does in the beginning of the year." For Jeff Pearson, a key recollection is that "Holtz started with the little things and he carried it on over. All the way from two-foot splits to three-foot splits. Periodically he would come out with a ruler that was exactly two feet long and he would check."

"If perfection isn't your goal, then I think you've got a flawed personality," says Holtz.

On another occasion, Holtz told the *Cleveland Plain Dealer,* "Perfection is the goal at Notre Dame and that's the way it should be."

Because Holtz was so into perfection, it's no surprise that one of his favorite drills was the 99-yard drill. Jim Baugus explains: "It would be no pads. You would start on the one-yard line and you'd have to run plays until you got down to the goal line. If you made any mistakes, you'd have to come back. You could be out there forever. Or you could accomplish it in five minutes if everything went well. Everyone had to have their steps right. No one could jump offsides, the backs had to do what they were supposed to correctly. Everything had to be perfect for you to get a yard or five yards. They'd gradually move the ball up. It really made you concentrate on exactly what you were doing, because you sure as hell didn't want to get down to the other twenty-yard line and screw up and have to come back. If you really started screwing up, Holtz would take us all the way back to the one-yard line. One day, I think it took forty minutes to do it and that week was when we lost to Pitt. The mental part just wasn't there."

To achieve perfection meant putting a different slant on things, as Bill Bilinski writes in his book *Champions:* "Nice doesn't cut it on a football field and Notre Dame now knows better." Isn't it strange that the fact Faust was a nice guy and treated the players decently probably was, in the final analysis, yet another minus for him? Perfection on the field matters more than anything else to Holtz—more than your grades, more than your health, more than your family, more than your religion. Line up the stripes on the shoes.

Baugus says another part of what makes Holtz a superior coach is that he "always knows what to say. It's really amazing. He definitely makes you want to be your best. I remember when we were doing sprints during summer camp before my junior year and it was hot as hell. We had been at it for two or three days, and everyone was dog tired. So Coach Holtz said, 'You guys do sprints. We're [the coaches] gonna go inside. When you feel you've done enough and you're tired, then just bring it in.' So the coaches walked off the field and we started doing sprints. I just kept doing them and doing them and everyone was dying. Everyone kept sprinting and it seemed like five hours. It probably was ten minutes. Holtz came out and said, 'Come on in.' Then we all came in. I guarantee if Faust had said, 'You guys do what you need to do,' the players probably would have beat him to the door. It's amazing what Holtz can do. I don't know how he does it. But I do know if you could bottle it, you could make a million."

In Tom Byrne's view, Holtz's concept of practice was that he would "just work you to death. It's kind of like breaking somebody down. You break them down and you build them up. You get someone down to their lowest and you build them back up. At practices, you just beat the shit out of each other all day long. You constantly do it and do it until you're at your wits' end with the person across from you. When you got out on the field in a game and you saw someone else across from you, you thought, 'I'm gonna take every bit of aggression I have against the coaches, against the guy I've been pounding on all week long, I'm gonna take it out against you.' Holtz had this uncanny ability to get people at their wits' end by the time Saturday came around. It would just explode."

Falling victim at practice to Holtz's slashing tongue is never a wonderful experience. Pat Terrell, who was a wide receiver when he was recruited to South Bend, but who was having troubles catching the ball, knows. He tells his story:

"Right before the Cotton Bowl game in Dallas, we were practicing and Holtz blew his whistle and was waving his hands, stop everything. I was like, 'Oh, my gosh, he is gonna come yell at me.' But he went right past me and started yelling at Tony Rice. He said, 'Tony Rice, I don't care if Pat Terrell is wide open, take the sack. Take the sack. I don't care if you can walk up and hand him the football. Take the sack.' I remember thinking that I've never quit a sport in my life and I wasn't about to quit, but it was the first time I ever had just given up and I didn't want football anymore. I was walking back into the locker room and Holtz walked up to me and said, 'Pat, we're moving you to free safety.' When he said it, it didn't spark. I didn't really care at that point. I was like, 'Well, I'm gonna work hard because I always give a hundred percent no matter what I do, so I'm gonna be the best free safety I can be.'"

For a receiver to be shunted off to the defense is never a promotion. Yet somehow Terrell was able to dig deep down into what he is and make the best of it. Behind Holtz's painful outburst was a solid football perception: Terrell was ultimately drafted by the Rams in 1990 and has been playing in the NFL and enjoying nice paydays—as a free safety.

Given this fortuitous turn of events, it's not surprising that one of the most thoughtful appraisals of the Holtz style comes from Terrell when he is asked what he would tell players who are thinking about playing for Holtz: "I'd tell them to expect to be broken down to nothing, and to be rebuilt, but at the same time keep your integrity, your personal pride and your confidence. Take some of that with you, because it's a rough road."

One thing about a Notre Dame practice, says Terrell, is "that the talent I saw on the other side of the ball far exceeded any team I ever played against. Covering the Rocket [Raghib Ismail], Ricky Watters, Derek Brown, Tony Rice. That's why Notre Dame is so good."

Thinking back to those days on the practice fields, Jim Baugus says of Holtz, "He always said it was a great day for football, whether it was hot or cold or sunny or rainy. He's a great observationist. He'd say,

'Isn't it amazing that a dog can lie under a porch for two hours and jump up and run after a car and nothing will happen to him, yet we have to lie on the ground for a half hour and stretch before we jog around the field?' "

On days when the offense would continue looking awful with the defense winning every battle, Holtz would start running through players. Recalls offensive lineman Mike Harazin: "He'd say, 'Get out of here,' and he'd put in the next guy in line. I remember one time I was about fifth or sixth down the line and I finally got in there. I was in with the first team and I think I messed the snap up or something. It was my glory, my one play with the starters. Holtz screamed, 'Get this kid out of here. I don't want to see him anymore.' He was really upset and mad. He was just trying to motivate people. But there's no doubt he'd snap every once in a while."

Another practice tool often employed by Holtz, according to Tom Freeman, is that he puts the player in a "humiliating situation. I mean, that's the way he does it. He wants you to get back up and be so pissed off at somebody that you were gonna perform higher than you would normally. It worked. Lou was a tough person to play for. He's extremely demanding. . . . He would motivate you. He'd say, 'You had a shitty game last week, and if you don't improve this week, then you're not playing.' And that means almost everything to you at the time during the season.

"This stuff worked my junior year. But by my senior year, it made me kind of mad. I mean it just insulted my intelligence."

It was Holtz's practice-field awareness that impressed Chris Kvochak, a defensive back from Vancouver, Washington. "He was always aware of what was going on anywhere," says Kvochak. "It was like he had eyes in the back of his head. Whenever he would make his rounds during practice, you'd always have to be on guard, always trying to do your best, because he's watching somewhere. He's going to see it. It always seemed to be the times when you'd let your guard down that he'd catch you."

There were many times, says the Chiefs' Tim Grunhard, "when if you were doing bad in practice, Coach Holtz would take you out of the line and say, 'Hey, we don't have a right guard. He's not good enough to play right guard and we don't need him in the game. He can't block anybody in practice, so we're gonna run the line with four players.' So that left the guy across from you totally unblocked, making the tackle on the running back every play. Everyone was looking at you and your spot where you're supposed to be, and there's only four guys on the line and the guy runs in there and makes the tackle and Coach Holtz says, 'Well, that's what he was doing anyways, so it doesn't matter if you're in there or not.' That sort of thing. That's the kind of thing that was a psychological ploy for him. He really did it to a perfection and that's his way of teaching. Everybody has his way of teaching and that's the way he did it."

John Carney knew that at every practice, Holtz had a trick in his mind. At some point, he would suddenly call on Carney to kick two field goals. If he missed one, the entire team had to run seven wind sprints; if he missed both, fourteen sprints. The trick was that Carney never knew when he might be called on. It could be today. It might be never. One day, near the end of practice, Carney decided he would get in some running: "I ran a pretty quick mile. Just as I finished, suddenly Holtz calls for me to kick field goals. I run out there and miss two." The team was neither amused nor impressed. Says Carney, "It didn't do much for my confidence or the team's confidence in me, in the short run. But there was a lesson learned. It taught me to always be ready, because there would always be a chance I'd be kicking for sprints. It taught me to be ready to go from then on. I was, and he never called on me again."

Lou Holtz can truly be funny. After one practice, he told reporters, "We looked great against dummies. Too bad we don't play Dummy University." He loves to tell about the time, in 1963, when he was an assistant coach at William and Mary. He desperately needed a summer job even to make ends meet. There seemed to be nothing available. Finally, he secured a position selling cemetery plots, and his wife, Beth, scoffed, "You won't sell anything." Holtz points out she was dead wrong. "That summer, I sold our car, I sold our stereo . . ." Once asked why he doesn't work out, run, or do anything physical like that, Holtz said, "Because I want to be sick when I die."

Each winter, Holtz likes to tell listeners that "I took my flu shot in front of some players and never flinched. Passed out, but never flinched." He is pathetically weak looking (Sally Jenkins once wrote in the *Washington Post* of this "stringy little man"; *New York Times* columnist George Vecsey referred to him as "the wispy little door-to-door master-encyclopedia-salesman") and speaks with that now famous lisp.

Lots of his humor comes from situations that were light-years from being funny at the time. For example, he tells the story of playing Michigan State his first year as coach of the Irish. Things seemed to be in hand when he called his quarterback to the sideline and instructed him to run a play called Right 324 SXP Pass. "I understand," intones Holtz to his audience of automobile executives, "that means absolutely nothing to you. What I did not realize at the time was it meant absolutely nothing to our quarterback, either." The player ran it all wrong, the pass was intercepted, and Notre Dame lost.

If you can listen to Lou Holtz and not laugh, the problem is you, not him. By any and all definitions, he is funny, and sometimes hysterically funny.

Not long ago, he was in Denver to speak to the Regis Jesuit High School Ignatian Dinner. He said he had looked forward to coming to Denver because the weather isn't so good in South Bend; when he arrived in Denver, it was -8 degrees. That got him to telling how it was that Notre Dame ended up in South Bend, where the weather ranges from atrocious to worse. He says the Catholic priests were on their way from Baltimore to San Diego, where they would establish Notre Dame. They were stopped by a terrible storm in South Bend, and the leader said, "Let's put up our tents here and we'll leave when the weather gets better." The rest, as Holtz said, is history.

Then he's off telling this worshipful crowd of some 1,300 ($100 a plate) of a priest who had two parrots, Peter and Paul. All Peter and Paul did was say the rosary. A friend had a female parrot, and she would say, "Hi, my name's Sally and I want to party." In order to expand Peter and Paul's horizons, it was decided to bring Sally over for a visit. She was put in their cage and she said, "Hi, my name's Sally and I want to party." Peter looked at Paul and said, "Lay down your beads. Our prayers have been answered."

Soon he is telling of seeing the all-time Irish speedster, Raghib Ismail —The Rocket—for the first time on campus. Holtz went home and told Beth that he had seen Rocket, a flanker from Wilkes-Barre, Pennsylvania, playing tennis, and he was really impressed. When Beth asked what was so special about that, Holtz said, "He was playing by himself."

Football does provide endless stories, whether real or imagined. Holtz got lots of grist when he was coaching at Arkansas. He tells his Denver audience that after Arkansas upset mighty Oklahoma in the Orange Bowl, a stamp with his picture on it was put out. "I can tell that doesn't impress you," he sniffs, "but it impressed me." Anyway, the next year Arkansas got beat by Texas, and Holtz said they had to retire the stamp "because people were spittin' on the wrong side." That in turn reminds him of his first meeting with Dan Hampton, a huge lineman, who was doing nothing for the Hogs, going nowhere, and certainly was not close to being a starter. Holtz kept asking him what he wanted to do, what would motivate him, what did he want to achieve. Hampton could think of nothing. Hampton shrugged a lot. Finally, a light went on inside Hampton and he said, "Coach, what I'd like to do more than anything in the world is play in the marching band." Since Hampton played the piano, Holtz pointed out that might be a little difficult, but it was a start on goal-setting; Hampton became an all-pro with the Bears in the NFL.

Even by getting the head job at William and Mary—where Holtz likes to say he had too many Marys and not enough Williams—he was way down in the coaching pecking order. And when you are down and hurting and scraping, humor can put up a nice facade. So it was natural that since Holtz knew he could make people laugh, he gravitated toward magic tricks. He learned how to tear up a newspaper and then put it back together; he has done that approximately 40 billion times. Former player Jim Dadiotis is asked about Holtz's weaknesses. "His magic tricks," says Dadiotis. "He just keeps doing the same ones. Yeah, I'd say that's the main thing he needs to work on."

What Holtz learned over the years was that, indeed, style can count for more than substance. "Some football players," Holtz says, "run forty yards toward somebody in five point one seconds and away from somebody in four point three seconds."

In 1986, Holtz told the *Los Angeles Times,* "I'm insecure about a lot of things. That may be why I try to make people laugh." Of course, the humor sometimes isn't genuine. It's playacting. At the core, Holtz is rough. Back in 1988, he admitted to a *Newsday* interviewer, "I'm rather tough and I'm not very popular. There's no doubt about it."

Make no mistake, a key to understanding this enigmatic personality is understanding where his humor came from and how he has figured out ways to use it. Holtz was born January 6, 1937, in Follansbee, West Virginia, and grew up in East Liverpool, Ohio, which, he says, "was on the river except for [in] the spring when it was in the river."

Growing up was not a joyful family time for Holtz. In *The Fighting Spirit,* Holtz criticizes his mother for always threatening to tell his dad about something little Lou had done. And in criticizing his father, who through hard work was able to buy part of the bus route of a company he used to drive for, Holtz uses words that many could apply to him today: "Unfortunately, my father changed in some ways. Like so many others, he had a hard time handling success. Successful people think they become invisible and invulnerable."

Lou went to St. Aloysius Grade School, where he insists the Notre Dame "Victory March" was one of the school's daily staples. Then it was on to East Liverpool High School, where he didn't date much. "Once I had a date for the senior prom," he recalls, "but the girl broke it. I wasn't too disappointed. It saved me money."

He says he graduated 234th out of his high school class of 278, in 1955. What bothered him, he says, was not his rank but that the principal said it was a "rather stupid class." Holtz contends he wanted to go to Notre Dame—"Imagine, I wasn't smart enough to come here as a student but I'm smart enough to coach"—but that because he was a flickering dim bulb, he had to go to Kent State. Kent had an open admissions policy then; for Ohio residents, the only requirements were a high school diploma and a measurable pulse. He shrugs off his academic nonachievement, saying, "I went to school primarily to eat lunch."

At Kent, he continued building his generally undistinguished record. He played football for a couple years, but had no particular accomplishments. Holtz received his bachelor's degree from Kent in 1959. His résumé would do any gypsy proud, yet he had no trouble telling the *Wall Street Journal,* "I'm not the kind of person who jumps from one thing to another." He has had eleven football coaching jobs in thirty-two years. He meandered through the lowest levels of coaching, including the Iowa freshmen in 1960, the offensive backs at William and Mary 1961–63 (he married the former Beth Barcus July 22, 1961; subsequently they had four children, "all boys except for the two girls," he says), the defensive backs at Connecticut 1964–65, then on to South Carolina 1966–67, Ohio State in '68, and finally, he nabbed that first elusive head job back at William and Mary in 1969.

Holtz for years has been telling—and embellishing—the story of when he found himself out of work after a stint at South Carolina. Having plenty of time on his hands, he says he made a list of his goals that grew to 107—meet the president at the White House, appear on the "Tonight" show, and so on. His wife looked over his list and suggested a 108th goal: get a job. He considered that a good idea in view of the circumstances and so he ended with 108 goals. Holtz claims he has achieved more than 80 of them.

Against this ordinary background, it's easy to see Holtz gravitating toward humor. Once Holtz admitted, "Because of my size and stature and the fact I wasn't a very good athlete, if you listed my accomplishments as a person—if you didn't list speaking or coaching—there would be absolutely nothing to it."

Over the years, Holtz's humor has deflected much criticism. Yet, conversely, his humor and his jokes sometimes wear thin, sooner rather than later—not with fans, who by and large would laugh at Holtz if he stepped onto an elevator and said, "Good morning," but with those who matter most: university presidents, athletic directors, assistant coaches, players, and the media. Riding along in a car late one night in North Carolina, he mused to a fellow traveler, "The problem with having a sense of humor is that most people you meet are not in a very good mood." One veteran Arkansas athletic-department official says, "His routine gets real old. He's like a comic who doesn't have new material."

This is Louie One Note. But it's a very funny one note.

So how does Holtz treat the people closest to him, including those he works with? Well, remember, Holtz admits that he's tough on folks.

"I think one of the funniest stories I ever heard was from a graduate assistant," says Joe Allen. "Every day for lunch, Holtz would get a double cheeseburger from Wendy's and it would be with mustard, and it would be $2.48 and he would give the office kid $2.48 to buy it. One day, the kid comes back and he forgot the mustard on it. Holtz threw the hamburger against the wall and stayed in his office the rest of the day. All the coaches were kind of laughing about it.

"There were a couple of stories about his shakes, too. One of the managers got chocolate shakes one time instead of strawberry, and he kicked the shakes and went back to his office. He was really weird with things like that. He was very demanding." Allen also recalls that "Holtz would have six strawberry shakes brought in every game day. That was his thing. I remember [defensive coordinator] Barry Alvarez one time was drinking one of his shakes and Holtz just blew up. 'Hey, Barry, what the hell are you doing? Those are mine.' Alvarez had to put it back."

Treating others without kid gloves can create a ground swell of frowns. Understand that Dan Devine loves Lou Holtz. Holtz, he says, goes out of his way to be kind. Holtz returns his phone calls. When Devine needs a football or some other Notre Dame item for charity or for someone in a hospital or whatever, Holtz has it there the next day. Devine cannot praise Holtz enough for the record he is compiling in South Bend. Lou Holtz does not have a better friend than Dan Devine.

So what does Devine think of Holtz? Devine doesn't squirm: "Well, his reputation with other coaches is not very good. They think he cheats and they think he's hypocritical. They don't think he's a good winner. He's just an unpopular guy. I guess I would say that he is perceived by his enemies as being ruthless and his friends as being determined. Lou's strength is selling Lou Holtz. And the one thing I know for sure is that he can get from here to there as well as anyone."

But so can steamrollers, which operate without wisdom, compassion, or humanism.

A footnote: After Notre Dame beat West Virginia 34–21 in the 1989 Fiesta Bowl to win the first Irish national championship since Devine won one eleven years previous, the coaches association voted on the coach of the year. The winner was West Virginia's Don Nehlen.

Holtz thinks he knows one of the reasons he has trouble with his relationships with others. He once told the *Chicago Tribune,* "I have a real shortcoming, and that is I don't compromise real well. I just don't compromise."

In spite of this, Holtz does have admirers, in addition to Devine. For example, Faust gushes uncontrollably, "He's one of my best friends. God bless him. We call each other and talk about what we should do. Well, really, I call him more to ask him what to do. You have to understand. Lou is different. He talks when he wants to talk. He hangs up when he wants to hang up." Faust laughs. That's okay with him. Then Faust lowers his voice and says, sadly, "I may be the only football coach in America who likes Lou Holtz."

•　•　•

According to the Bible, Joseph died leaning on his staff, and I think the same will be said of me.

　　　　　　　　—Lou Holtz, repeatedly

Nobody truly knows the meaning of being picked on unless they have worked under Holtz. To live inside the Holtz staff is to live in ferment and torment.

From 1986 through 1990, Lou Holtz averaged two losses a year from his coaching staff. Then, in 1991, five left—and arguably, not one left for a better job. By comparison, in eleven years with Ara Parseghian, four assistants left—and not one departed in five years from 1970 to 1974. Says Parseghian, carefully, "He has had quite a turnover in assistants, hasn't he?" And Ned Joyce says, "I'm sorry it happens."

Even *Blue & Gold Illustrated* conceded that "throughout the 1980s, assistant coaches have come and gone from Notre Dame at a disturbing rate." George Williams thinks the short shelf life of a Holtz assistant is because the boss "is a hard man. He's basically a tyrant."

George Marshall says a big part of Holtz's problem with his assistants is that "he has no understanding of respect. I mean, when we're on the football field, he suddenly steps in. He's the smallest man out there. He doesn't hesitate to push a coach aside and say, 'This is the way it's supposed to be done.' Even if it's not. With him blasting an assistant coach, who am I supposed to talk to? It really does take away from their credibility. How am I supposed to listen to him when Holtz is telling him he's wrong?"

Says Mirko Jurkovic, "I know that since I came in [1988], there are only two coaches that are left and a lot of them have changed."

Did you ever see him treat an assistant coach poorly?

"Sure, he yells at them."

Has he embarrassed them in front of everyone?

"That's part of his manners."

Dan Quinn remembers that "during practice [assistant coach Foge] Fazio called some play in the coverage and Holtz came up and said, 'No, no, no, no, that's not what we do.' And Fazio's kind of off to the side listening and shaking his head. Then Holtz said what we had to do and left, and Fazio goes, 'That motherfucker, that motherfucker. I've got more all-Americans and more motherfuckers in the pros than he ever has, and he's coming down here to tell me how to run my defense.' We just kind of all looked at each other, like, Jesus Christ, because he's like almost the assistant head coach. He didn't have that title, but everybody knew who Fazio was. [Holtz] treats his assistant coaches like shit."

Mike Kovaleski says that the first year there Holtz devoted himself, at the beginning, to the offense, "spending time with his quarterback, spending time with his offense to make sure everybody was reading off the same sheet of music. Our record grew to one and four and it was really pathetic for Notre Dame. Changes needed to be made, and Lou started looking at the defense and came over and started spending more time with the defense, and that was probably the beginning of Foge's problems with Lou." Fazio left after just two seasons under Holtz.

Jeff Kunz recalls the time "the defensive line messed up and he just jumped all over Coach [Joe] Yonto. Just went nuts screaming and yelling. He'd just fly off the handle." Erik Simien says that "one time, my coach, Jay Hayes, was doing something Holtz didn't like and Holtz jumped up and pulled him down to his size by his neck. Life's too short to put up with his shit. That's why I think so many coaches leave."

Holtz's attitude toward his assistants borders on imperial. For example, Linc Coleman talks of Holtz riding around "in a golf cart to each field, stopping with his pipe in his mouth, and looking." Says Coleman, "I felt like if you're gonna get on your coaches, you should do that in the office, in private. But he would tear their ass up right there. One time at practice, the defensive linemen and defensive backs or whatever were having a little practice. Coach Fazio was telling the defensive linemen to do one thing and Coach Holtz was trying to tell Coach Fazio to tell them to do another. I don't think he heard Coach Holtz trying to tell him. After the play was over with, Coach Holtz screamed, 'Goddammit, Coach Fazio, I tell you, you listen to me, I'm the head coach here. I want those linemen to do this and that.' And Fazio says, 'Okay, I'm sorry, Coach, I didn't know.' This was in front of everybody. That's nothing for him to curse out a coach in front of all the players."

Matt Dingens says that "Foge did a very good job, but he suffered underneath Holtz."

Therefore, it's no wonder "there were a lot of coaches looking for other jobs trying to get away from Holtz," says Coleman. "Sometimes they'd slip up and say things behind Holtz's back like, 'Oh, that son of a so and so.' Coach Fazio would be the one that would really say things about Holtz behind his back to some of the players. Call Holtz a 'son of a bitch' or something like that."

Fazio, who still wants to coach football and thus is not eager to bring Holtz's wrath down around his ears, chooses his words carefully: "He's demanding, there's no doubt about that."

But former Irish assistant Schottenheimer, who admires Holtz and worked for him at Notre Dame in 1986, gives Fazio low marks for how he handled the abuse from the boss.

"If Coach Holtz did something like that to me," says Schottenheimer, "I tell you what, we would have gotten it worked out right then and there."

You mean in front of the players?

"You bet your ass."

You wouldn't have walked away?

"No, you better believe I wouldn't have walked away. Respect is a two-way street. I mean, you get it and you give it."

What's it like to work for him?

"Tough."

Former Irish defensive coordinator Gary Darnell knows what it's like to experience the slashing Holtz tongue. Erik Simien grimaces when he thinks back to Darnell's troubled days. Darnell arrived for the 1990 season from Florida, where he had built a first-rate defense; in fact, during 1989, when he served seven games as interim head coach, the Gators were third in the nation in total defense. All fall in 1990, says Simien, "we practiced his defense." In the first game, against Michigan, the defense struggled and Holtz immediately told his team to " 'forget Darnell's defense.' So our respect for Darnell was immediately gone." Shawn Smith sees the same abuse. "He was really bad with assistant coaches," he says. "Holtz doesn't know too much about defense and it [the Darnell episode] made it look bad on Holtz, too. But you're a player. What could you do? Holtz was mad."

In the 1990 Tennessee game, Scott Kowalkowski says that "it was a crucial point in the game just before Rod Smith [a cornerback from St. Paul, Minnesota] intercepted the ball for us to wrap up the game. We had time-out on the field, the whole defense was huddled up, the game was on national TV and the cameras were there, and Coach Darnell was trying to say something to us. Holtz comes in and he says to Gary, 'Listen, you just shut up,' and then he told us what to do. At that point I knew that that was it. Obviously, it has an effect on you mentally and the respect you have for a coach and the confidence you have in a coach. If the head coach doesn't believe in an assistant coach, how can the players? Something like this takes away the team's energy."

All of this is not to say that Darnell was blameless. At *Blue & Gold Illustrated,* editor Tim Prister wrote that "the defense under coordinator Gary Darnell was abysmal in 1991. No lead was big enough with a defense that allowed 205 yards rushing per game and couldn't generate a pass rush under any circumstances." Giving up 42 points to Hawaii in 1991's last game doesn't look good on anybody's résumé. Yet Darnell had done extremely well in Florida, and the Gators play the same level of big-time football that the Irish do. So what happened?

Darnell says he feels he shouldn't comment on his situation with

Holtz. But those who know the situation point to two things: first, Holtz was far too intrusive and so the players began to lack confidence in Darnell. Next, Darnell began to lack confidence in Darnell. It's that simple. But anybody in football knows that if you need somebody to coach your defense, and your choice is Holtz or Darnell, take Darnell in a heartbeat. After all, while Holtz has a lot of offensive ability, defense is not his game. It is Darnell's. Darnell is now an assistant at the University of Texas.

Andre Jones, who hooked on briefly with Detroit, says, "You have so much to do I didn't have time to worry about Darnell. Darnell was like the third defensive coordinator to come through here. I had four defensive coaches my four years."

How difficult is that as a player?

"Damn difficult, because you get coached under one person and you learn his ways, and then you've got to learn somebody else's ways," says Jones.

Why do you think so many assistant coaches come and go there?

"I think the man just demands perfection to the hilt and just feels if he's not getting it, you're gone. That's just the way it is and I think he tells them that up front. But I don't think a lot of people understand that Holtz means it."

James Bobb, a free safety from Port Arthur, Texas, shrugs off criticism of the way Holtz handles both players and assistant coaches: "He's the head coach. He calls the shots."

Another former assistant coach, Tom Beck, who was fired by Holtz, went to Illinois, and then left there in the spring of 1993 to be head coach at a Chicago-area high school, talked to *Blue & Gold Illustrated* for an April 1992 story about Holtz's changing cast of assistants. "This is one situation that it's best I don't say anything. Just clichés. You won't get a lot of people who'll tell the whole truth and nothing but the truth. You're just going to get some things that are safe. If people really told the truth, it would shock you. I'm probably better [off] not saying anything than being dishonest." Asked whether he told Holtz he was dissatisfied with his role, Beck said, "You don't say that to Coach Holtz." Beck told *Champaign* (Ill.) *News-Gazette* columnist Loren Tate why he left Notre Dame: "It was the same reason that nine assistants left Notre Dame over the past two years—and twenty-six over the last six. I was the quasi-coordinator at Notre Dame. Holtz coordinates the offense, the defense, and the special teams." *Blue & Gold Illustrated* says, in fact, there were sixteen, not twenty-six, coaching changes over six years. Beck declined to discuss Holtz for this book.

In 1984 and '85, Larry Beckish was offensive coordinator at Minnesota under Holtz. He was subsequently out of coaching for three years —he tried to survive when nobody would hire him by marketing a quarterback training tape for high school coaches—before being hired at Ole Miss prior to the 1992 season. Beckish calls himself one of Holtz's best friends. Yet, when asked to comment on Holtz, he said, "There ain't nothin' to say."

Don Lindsey, who once was assistant head coach and defensive coordinator for Holtz at Arkansas, says that "Lou can be very persuasive and convincing, both ways. By that, I mean he can be convincing in an uplifting way or he can be convincing when he is putting you in your place."

Now an assistant at USC under coach John Robinson, Lindsey quit in protest when Holtz, near the end of his stormy reign in Arkansas, summarily fired two of Lindsey's defensive coaches, Rich Olson and Harvey Hampton. Lindsey, a Holtz admirer, says that "it just blew me away when he flat out fired two coaches without discussing it with me." Understand that Lindsey is the first person to agree that Holtz was the boss and if he wanted to outfit the team in flowered tutus and matching beanies and send them out against Texas, he could do that. It's just that Lindsey felt, correctly, that he should have had some input into the decision.

The talented Lindsey insists that "Lou Holtz's professionalism is top of the line," but that particular action tore at Lindsey's concept of team play and working together. He says, "I am most interested in being a part of something, and what happened wasn't something I could feel good about. I thought, if this is what coaching football is about, I don't need it." He dropped out of coaching for a short period.

This, again, goes directly to what it's like being an assistant under Holtz. You get no respect. Lindsey was Holtz's right-hand man; the defense for which Holtz had given him responsibility had the previous year led the nation in scoring defense, and without warning, Holtz cut him out of the loop and sliced him up in the process.

(Rich Olson, one of those fired by Holtz at Arkansas, is now an assistant at Miami. He is one of the nation's top assistants and will almost certainly get a head-coaching job soon. Yet, he is also too concerned with Holtz's power and influence to talk about his former boss. "It just wouldn't be good for me to comment," he says.)

Former player Arnold Ale thinks the turmoil within the assistant coaching staff is caused by the pressure because Notre Dame "is expected to win so many games. Pressure gets on Holtz and Holtz puts the pressure on them." Ale is right; pressure always rolls downhill. Continues Ale, "You feel like you've got to go out there and uphold the tradition. You've got to win national championships every year you go out."

Is that a lot different from UCLA?

"Yeah, it definitely is. Definitely. Out there it's national championship; out here it's Rose Bowl."

Holtz often shoots himself in the foot because of his lack of sensitivity. For example, his offensive coordinator is one Skip Holtz. Imagine the odds against scouring the country for the best possible offensive coordinator, having the pick of almost anybody, and finding that the best possible person is your own son. Skip's background includes two seasons as a graduate assistant at Florida State with Lou's longtime buddy Bobby Bowden, then a year as receivers coach at Colorado State under since-deposed Earle Bruce. Assume your last name isn't Holtz and this résumé hits the desk of the head coach at Notre Dame. What happens?

It is safe to assume, however, that Skip might be the only assistant who won't leave in disgust. The problem for an assistant is that any move away from what is considered the pinnacle of college football in South Bend is a move down, except for a significant head-coaching job.

So, for example, when former assistant Peter Vaas moved to become head coach at Holy Cross, a Division 1-AA school that is a level below more than a hundred major schools, that was not considered a move up in any sense. Darnell went from defensive coordinator at Notre Dame to offensive line coach at Texas; Dick Bumpas from defensive line coach to always struggling Utah State as defensive coordinator; Jay Hayes, outside linebackers and special teams coach to Holy Cross with Vaas, then quickly to Cal as outside linebackers coach. The fifth, Tom Beck, went from Notre Dame running backs coach to Illinois offensive coordinator—possibly a step up, except that he was at Notre Dame and he went to Illinois, which makes it a step down. Then it was back to high school coaching for Beck.

Among the sixteen coaches who left the Holtz staff over six seasons, only one got a clearly better job: Notre Dame defensive coordinator

Barry Alvarez, who was named Wisconsin's head coach. (Jim Strong got the head job at UNLV, and Pete Cordelli, who may have jumped from the Irish staff moments before he was pushed, got the Kent State job.)

Because of the flood of coaching changes, Cedric Figaro says he had three different outside linebacker coaches. Given Holtz's feeling that his assistants often don't measure up, there is no reason to think the revolving door will stop spinning.

Still, while Holtz's relationship with his assistants and other staff is generally poor, it's not entirely poor. One shining star is the offensive line coach, Joe Moore, sixty-one. It was a stroke of genius when Holtz got him to South Bend in 1988. He was a veteran assistant at the University of Pittsburgh, coaching a string of good offensive linemen, many of whom became great. He's crusty and tough and irascible and the players love him. Marty Lippincott rhapsodizes: "Joe Moore could tell you every bar in Philadelphia. He was a drinker, partyer. He's a fantastic coach and individual. They don't care what the fuck he does. One-on-one, every player loves him. When he had to be mad, you didn't get mad at him, because you knew you were fucking up. I always tried to do good for him, but I never started with him, either. Maybe I just sucked." Moore, who developed a great fondness for Greek food while working in Pittsburgh, is one assistant—maybe the only one—who can stand up to Holtz and never even consider folding up like a cheap paper fan.

While most of Holtz's former assistants beg off commenting on him publicly, one who doesn't is Schottenheimer. "I loved working for the guy," says Schottenheimer. "He was tough, he was demanding as hell, but you had your say. If you believed in something strong enough, you could argue with him and fight him on anything that you wanted to fight him on. He appreciated that, he liked that in a coach, and that's what I liked about him. He pushed it and he pushed the players and that's the way you're successful. There are no shortcuts in any business, and college football is difficult. You have to work on the little things all the time in detail. He was on top of those things all the time.

"My own feeling is we probably spent more hours working there than I had to, and there were many times that we stayed later in the evening than I thought was necessary. When my work is done, I'm not embarrassed to walk out the door. But if the head coach wasn't going, I wasn't going either."

Still, even an admirer like Schottenheimer thinks that the revolving door on the assistant coaches' offices whirls partly because Holtz is "not always fair." The key to coexisting with Holtz, even lasting and prospering, is, according to Schottenheimer, self-confidence: "I don't think anybody would ever be disloyal to the man because all he wants to do is win and be successful, and you can't find fault with the man for that. But if you weren't a very confident person yourself, then you can have problems. You better be the kind of coach that you are. Don't always worry about what he thinks all the time or what's going through his mind. Don't worry about whether he likes me or not, or does he think I'm doing a good job? Shit, I'm a good coach, I'm going to go and do my job as Kurt Schottenheimer and appeal to him. If he likes it, great. If he don't, then I'll go and find another job."

Part of the problem is that unless—as Schottenheimer suggests—the offended party draws a line in the sand, the Holtz pattern of behavior will continue unabated. Even though it affected the players enormously, it was hardly the players' place to set things straight. When Holtz was routinely dumping on Gary Darnell, George Williams recalls that Holtz "just humiliated the man and that wasn't called for. I don't think that was right."

Mike Crounse says that Holtz is "insecure in a way. He likes to have control over everything. He wants to be the power figure. I know he's not an easy person to be around, and these guys are there fourteen, fifteen, sixteen hours a day."

How fast Holtz runs through assistants spins Jeff Pearson's head: "Oh, Jesus Christ, it's never his fault. It's always the assistant coaches. He goes through assistant coaches like glasses of water."

Did he treat his assistants pretty badly?

"Yeah, compared to other coaches."

Like what?

"He just talked to them like they were goddamn school kids."

What do you remember?

"I can remember my old line coach, Tony Yelovich, and how Holtz would get down on him and just blow up. 'Jesus Christ, Tony, I told you it's got to be this way,' and poor Tony would not even remember discussing this with him. He just agreed with him."

During halftime of a Michigan game while Holtz was at Minnesota, Dr. Rob Hunter says that the coach "sent [head trainer] Jim Marshall out for a strawberry milk shake. He did it for two reasons: he wanted a milk shake, and he wanted to make sure everyone knew the trainers weren't worth shit." Indeed, he often leaves his staff feeling as if they're not worth, well, much.

This creates discontent because, Hunter says, it dramatizes how Holtz "sees himself as the center of the universe. Lou is centered firmly on himself. He makes sure the light is always brightest on Lou. Now, Bobby Knight is a flaming asshole, but at least his focus is the players."

Says Joe Allen, "When Holtz would tear down a coach or some other assistant in front of you, I just never respected it. I couldn't see it now in the corporate world. Say you are a president chewing your vice president in front of the whole company. No."

Like most football coaches, Holtz is given to expressing himself in language unfettered by concern for tender ears. Unlike most, Holtz lies sanctimoniously about it.

In his book, Holtz notes that the players are not "allowed to use profanity. We are allotted so many words of profanity per team, and I will use our entire quota. Incidentally, our quota is ten words per year." Huh? Holtz has gone way past that before he even settles into his office chair each morning. Or, more likely, even before his head has dismissed his pillow in the morning.

Linc Coleman says, "The cursing got worse as time went on."

Back in 1984 when Holtz was at Minnesota, he decided that one day he would give $50 to charity—diabetes—for every profane word he uttered that day. The reason, the coach said, was "there's no place in football for it." The official accounting wasn't disclosed, but if he stuck to his pledge, the diabetes people would have been thrilled to get a check for approximately $4 billion.

Tom Riley recalls the time Holtz said to an Irish player who was giving him problems, "I'm the best sideline coach in football, and if you fuck with me, I'll ruin you. You won't get a job." Yet, no matter how raunchy the words that spew from Holtz and from his players, he was still able to tell USA Today on August 24, 1990, "The real pressure is when a rector calls and tells you one of your players used profanity."

In fact, Holtz spends a lot of time trying to pretend the Irish vocabulary is up on the curb and not down in the gutter. "Profanity," he says, "is a crutch for conversational cripples." John Carney, however, takes the calm road in evaluating Holtz's profanity: "Sometimes if a coach is very passionate about what he believes, he has a hard time getting across what he means in Sunday school language."

. . .

The crafting of the Lou Holtz image takes almost as much of Holtz's time as coaching. His book, his motivational videos, his public speaking —it all adds up. And the man portrayed in his public utterances is often very different from the one his players see on a daily basis.

"Every time he'd come on TV," says Erik Simien, "we'd wait to see what he'd say next. He'd say anything, if he thought it was what the public wanted to hear. He can manipulate words, make a lie seem like not a lie."

Holtz doesn't sneak his phoniness past the players. A classic example is Holtz's decision to put his son, Skip, on the football team. Skip in no way measured up to the football ability required of an Irish player, yet, suddenly, he was on the squad. Says John Askin, "Holtz told me that Skip would be on the team, but that he would never play in a game and all this other stuff. [Then] the guy starts. He started on the kickoff return team and played in every game. Holtz told us he wouldn't letter. He did. It was bizarre."

Did that cause a lot of friction on the team?

"Yeah, because the guys that were smarter knew right away what we were dealing with. Same ol' same ol'. You're dealing with somebody that is promising something and doing something else. Like a politician."

In California, Joan Quinn, mother of the former player Dan Quinn, pulls nary a punch.

"He's a hypocritical asshole," says Ms. Quinn.

Is that what you think of Lou Holtz?

"Well, let's take away *asshole*. I think he's a real hypocrite. He's very successful, but I think hypocritical would be my main description of him."

What makes him a hypocrite?

"Because he's always saying Notre Dame's so perfect. Put *asshole* back in. . . . He's a cruel, self-serving son of a bitch."

"I think," says Linc Coleman, "that he's a hypocrite because he's always telling you about Christian values and telling us we've got to do the right things—and he does it all so backwards. He's a lunatic, crazy, cursing on the field and in private. He sat there in my house during recruiting and told my mom, 'Don't worry about Lincoln. Any problems he has, I'll take care of them. If he's getting homesick, I'll have him over to the house for dinner. It's no big deal.' No one went out to his house."

Says Jason Cegielski, "When I think of Holtz, I think of him being a preacher such as a Jimmy Swaggart or a Jim Bakker. That's what comes to mind. Say one thing, do another." Mike Harazin saw the same thing. "It's kind of funny," he says, "because it was almost like a dual personality."

On the one hand, Holtz says, "You cannot give me one reason in the world why we should ever lose a game at Notre Dame—not a one." Then, another time, another place, he says, "In some respects, Notre Dame is the most difficult place in the world to win." Then he writes in his book, "Notre Dame is the easiest place in the world to win." So what does he really think?

Too often, the answer to that question is, what Holtz really thinks is whatever he isn't saying. Take his quote to *The Boston Globe* cited earlier: "I'm not concerned about being No. 1. My mandate is not to win a national championship." Why then, just a week later when Miami was voted No. 1 after both teams finished 11-1 (Miami had beaten Notre Dame 27-10 earlier in the season), did Holtz whine, "I have no qualms with anyone picking Miami. But I want them to justify not picking us." *Globe* columnist Bob Ryan pointed out, "Lou Holtz thinks it's very important to be No. 1, which is fine. But in the future, let's leave out the hypocrisy part."

Holtz often speaks with a veneer of modesty so thick and false that you have to go at it with a chisel. Of his own coaching abilities, he says, "I've never won a football game because I outsmarted or outcoached somebody. The only person I've ever outsmarted is myself. . . . I try to keep things simple. I'm not smart enough to keep them complicated. . . . The biggest liability I have is I'm emotional." If you think he believes all that, try to imagine his reaction if someone wrote of him, "He's not very smart, nor has he ever outcoached anyone. His approach to football is naively simple, and in tight moments he gets too emotional." Would the reporter receive a call from Holtz congratulating him for his insight?

Holtz's poor-mouthing sometimes reaches epic proportions. To hear him talk before a game, you would imagine that Notre Dame was about to face the '75 Steelers with a squad recruited from the St. Mary's Home for the Aged and Infirm. In *The Fighting Spirit*, he talks of the Rice Owls as "a very explosive offensive football team." *Rice?* He further says, "I am aware that when I came [to Notre Dame], our opponents were telling prospective athletes we were deemphasizing football. Likewise, I read all the comments about how Notre Dame could never be one of the better teams in the country." Who exactly was saying this? Certainly no one who was paying attention; the hiring of Lou Holtz alone made it clear that this was not the case. And even those who deride the Gerry Faust regime speak of their frustration that he couldn't do more with all the talented players he was bringing in—not that he couldn't get good players to come to Notre Dame.

It's all part of the Lou Holtz image: the more you deny your talents, the more people will praise you for them; the more you talk down expectations, the more you're honored for exceeding them.

The image crafting gets a further boost during recruiting. Early on, George Marshall got a quick understanding of how Notre Dame works: "It's very political, and Holtz is full of shit." Marshall doesn't say this in a mean way, but as if stating a simple fact. And he acknowledges the role the players take in supporting the illusions. "A lot of guys go to Notre Dame to play for him because we [the player hosts on recruiting visits by high school seniors] tell them when they're being recruited that 'Lou Holtz is a great guy, he's like a father, he'll do anything for you. He'll bend over backwards for you as long as you bend over backwards for him,' and all that stuff.

"It's not necessarily something he writes down, and he doesn't send out a memo and say, 'All right, you say these things about me.' But a lot of guys know that for them to have a good team, they have to have good recruits. And if I am going to be a senior and on a national championship team, I want my junior class, my sophomore class, and my freshman class to be as good as they can be. Because when there's more talent, that's more of a chance for me to get a [high ranking]. And you say it not because you want them to come and play for Lou Holtz, but you want them to come and play with you. You want to put as much talent together as possible. We're not doing it for him, we're doing it for us.

"I personally think that Lou Holtz is Lou Holtz. He's just very two-faced. I think Faust was a really nice man, a really good man, but he carried that nice man, good man onto the field and it didn't work. The players loved him, but there was no performance, so I think Holtz gets the performance and he has the public loving him. I respect that. I didn't say that I like him or I want to be around him anymore, but I respect him."

There's no confusion in John Carney's mind about Holtz: "His priority is winning. If he steps on a few toes to reach that end, there's nothing wrong with that—depending how hard he steps on the toes." Indeed, if *USA Today*—the inventor of the short, short, short, short story—were to write about Holtz's philosophy, it would say: "Holtz's philosophy: win."

And, in some ways, that may be enough.

Holtz is not a philosopher, although he tries to create the impression he is. Most of his theories sound like they come out of Chinese fortune cookies, or maybe off the "Regis and Kathie Lee" show. Yet there is a certain charm to what Holtz tries to pass off as his intellect. And, in fairness to Holtz, it can sound a lot more thoughtful when he says it into a microphone than it does when spelled out on paper. Examples:

"Happiness is nothing more than poor memory."

"We aren't where we want to be, we aren't where we ought to be, but, thank goodness, we aren't where we used to be."

"Life is really quite exciting. One day you're drinking the wine, and the next day you're picking the grapes."

"The man who complains about the way the ball bounces is likely the one who dropped it."

"The only place you can start at the top is digging a hole."

On one of his videos, Holtz says:

"In adversity there's opportunity."

"Around every corner is always a corner."

"When we need love and understanding the most is when we really and truly probably deserve it the least."

"Great players come. Great players go. The graveyards are full of indispensable people."

"A majority is one man with courage."

However, people who incur his wrath should never forget that following the 1988 season, he reread Sun Tzu's *The Art of War*, considered must reading for the corporate cutthroat.

Still, the only way philosophy ever sells is if the listener is buying. And Holtz has a definite talent for making people buy.

Tom Byrne is one listener who bought, and he says, "What I tell people about Lou Holtz is, he taught me more about my life after football than when I was there. I've implemented more of his philosophies in my business life. . . . When I left Notre Dame, I did a lot of soul-searching and I took a real hard look at myself, and I said he was right about a lot of things. He really was. There's no way in hell I'm gonna let opportunities like that pass me by again. I'm gonna focus the energies I have or thought I had for football towards my business life.

I'm gonna do the little things. It's the little things that count. I'm gonna be consistent in everything I do. That's real important when you're playing football. When you go on the field, the coach has to know exactly what he's gonna get out of you every time you go on the field. Consistency is key."

When Holtz makes his frequent appearances before business groups, he reduces his philosophy to:

1. "Do what's right." ("It's right to be honest," he offers as a for-instance. Please see the chapters on Minnesota.)

2. "Do the best you can."

3. "Treat others as you'd like to be treated." Then, he promises with a straight face, "These three rules guarantee success."

Then, in his "Do Right II" tape, he dwells on what he says are three universal questions: "Can I trust you? Are you committed? Do you care about me?"

Holtz's players never doubted the answer to the second of these three questions. Their doubts lingered on the first and the third.

Says Crounse, "Everybody asks, 'How is Holtz? He's great, isn't he?' No. He's a prick to play for—but he knows how to win and that's what most everyone is there for. When I was there, I was miserable at times, but he was turning the program around, although maybe at my cost." In fact, Holtz once confessed, "There is no way you can establish a relationship with players on the field when you act the way I do sometimes."

Dan Hampton says, "I don't think there's any doubt he's a very gifted man in his ability to generate esprit de corps, the way that he can inspire young minds to aspire. But anytime his ego would not be kept in check, it would get him in a lot of trouble." Even Hampton, who likes Holtz a lot, picks his words carefully when asked about his former coach: "He's, uh, a very complex guy." Shawn Smith backs up Hampton, pointing out that "when you see TV and they advertise Notre Dame football, it's always 'the Michigan Wolverines meet Lou Holtz and the Fighting Irish.' It's not Notre Dame; it's always Lou Holtz this and Lou Holtz that."

Do you think he has become bigger than the program?

"Yes, definitely, definitely."

For his part, John Foley says, "I was scared shitless of Holtz. I still am. He's a very intimidating man. Lou Holtz is very low-key and kind of keeps to himself all the time. I think it's that control thing. He doesn't want people to know what he's thinking. He doesn't want people to know what he's doing."

No wonder former running back Roselle Richardson—from whom we will hear much more later—recalls his days at Minnesota under Holtz with wonder: "It was like you couldn't really trust what he had to say." Muses former player Tom McHugh, "I wonder who is the real Lou Holtz. I just think he is such a mix of motivator and manipulator, along with being a showman and an actor. I always got the impression that everything he said was for subliminal effect on the players."

Others are not so philosophical. Outspoken Tom Riley erupts on the subject: "Lou Holtz is an asshole. Lou Holtz would use any technique or means he could to win. What offended me most was how he took young guys and played mind games with them. It was like a psycho way of coaching—molding players into one of his machines. It bothered me because he knew we wanted to play so much we'd do anything. He wasn't honest with players. As a football coach, he's a genius. But with people, he leaves a trail of people who've been hurt and degraded."

Marty Lippincott adds a bizarre story of a postcollegiate encounter with Holtz: "I was on a plane leaving South Bend, and Holtz came on the plane and [sat nearby]. I said, 'Hey, Coach Holtz, how are you doing?' And he goes, 'Hey, Marty, how are you?' We had a two-minute conversation. It was an hour and ten minute flight since we were only going to Detroit. We're talking, and then all of a sudden he takes his suit jacket off, sits down, puts the suit jacket over his head and leans against the window. He didn't talk to me for the rest of the flight.

"Maybe he was worn out, I don't know. But would it have killed him just to bullshit about anything, anything at all? But instead, to put his suit jacket over his head? I don't think I felt real bad [about my time at Notre Dame] until that day with the suit jacket. What am I, a piece of shit? Would it have killed him to talk to me for ten minutes—just out of courtesy, out of spending three years with you, to give you an hour? Instead, he just crawled into his shell like a turtle."

John Askin recalls one team meeting when Holtz "went off and said, 'How many of you people have slept with rats and cockroaches and how many of you people have had your own dad pull a gun on you?' I mean, you could tell, there is something wrong with him." Tom Riley remembers the same story and says, "Of course, after playing football for him, I know why his father pulled a gun on him."

• • •

Holtz told the *Chicago Tribune,* "I couldn't describe myself. I'm a very complex individual. I don't think people really know me."

True enough. What they have seen is the work of a master illusionist, with no sleight of hand more important than the way he turned disaster to personal triumph in his first year at the University of Arkansas.

CHAPTER 8

Arkansas: Trouble in Hog Heaven

If the University of Arkansas and its fanatical football faithful wondered what they might be getting into by hiring Lou Holtz as head coach on December 11, 1976, they got their first solid clue on the same day. It was an ugly start to what, seven years later, became an ugly finish in Fayetteville to the iron rule of King Lou.

There was no suspense the day the Board of Trustees gathered to give rubber-stamp approval to former coach Frank Broyles's choice to follow in his giant footsteps. Giant footsteps? That grossly understates. Broyles, who stayed on as athletic director, coached nineteen years at Arkansas, from 1958 through 1976. He achieved a record of 144-58-5, won a stunning seven Southwest Conference championships, and even earned a No. 2 national ranking from the Associated Press in 1964, when the Hogs went undefeated and recorded an astounding five shutouts. Ten times Broyles took Arkansas to bowl games. Actually, he was even better than this, when you consider that in the history of Arkansas football prior to Broyles's arrival, the Hogs had the worst overall record in the Southwest Conference. If Broyles wasn't a genius—and that word is tossed around much too easily, since close inspection almost always spots wobbles in the spiral—he at the very least performed geniuslike acts for the long-beleaguered Hogs.

Who could succeed Broyles? The question was further complicated by the fact that the legend would remain on the scene to be the new coach's boss. But Broyles believed he had found his man, declaring, "Lou Holtz will take this state by storm." Holtz did, too, although storms very often are not things of beauty.

Even though the Holtz selection was a done deal, the university's Board met for more than an hour in executive session in order for Broyles to introduce the new coach. Never was there any question that the Board would offer Holtz the job; the only question was how quickly he'd accept. Not, as it turned out, so quickly.

There was a minor complication to the whole process: Holtz already had a job. He was thirteen games into a five-year contract with the New York Jets. Holtz handled this impediment in a way that would become familiar to the people of Minnesota years later: he lied.

Earlier in the week, when his name first surfaced as the Arkansas front-runner, Holtz flatly denied any interest and said he was staying with the Jets to "honor my commitment." The next day, Holtz said he awakened with the feeling he shouldn't be coaching professional football. His commitment quickly fell by the wayside and Holtz resigned— with one game still left to play in that miserable 3-11 season for the Joe Namath–led Jets.

"He told me often how disappointed he was that it didn't work for him in New York," says the Arkansas superbooster Pat Wilson, who became one of Holtz's closest friends. "The fact about Lou Holtz is Lou Holtz is not a coach. In reality, he should not be called a coach. He's a teacher. That's his forte. That's what he wants to do, and you can't do that in the pros. They already think they know more than you do because they get these high salaries and they don't want anybody telling them what to do. That's what he felt, anyway."

The Board meeting was scheduled for nine A.M., but treacherous weather closed the Fayetteville airport and several trustees couldn't fly in, so the meeting was rescheduled for two P.M. At two-thirty P.M., the Board went into executive session to talk to Holtz. About an hour later, Holtz left the meeting and went into a nearby office to make some calls, telling the Board he couldn't officially accept until the calls were made.

Some of the most influential people in Arkansas had to sit and cool their heels for about an hour and a half. Even though Holtz had re-signed his Jets job two days earlier, he felt compelled to tell Jets owner Phil Iselin about his new job before he stepped in front of the media in Fayetteville.

Raymond Miller, a veteran Board member, still fumes when he recalls the scene: "The thing I remember most about Lou Holtz is the day we hired him. It was raining, cold, overcast, a foggy day in Fayetteville, and as he said all the time, it wasn't the end of the world, but you could see it from there. When Lou called Iselin, the guy was asleep and Lou would not allow them to wake the man up. So the whole Board had to sit there until this man could finish his nap before they could put a phone call through to him from Lou. I guess that should have been a tip-off right there. Maybe that was Lou's gentle side. But it wasn't very gentle to all of us who were sitting in that room, who had flown up in bad weather just to do this. Actually, it was kind of rude."

After all the calls had been made and Iselin had awakened and the deal was sealed, Holtz met the press and promised the Arkansas disciples—as he has at every stop in his well-traveled career—that "this will be my final move, the place I'll be happy the rest of my life."

When Holtz took over at Arkansas, he had the good sense to point out there is one person the coach needs to get along with: the athletic director. Holtz repeatedly said, early and often, "It's Lou Holtz's job to get along with Frank Broyles, not Frank Broyles's job to get along with Lou Holtz. My job is to please him. His job is not to please me." In retrospect, that little homily would have been a good one for Holtz to reflect on from time to time.

Early on, people couldn't stop laughing at Holtz's jokes in Fayetteville. He would tell them, for example, that he teaches his running backs, "Just run as hard as you can, and if you keep hearing people cheering, keep on going. If you hear them booing, turn around, because you're probably running the wrong way." Not long after being hired at Arkansas, Holtz said, "If I were ever to leave Arkansas, it would have to be without my family. My wife goes into a state of shock every time she sees a moving van." He once told the *Miami Herald* that he doesn't mind playing in a bowl on Christmas because "after going to church and opening up the gifts, let's face it, Christmas is a very boring day. My family has always lived a thousand miles away—and even when we lived close, they didn't invite us." Asked why his Arkansas players didn't carry him off the field after winning, Holtz cracked, "They're smart. They realize they won the game, not the coaching."

People in Fayetteville were understandably jittery about how long Holtz might stay—after all, this was his ninth coaching stop in just seventeen years—and he did little to ease the situation when he said two years into his tenure, "I made a commitment to our players, and I plan on keeping it unless something happens to change my mind."

Pat Wilson, who lives in Jacksonville, Arkansas, says he recently gave the Razorback Foundation $100,000 for scholarships, "and I've done that several times." He is clearly a man who puts his money where his mouth is. Says Wilson, "I have had pretty good luck in judging people, and I've always considered that one of the strong points of my life was that I was able to judge people. My first meeting with Lou, I was impressed with his frankness, his honesty, and his desire to do good."

The new coach with the quick quip and the desire to do good spent many of his early days in Arkansas convincing boosters that he needed to "take a chance" on some risky athletes. An example of such risk-taking was wide receiver Bobby Duckworth. In his time at Arkansas, Duckworth was involved in a number of incidents: he was given a disciplinary warning for his part in an alleged rape in December 1978, was arrested for another action, and took a "voluntary one-game suspension" in 1978 for violations of team rules. After one of Duckworth's many run-ins with trouble, Pat Wilson recalls, "I said, 'Lou, why do you put up with a guy like him?' He said, 'Pat, I recruited that kid, I went into his home, saw the life he was living, his family values, and it was the worst case I had ever seen. Neglect, you name it. I mean, he didn't have any support anywhere, and I made up my mind if I could keep that kid out of the penitentiary, I would be doing a good deed, and that's what I'm trying to do.' "

Duckworth's football career at Arkansas was successful, though his academic career was far from it. And if Holtz's goal was to keep him out of prison, he was successful only temporarily: Duckworth was convicted in 1992 of raping a woman in San Diego County, and was sentenced to three years in the California state penitentiary.

Of course, Holtz wasn't just trying to help Duckworth stay out of the penitentiary; he was looking for a great wide receiver, and he got one. But his rationalization for recruiting Duckworth demeans the university by turning it into a glorified social worker/baby-sitter. Holtz's words are the classic cry of the outlaw coach trying to build a winning team without being hampered by bothersome academic restrictions.

Holtz, however, immediately had the impact Broyles had envisioned. Says Dan Hampton, "From the first day, he demanded our respect, he focused us, we started working. I thought he was the greatest goddamn thing that ever hit the pike."

Picked to finish sixth in the conference, Arkansas won its first four games, then stumbled 13–9 in a battle with highly ranked Texas. The team didn't fold, though—yet more testimony to Holtz's ability as a coach—and won its next six games to finish the season 10-1 and ranked tenth in the nation. Playing with basically the same team that Broyles had gone 5-5-1 with the year before, Holtz's Razorbacks were selected to play No. 1–ranked Oklahoma in the Orange Bowl.

But as that first successful season wound to a close and the Orange Bowl date loomed in December 1977, Holtz found himself at the center of a controversy that became a defining moment in his career. A woman student told police that she had been sexually molested and raped by several Arkansas football players in a campus dorm room. The next day, December 21, Holtz suspended three of his star players, which precluded them from playing in the Orange Bowl. The three were:

—Ben Cowins, a slashing-style running back who in 1977 led the Southwest Conference in rushing for the second straight year (1,162 yards in 1976 and 1,192 yards in 1977). Cowins, a junior from St. Louis, was also a fine receiver (14 catches in 1977) and a first-rate blocker. Assuming a strong showing in the Orange Bowl, Cowins was expected to be a Heisman Trophy candidate in 1978.

—Donny Bobo, a sophomore wide receiver from Atkins, Arkansas, who led the Hogs in receptions in 1977 with 22, with an average of 20.6 yards per catch.

—Micheal Forrest, a junior fullback who averaged 4.9 yards per carry.

Among them, the three had accounted for 23 of the 43 touchdowns Arkansas scored in 1977.

Precisely what happened in that dorm room will never be known for certain. The victim's identity has never been made public, nor has the statement she made to police.

However, for the first time, one of the suspended players, Forrest, has given his account of what happened that night. In lengthy interviews for this book, Forrest did not paint himself, Holtz, the victim, or the other players as all good or all bad. What makes Forrest believable is his attitude about the event. He spoke very matter-of-factly about the circumstances, remembering details clearly and calmly. He doesn't brag about it and he doesn't try to dismiss it as boys-will-be-boys. In no way does Forrest place himself on the side of the angels.

For openers, says Forrest, it wasn't as if a female student spending the night in a dorm room with a football player was unusual. Explains

Forrest, "You would get up in the morning—the athletes that did go to class—and you would see females leaving the athletic dorms going to class, too."

On the night in question, Forrest says somebody knocked on his door and said that there was "a groupie going on. This was happening two or three times a week in the athletic dorm at Fayetteville. Everybody would go down there [and] if they wanted to fuck or watch or you know, they do it. If not, they don't. Donny [Bobo] had been dating this girl, and so had Bobby Duckworth [then a freshman, from Hamburg, Arkansas]. I guess now you can say it. She was a type of groupie girl. As a matter of fact, [she and] my wife Kim, the one I'm married to [now], they were real good friends. She used to always come home [with us] when we would visit my wife's parents." These family visits continued on in the years after this incident—which would be very unusual behavior if Forrest had been involved in molesting and raping her.

Getting back to that evening, Forrest says, "So several of us went up on the third floor, and when we went into the room, she was laying on the bed or something. So were Ben [Cowins] and Bobo and Duckworth." Forrest describes the scene as involving a lot of joking, kidding, laughing, and—however despicable—business as usual in the Arkansas athletic dorm. Even when the alleged victim picked up a phone and called a girlfriend—"Call security," Forrest remembers her saying, "they are trying to rape me"—he says it was all in "the sense of kidding. Everything at first was like a big game, and then all at once, the next thing we know, the security was there. They rushed her off, and I think out of all of it, the thing that really gets me is that when we talked to her a couple days after this had happened, I said, 'Well, Laura [not her real name], why did you press charges?' She said they called the rape crisis center and Lou Holtz got involved and then her pastor got involved. I guess she was Baptist. She told us all [of] them prayed, and it was like they in a sense forced her to say that we assaulted her. She said that she didn't want to. All of us were such good friends. It was just a groupie thing. Like I said, it was a pretty common thing maybe two or three times a week, players would have a girl in the room and everybody just would come in and have a good time and nothing had never been done about it."

The situation further escalated when Holtz showed up, around midnight, and pounded on the door of the room occupied by quarterbacks Kevin Scanlon and Mike Scott. The trouble had occurred in the room of Trent Bryant, a freshman cornerback from Arkadelphia, Arkansas, and Holtz wanted to know the location of Bryant's room.

That's when, according to Forrest's account, Holtz and the other authorities took the woman and "went and prayed with her." Later on, Forrest says the woman, who is white, "told me that either the pastor or Holtz—I'm not sure which—said, 'Why do you want to socialize with blacks?' " (Press accounts after the prayer session differed greatly from Forrest's version. A copyrighted story in *The Washington Post* said Holtz had cut a deal with the woman, promising that he would enforce the Orange Bowl suspension if she agreed not to press charges. Holtz called the story "unfair," declining to call it "untrue.")

Forrest says, "I'll tell you one thing that really got me to thinking about Coach Holtz. The next morning we [Cowins, Bobo, and Forrest] went to his office, I guess around nine-thirty or ten, and for some reason he made a comment about his wife. Coach Holtz said something like his wife heard about it and 'she was so devastated that she ran in the bathroom and locked herself in the bathroom and wanted to flush her head down the toilet' or something like that. And to myself, I'm like, 'What does your wife have to do with this?' "

Holtz did not let the players give their account of the events, Forrest says; he had already made up his mind. It was at this point that Holtz said he was going to suspend them because of their violation of the "do-right" rule. Forrest says this was the first time that he or any of the others had ever heard of such a rule. It was, according to Holtz, simply a rule that required the players to "do right at all times." And since they had violated a team rule, they would pay the penalty. Although the "do-right" rule was to become a cornerstone of the Holtz coaching philosophy, Forrest was mystified and says, "There was no such thing as a do-right rule. The only do-right rule that I knew about is when Coach Holtz wanted to take action against players, then he would take action that he would feel was right. There was no do-right. There was white players going out and getting into bar fights and arrested and a number of things was going on at the time. No one really was concerned with what was right or wrong. I'm quite sure now if you look back, we should have been, but we weren't."

Anyway, Forrest says he thinks Holtz made up the do-right rule on the spot, but that the further point is that "the girl was never raped." Forrest insists that the goings-on in the room were consensual. And as a result of this common scene, "we were denied the chance to play in the biggest game of the season, as hard as we had practiced and played for Lou Holtz. When this happened, Holtz was not listening to our side and giving us [any] consideration and sticking with us. Instead, he goes and prays with this girl."

Did he ever pray with you?

"No, that's what I'm saying. Automatic, he went on her side. He never prayed with us. He didn't say when we walked in that morning, 'You all, let's all bow, hold hands, and pray.' They put words in her mouth." Forrest says he doesn't know what happened to the woman, "but she's a great person. I totally don't fault her. She got caught up with Lou Holtz and her pastor and they put words in her mouth. She was not going to file charges." Attempts by the authors to locate the woman were unsuccessful.

Quarterback Kevin Scanlon, who had been recruited by Holtz to go to North Carolina State and then subsequently followed Holtz to Arkansas, says, "I'll never forget the next morning when Coach Holtz came in early and addressed the team. He told us what had happened and what he had done. Everyone just kind of sat silent."

Everyone, that is, but Cowins, Forrest, and Bobo. They promptly hired the state's two leading civil rights lawyers—John Walker and P. A. Hollingsworth, both of whom are black—to make their case. Says Walker, "Usually people who are charged with crimes are presumed innocent until they are proven guilty. In this situation they were seen as guilty from the beginning. Consequently, if you want to say there is a do-right rule, there's a competing do-right rule that students are entitled to some procedure for having all the facts fully developed before they are subjected to punishment. And that didn't happen in this case."

Even with the three stars in good standing, Arkansas was an 11-point underdog. Without them, the game was virtually unbetable.

Holtz came up a big winner in the public relations battle. *The Arkansas Democrat* reported that an employee of Western Union in Fayetteville said Holtz received 125 telegrams within forty-eight hours of the announced suspensions, and "99 percent plus" were in favor of the decision. "When this became a national story and when everybody started jumping on the story, then he started being Lou Holtz," Hollingsworth says. "He started wondering, 'How can I come out of this a saint? I want to maximize it.' Holtz is a very ingenious person. I mean, he can take something and steer it the way he wants to steer, and that's what he did. He was good and had a lot of damn resources."

Hollingsworth says that part of the problem is that there was "a lot of admiration" for the football players and so "they could do whatever they wanted. If they would just see somebody, they would say, 'Come on, I want you to go to bed with me.' It was okay. I mean, that's terrible, but that's just the way things were." Hollingsworth says it's his opinion that the woman had sex voluntarily with Bobo. Explains Hollingsworth, "She was very willing to forgive, primarily because she really did care a lot about Bobo. I'm not saying it was any love, but you know how when you are young, she didn't want to do anything to hurt him, and she knew that there were some other players that were subject to being hurt. Bobo was a very bright kid. He had a lot of maturity and feelings about the danger [the players would face if charges were filed]. He was more realistic than Ben and Mike."

The players' attorneys knew that regardless of the legal issue of consent or nonconsent in this case, an overwhelming problem for the players was the fact that, as Walker notes, "in the history of [Arkansas] up until that time, every black man who had been accused of rape by a white woman had been convicted. And until that time, most of them had been given death and the rest life, so what we were looking at was the ultimate penalty in the event that she chose to charge them with rape."

So, while it was clearly in the players' interest for charges to be dropped, Hollingsworth sees much to find fault with in Holtz's actions: "Holtz was their coach and he was their teacher, so he had an obligation to teach them values outside of playing football. He didn't do that. He had no regard for the complete development of these black athletes. All he wanted was for them to perform on the field, and that's all that Lou Holtz cared about. I'm saying that to me that is a very tragic flaw in Lou Holtz's character. He exploited this situation to his advantage and made three young men look very bad. While in the overall scheme of things, their acts [using a woman sexually, however consensually] were reprehensible, they weren't criminal. When it's going to catch up with him, I don't know. You have to give him credit, though; he knew how to use this in just the right way just before the Oklahoma game to get all the attention."

But Oklahoma was the least of Holtz's problems at that point. Forrest, who failed to earn a degree at Arkansas, says, "Once they [athletic department officials] knew we was going to bring in John [attorney Walker], local alumni there in Fayetteville made calls to us telling us that 'you are making a big mistake getting John Walker involved. He's a racist and he wants to make a big thing out of it, he wants to make his name. Why don't you all just take the punishment and look forward to next year?' They didn't understand. There was no such thing as a do-right rule. We didn't know about the do-right rule until we read it in the paper like probably a hundred thousand, two hundred thousand other people. It was something Holtz made up to sound good."

Attorney Hollingsworth, an Arkansas law school graduate, smiles when remembering Holtz's first mention of the "do-right" rule. "Well, I had a law professor named Al Witte," Hollingsworth says. "He was one of my favorite professors. I had a lot of respect for him. Al was the Southwest Conference faculty representative [for the University of Arkansas] at the time, and he sat in on all the discussions. And at one of them, I said, 'Lou, what rule has been violated?' And Lou looked at me and said, 'The do-right rule.' And I said, 'The do-right rule? What is that?' And Al looked at me and said, 'Hell, you know what the do-right rule is.' And I said, 'Look, if I had come up with some bullshit like that in your class, you would have kicked me out or laughed me out of class if I had told you that there was such a thing as the do-right rule, a rule that I wasn't aware of.' So it was a big joke, I mean, all of a sudden Holtz just came up with this concept that they had violated something."

Of course, something had happened. Holtz, like many others, tried to ascertain what it was. The problem is that, regardless, he acted summarily and precipitously, ignoring any input from the players and severely damaging their reputations. The "deal" he cut—the dropping of charges in exchange for the players' suspension—was made without any involvement of the players or their representatives. He ran rough-shod over the players and over all legal niceties and in the process achieved great personal gain for himself. The "do-right" rule became the cornerstone of Holtz's fabulously successful speaking career. He made this situation one of the benchmarks of his career.

But John Walker counters, "I know what the players told me, and it was my attitude that it was a consensual act. The investigation showed no rape." Hollingsworth is less sure and says, "I think the woman might have consented under a straight legal interpretation. But there's no doubt in my mind she could have pressed charges. And if she had, she probably would have won. If [Mike] Tyson got convicted, they would have gotten convicted. Tyson got convicted in 1992; they would have certainly gotten convicted in 1977."

However, Walker says, "I don't know of a single situation in the history of the University of Arkansas where [black] athletes had been reported publicly as having relations with a black female. I cannot imagine that it is not happening in the athletic dorms. In fact, it happens frequently, I'm told, and it has happened between white athletes and white females over a long period of time."

Micheal Forrest says he remains convinced the "crime" the three committed—at least in Holtz's mind—wasn't rape; it was being black and being with a white girl.

Meanwhile, in support of their teammates, eight other Arkansas players—all black—announced that they were going to boycott the game.

Suddenly, it looked as if Holtz would be lucky just to field a team in what was to be the biggest game of his life. With all this on the line, a poker game broke out. The three suspended players filed papers in U.S. District Court in Little Rock requesting a restraining order that would prevent Holtz from suspending them. This forced a tense negotiation. Holtz knew he couldn't give in to any threat that challenged the suspension of the three principals; the nation, after all, was hailing him for the decision. If the players continued with their legal battle, then Holtz could be placed in the embarrassing position of having a court say he violated the due process rights of his players. But the other side had one extremely valuable hole card: then state attorney general Bill Clinton's office argued that if the players persisted and the young woman was called to the stand as part of the lawsuit, she'd be forced to counter by filing rape charges. If the players backed off, the threat of rape charges would be dropped as well.

Hollingsworth explains, "In the attorney general's office, the chief deputy, Royce Griffin, was representing the university. Royce said, 'This woman wants to press charges.' And I said, 'I don't think she does.' He said, 'If you all go forward, we're not going to have any choice, because we're going to have to call her in as a witness. As to what rule they [the players] violated, what rule they violated was they took advantage of her, they raped her. And once she takes the stand, we're going to have to press charges.' This is serious because they were going to bring her in to testify against our injunction. He said her testimony was going to be really implicating to them as criminals. So we [Walker and Hollingsworth] talked to her. We called her and she was very, very upset. She didn't want to do it. And she was under a lot of pressure. It became obvious that if she was going to have to testify, they were certainly going to insist that she press charges, because it was going to make them look like they were allowing something to go on and then turn their head."

Shortly after his 1992 election as president, Bill Clinton told Don

Yaeger in Little Rock that handling the Holtz case was one of the most delicate matters he faced as attorney general, simply because Arkansas football was so important to the people of his state. "I was in Miami for the game when the lawsuit was filed, and I spent practically two full eight-hour days on the phone to my attorneys trying to work this thing out," the president said. "I also was busy trying to convince Coach Holtz everything was going to work out. I really believed there for a while that he was going to resign. He felt like he was under so much pressure, everyone was calling him a racist. I thought he was going to quit. It was tough on all of us. Fortunately, it all worked out."

It all worked out because the players dropped their legal challenge, deciding not to risk the chance of rape charges being filed.

That very sticky wicket now finessed, Holtz then asked for a meeting with the boycotting players. Raymond Miller agreed to arrange the get-together at his Little Rock home. During the meeting, Holtz talked about the need to become a team again. Led by freshman offensive lineman George Stewart from Little Rock, the group began, one by one, to agree to play. By the time the meeting was over, Holtz had a commitment from each of the players that they would show up ready to play in Miami. "I guess we should have known that a football coach who provides scholarships for his players would have much more influence than we had," Hollingsworth says of the failed attempt to rally teammates around his clients. "I think the boycott fell apart because you had black seniors who were willing to do it, but you had a lot of underclassmen who were not willing."

When Holtz later became coach at Minnesota, he hired George Stewart as an assistant coach, then hired him again, at Notre Dame.

All that behind him, Holtz was finally able to focus on Oklahoma, a team Arkansas hadn't beaten in more than fifty years. Nobody loves a crisis like Holtz, who always has done his best coaching as an underdog. He had no problem convincing his players that the Orange Bowl game was all about respect. "Nobody except us believes," Holtz told the team several times. At game's end, with Arkansas an amazing 31–6 victor, others believed, too. "No matter what adjustment I called," Oklahoma defensive coach Larry Lacewell told reporters, "we wound up wrong. It was the first time I ever feared a coach."

Forrest says that the Orange Bowl win over Oklahoma "just put icing on the cake for Lou Holtz. It made him look like he saved the three black players that got suspended for raping a white girl from going to

Young Lou Holtz, during his football-playing career at Kent State

1.

2.

Holtz on the day he was hired as head coach at the University of Arkansas.

3.

Michael Forrest, one of three Arkansas
players suspended by Holtz before the
1978 Orange Bowl.

Donny Bobo.

4.

Ben Cowins, running for Arkansas in 1976.

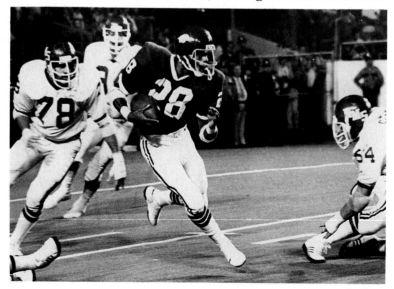

5.

6.

Holtz is carried off the field after Arkansas's 31–6 victory over No. 2–ranked Oklahoma in the 1978 Orange Bowl.

The suspensions of Forrest, Bobo, and Cowins, coupled with the Orange Bowl win, made Holtz a very popular man in Arkansas in 1978.

7.

8.

Holtz, on the set of his TV show during the 1978 season.

9.

Former Arkansas star Dan Hampton, one of Holtz's staunchest defenders, went on to an all-pro career with the Chicago Bears.

10.

Frank Broyles, at the press conference on December 19, 1983, after he fired Lou Holtz.

11.

Holtz, at the same press conference, explains his "resignation" because of "burnout."

12.

Holtz, during August practices
before his first season at the
University of Minnesota. He took
the job there just two days after
leaving Arkansas, his case of
burnout miraculously cured.

13.

Dr. Rob Hunter, who clashed repeatedly with Holtz at Minnesota over
the proper treatment of athletes'
injuries.

14.

16.

Roselle Richardson, who received money from Lou Holtz while being recruited to come to Minnesota—and received a phone call from Holtz years later asking him to lie about it.

Luther Darville, who was convicted of embezzling from a slush fund used to pay minority athletes at Minnesota—with, he says, Holtz's knowledge.

15.

Richardson in action for the Golden Gophers.

17.

Theodore Hesburgh, former president of the University of Notre Dame.

18.

Father Edmund P. Joyce, longtime number-two man at Notre Dame, who takes credit for the hiring of Lou Holtz.

The scoreboard reads:

NOTRE DAME 1:28 USC
0 QTR. 0
TIME OUTS LEFT 3 — 3 TIME OUTS LEFT
DOWN 2 TO GO 8 BALL ON 46

19.

The field at Notre Dame Stadium is watched over by the library mosaic long ago labelled "Touchdown Jesus."

20.

21.

(*Above left*) Gerry Faust, Holtz's predecessor at Notre Dame.

(*Above right*) Former Notre Dame coach Dan Devine.

Students playing touch football against a backdrop of the famed Golden Dome.

22.

Tony Rice (9), star quarterback of the 1988 national championship team, was the focus of concern about declining academic standards when Holtz brought him in.

23.

24.

John Foley (49), who with Rice were the first two Prop. 48 players ever at Notre Dame, salutes the home crowd after an Irish victory.

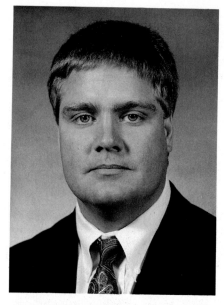

(*Above left*) Marty Lippincott, whose alleged mooning of Holtz became a Trivial Pursuit question, poses before the Golden Dome.

(*Above right*) Former Notre Dame strength coach Scott Raridon.

27.

Lou Holtz faces the press—a situation in which his words are not to be treated as uttered under oath.

Wide receiver Rob Carpenter, who tranferred from Notre Dame to Syracuse when the Irish tried to redshirt him— after Holtz told him during recruiting that Notre Dame doesn't redshirt.

Tony Brooks, now with the Philadelphia Eagles, is cited by several Notre Damers as not fitting in with the image of the Notre Dame Man.

30.

Tony Smith, now with the Kansas City Chiefs, believes the medical treatment he received at Notre Dame dropped him down to the sixth round of the NFL draft and may have cost him a million dollars.

George Marshall (68), a defensive lineman under Holtz.

32.

Holtz addressing his team in the locker room at Notre Dame.

Notre Dame Athletic Director Dick Rosenthal, who oversees the athletic department with, many feel, an excessive concern for the bottom line.

Mike Golic, now an NFL lineman, is one of many Notre Damers upset over the school dropping its wrestling program while it brings in big football money from NBC.

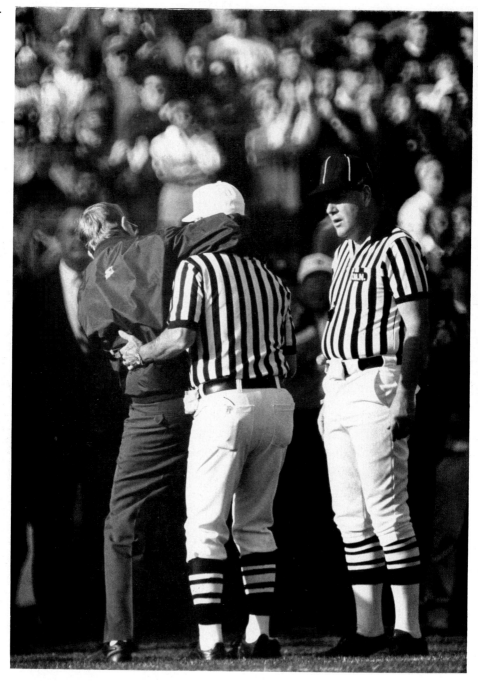

Lou Holtz puts a stranglehold on an official during a 1992 victory over BYU, one of many incidents leading to the question, Is Lou Holtz losing it?

prison. So it kind of made him look good on both points, to win and the fact that she did not press charges."

Holtz became such a nationally recognized figure that a New York company began making and marketing Lou Holtz dolls. Holtz received 14,000 letters and was receiving four dozen speaking requests a week.

While the do-right rule made Holtz a national figure, one of his biggest supporters makes the point that the application by its creator could be a bit slippery.

While Holtz was at Arkansas, money was being stolen from rooms. One player who had been victimized laid a trap for the suspect, according to Dan Hampton. The player left some money in his dorm room, went down to the shower, but quickly slipped back to his room and climbed up to the window, looked in, and saw the theft in progress. The thief, says Hampton, was a star on offense. Explains Hampton, "Holtz's two rules were [that] if anybody was arrested, he was kicked off the team, or if anybody was caught stealing from a teammate, he was kicked off the team. Well, the guys came in and said, 'Hampton, we caught the guy doing it red-handed.' "

And you were captain?

"Yeah, and I went and told Holtz. He said, 'All right, I'll take care of it.' But nothing happened. This guy didn't start the first game the next season." Hampton says that was the extent of the punishment.

Asked if it was because the guilty player was a star, Hampton responds, "Yeah. Oh, yeah. Holtz has got a lot of good ideas and is a good motivator. But on some of the other things, you've got to stand for something or you'll fall for anything. A lot of times in the crunch, Coach Holtz didn't stand for what he said he does."

Interesting, too, that Hampton notes Holtz's "two rules" without mentioning anything like a "do-right" rule.

After that unbelievable 11-1-0 first season, Holtz made all the right political moves, traveling the state and promising anyone who would listen that his second season as coach would bring even greater surprises. He promised—no, he guaranteed—that in 1978, the Hogs would beat Texas.

The Razorbacks opened the season as the nation's No. 1 team, and four games into the season it appeared the 4-0 Hogs deserved the billing. Then came the showdown in Austin, a contest that Holtz told friends had spurred him to prepare his best game plan ever.

Arkansas lost, 28–21. Holtz took it hard.

Then, the emotionally down Razorbacks lost the next week to Houston, 20–9. All hopes for a season of greater glories were gone. Yet, in still another tribute to Holtz's ability, he somehow managed to pull his disheartened players together; they won their final five games in a row and went to the Fiesta Bowl, where they tied UCLA. Still, naysayers were quick to point out that the Fiesta Bowl, especially back then, bore no similarity to the Cotton, Sugar, or Orange Bowl.

The next season, 1979, began with the Razorbacks picked to finish in the middle of the Southwest Conference pack. Again, Holtz surprised fans as the team finished the regular season at 10-1, its only loss a 13–10 thriller to Houston when a last-second Arkansas field goal attempt was blocked. The loss came a week after the Hogs upset No. 2–ranked Texas. The team went to the Sugar Bowl, but lost to Bear Bryant's last national championship team at Alabama, 24–9.

The Alabama game provided quarterback Kevin Scanlon, who today serves as one of Holtz's personal financial advisers, with a lighthearted memory. "Alabama was number one and they had won the national championship the year before," Scanlon says. "They had won something like twenty-three games in a row and we're playing these guys. It's big-time pressure. Before the game, Coach Holtz says, 'Does anyone want to say anything?' And Mike Massey, one of our linebackers, says, 'I do, Coach. Last night I had a dream that we lost the toss, so we kicked off to Alabama. I stuck the guy returning the ball and he fumbled and we recovered and we went down and scored. I just wanted to tell you that.' Coach Holtz says, 'That's great, Mike. I'm glad you shared that with the team. It's not exactly what I'm looking for, but, hey, thanks for sharing it.'

"The captains came walking back in and Coach Holtz says, 'Did we win the toss?' And one of them says, 'No, we're kicking off.' And Massey says, 'Told you this was gonna happen.' Coach Holtz says, 'Okay, Mike.' We kick off, go down the field on coverage, somebody hits the Alabama guy—it's not Massey but somebody—and he fumbles and we recover the ball. We're all in shock, so I walk up to Coach Holtz, huge pressure, eighty thousand people, and I say, 'What play do you want to run?' And he says, 'I don't know. Let's go ask Massey.' I just kind of looked at him, but it was his way of loosening me up and it was a great line, right in the midst of an important game."

Although Holtz has developed a well-deserved reputation for playing mind games with players that few of them ever appreciated, Scanlon says that that is what makes Holtz successful. "His belief is to put more pressure on the quarterback in practice, make it miserable for him, so in the game he relaxes because he [Holtz] is not out there," said Scanlon, who was all-conference in 1979. "He would tell me, 'In the game, I want you to look over at me and say to yourself, 'I'm glad he's not out here. Now I can relax and play football.' "

At this point, Holtz had been at Arkansas three years. His record of 30-5-1 was the best start of any coach in Razorback history. Fans should have been chipping in to erect a statue of Holtz on campus. That they weren't had much to do with Holtz's personality. He always seemed to be offending someone.

First, there was his inability—really, his refusal—to learn how to keep those faithful "soooweee"-chanting fans happy. Broyles had become famous for spending the summer and fall traveling the state and speaking to the many local Razorback Club Fish Frys. Standard fare at the events was always catfish. While making his first trip, Holtz reportedly asked what he'd be fed. "Why, catfish, of course," the host said. "Catfish are scavenger fish," Holtz replied. "Pull over and let me buy some Kentucky Fried Chicken."

The story of "The Insult" made the rounds in Arkansas quickly. Then came some of Holtz's patented one-liners:

"Fayetteville is fifteen minutes from Tulsa—by phone."

"I have never thought about leaving Arkansas since I got here. Suicide, yes; leaving, no."

People in Arkansas smiled gamely, but wanly. In fact, The Insult and The Jokes were rubbing almost everyone raw. "We didn't have just a hell of a lot to be proud of up until Bill Clinton got elected president," former trustee Miller says. "We really felt that we could be proud of our university, and so that was very special to the people here at Arkansas. When he started making fun of the state, it didn't sit well with a lot of folks."

The insults showed, in the eyes of many, that Holtz was insensitive. But what really bothered many Razorback fans was what they saw as Holtz's greed. Stories kept hitting the front pages showing Holtz trying to cash in on his name and fame.

In April of 1978, Holtz got into a sweet deal that allowed him to pay $3,000 for a 3 percent share of Riverside Cable Television, which holds the franchise to operate cable television in Little Rock. In 1980, an attorney for the cable company estimated Holtz's share would be worth $300,000 by 1985.

Then, in January 1980, it was revealed that Holtz was an investor in a proposed Coors beer distributorship in Arkansas. In the Bible Belt, many saw something wrong with such a public figure peddling alcohol. Holtz caught that drift and dropped out of the deal, releasing a statement to the press. One of Holtz's beer partners was quoted as saying, "The people who can put pressure on you can sometimes be so illiterate. I guess it's politics or something. I guess they [the people who talked Holtz into withdrawing] have more pull than I do." But, as always, the far larger point is: Why would Holtz even consider getting into the beer business in the first place, given his position of influence with young people? Did Holtz do right?

Holtz also raised eyebrows around the state when he made television and radio commercials and was pictured in newspaper advertising for Carrier air-conditioning. He also made a radio commercial for Lion Oil Company, which sponsored his daily radio program.

Innocuous as these actions sound, the *Arkansas Gazette* editorialized on the matter, saying it was "especially regrettable that Lou Holtz, insensitive to his almost unique place as a public figure everybody can root for, is now doing direct advertising." Holtz's excuse was that for most of his first year in Arkansas, he was carrying house payments for both his place in New York and the home he left in Raleigh, North Carolina. He said he was trying to earn the money to "alleviate a problem that has been a burdensome one." He said without those financial problems, "I would never have gotten involved" with the corporate advertising. Holtz, at his pious and inaccurate best, said in November 1977, "I can assure the people of this state that I will not get involved in any commercials in the future."

After the *Gazette* ran an editorial cartoon showing Holtz pacing the sidelines wearing advertising boards with space for rent, Holtz said the newspaper had "a comic page for the people who can't read and they have an editorial page for people who can't think." It was clearly time for Holtz to devote more time to the editorial page.

Greed. Lack of sensitivity. Too much self-promotion. Each charge was a buzzard circling around Holtz, surprisingly so for such a successful coach. And the biggest buzzard, ultimately, turned out to be Orville Henry, Arkansas's resident sycophant sportswriter who seldom had anything but praise for the Razorbacks in general and Holtz in particular.

When Henry wrote badly about an Arkansas coach, one of two things was sure: he was in real trouble or he must really deserve it. Further, because most observers saw Henry as being in Broyles's hip pocket, any criticism by the sportswriter implicitly carried the endorsement of the AD.

In a blistering "analysis" of Holtz's income package, written in May 1982, Henry pointed out that Holtz traveled as far as Saudi Arabia and Hawaii to make money giving speeches. Henry threw in that Broyles "did some speaking, seldom for money, and seldom out of state." Continued Henry, "It is true enough that Lou stays in Fayetteville in football season and spring practice, but on any other given day of the year, he is likely to be gone. This could not be said of any other head coach in the country." Henry pointed out that most head coaches take off the day after their last game to start recruiting. Holtz, though, had taken off the day after his final game of the 1981 season (when his team finished 8-4, following a 7-5 season in 1980) to head to Miami to give a speech. "He can defend this until doom's day," wrote Henry, "but the truth is, in each of the recent seasons, the Razorbacks have gotten a little slower, a little less quick. Those qualities aren't coached. They're recruited."

Henry's view was that after the Orange Bowl victory and the attendant national publicity, Holtz "was deluged with speaking requests and he filled as many as he could. He didn't cash in, recruiting-wise." Holtz was outraged at Henry's analysis and took a swipe at Henry in an interview a year after he left Arkansas. He said the recruiting situation was blown out of proportion. "That was just the concoction of one individual down there [Henry] who tried to make a case out of nothing. That individual needs professional help."

In college football, a coach needs to be especially good at recruiting blacks, since their often starry ability has formed—and does form—the heart of most football teams. One of the charges that has followed Holtz throughout his career is that he was a poor recruiter in general and is especially ineffective trying to recruit black players. Affinity for blacks is not in Holtz's background, and worse, it's the opinion of many who know him that it's not in his heart. In Little Rock, P. A. Hollingsworth recalls going to a bar with Oklahoma coach Barry Switzer. "We were drinking together," says Hollingsworth, "and Barry said, 'You show me any black home, you just show it to me and I'll go in and I'll win the mother and the father and I'll come out with that confidence that I'm gonna have that athlete on my team. I don't think there is anybody in the country who can recruit blacks the way I can.' And the way he was talking about it, I mean, he's right. I think he has a real empathy with the black people because he's from similiar circumstances."

What would he have done if Lou Holtz had told him that same thing? "I would have laughed, because it wouldn't have been true."

By 1982, Holtz was constantly rumored to be leaving Arkansas—for Ohio State, South Carolina, Michigan State, Florida, or back to the NFL. None of this helped his recruiting. The fact that Holtz continually lost top recruits to former Arkansas star turned Oklahoma coach Barry Switzer became a thorn in many a Razorback flank. One example among many was current Miami all-pro tight end Keith Jackson, from Little Rock, whom Switzer lured to Norman. Says Dan Hampton, "Frankly, Lou wasn't willing to commit to recruit as much as he needed to, not as much as Broyles wanted him to, and the reason was he was busy enough on his own circuit and the idea of going out and kissing up to some eighteen-year-old fullback didn't turn him on anymore."

Concerns about Holtz's recruiting came to a boil concurrent with the dreadful Jesse Helms episode. Helms, the conservative North Carolina senator, was leading a filibuster in Washington, attempting to kill legislation creating a national holiday honoring Martin Luther King, Jr. Holtz agreed to speak to a thousand people at a $1,000-a-plate fundraising dinner for Helms, and he taped two commercials endorsing Helms while sitting in the Arkansas football office. Though the commercials never aired, Holtz acknowleged his involvement. He apparently didn't see how endorsing Helms might worsen his recruiting reputation among blacks. AD Broyles and university president James E. Martin said Holtz did not tell them about the commercials in advance. Holtz was fired nine days later. Helms responded, "Lou Holtz will not be the loser in all this. The university will be."

Holtz tried to finesse the controversy by telling reporters that he was speaking as "Lou Holtz, citizen, not Lou Holtz, head football coach." He did not explain how that citizen just happened to be sitting in the football office for the tapings. Holtz said he "respected" Helms as an "individual of integrity in all my dealings with him." A Helms staffer said at the time that Holtz was asked to speak after Holtz wrote a letter to the senator saying that "if there was anything he could do to help, please let him know." Holtz said during his speech that "I've got so few friends, I can't turn one of them down when he asks me for my help." But a friend is surely more likely to ask for help once it's been volunteered. That's a different situation from the one Holtz continues to portray.

Holtz is full-bore defensive about Helms. In 1985, he told the *Chicago Tribune*, "It never ceases to amaze me that people continue to point that out. Senator Helms helped me at North Carolina State and I tried to help him when he asked. There is nothing in my background I'm ashamed of. I'll stand on my record."

P. A. Hollingsworth says of the Helms flap that Holtz "was willing to endorse Jesse Helms, and he's not the type of person I want impacting on my children. I think Holtz agrees with everything that Helms thinks. I think he completely bought into Helms's philosophy. When you endorse somebody, that is pretty personal. You're not holding back then. That says, 'This is my kind of person. I want you to vote for them because I'm supporting them. If you believe in things I do, help this person out by voting for him.' "

At one point, trying to explain the inexplicable, Holtz said his endorsement was of Helms's "character, not his politics."

Orville Henry was quoted by Minneapolis newspapers as saying the commercials Holtz did for Helms were "the straw that broke the camel's back." Raymond Miller agrees: "That Jesse Helms thing did not endear Lou to the black community, to say the least. Worse than that, I had assistant coaches talk to me, telling me they set up visits for Lou to come visit key recruits and he may not even show up. Lou may have been more of a problem for his assistants in recruiting than he was for the recruits. In other words, I'm the assistant, I go out and I get things straight with the family and pave the way, I roll the carpet out for Lou, he needs to show up and we need to tie this deal. I'm sitting here waiting and he doesn't show up. He may be off giving a speech someplace or doing a trick on the Johnny Carson show. But Barry Switzer, now he's in the backyard playing basketball with the boy's daddy. I mean, if you're a coach and can't recruit black athletes, you're gonna have a hell of a lousy basketball program and football program and you better stick with swimming, badminton, or golf. If you can't recruit a black athlete, you got problems. Lou couldn't recruit the black athlete."

Even Bill Clinton, who was by then governor of Arkansas, weighed in on Holtz's endorsement of Helms. Clinton told reporters he had "some very strong feelings" about Holtz's making campaign commercials for Helms, "but inasmuch as he has resigned and left, I think we should let it die." But something of this magnitude won't die, and the

Helms controversy haunts Holtz to this day. Still, Holtz apparently learned his political lesson. Asked in 1992 if he would endorse Clinton for president, the coach said, "I have absolutely nothing to say about who should be president of this country. I just don't believe personally that I should influence people."

Kevin Scanlon, a staunch Holtz defender, says he believes that Holtz's recruiting difficulties had nothing to do with any problems with black players. He says Holtz became frustrated by recruiting in the Southwest Conference, where every school except Arkansas and Rice was slapped by the NCAA for cheating during the seventies and eighties. "He realized that he was recruiting against SMU, that went on probation, so had TCU, that went on probation; he was recruiting against Baylor, which went on probation, Texas Tech, Texas A&M," Scanlon says. "He had a lot to overcome because he wasn't going to cheat."

But Micheal Forrest, one of the key players in that dormitory debacle —who offers to take a polygraph test to back up his statements—says Scanlon is naive. He says that the fact that Arkansas and Holtz didn't get caught doesn't mean they weren't cheating. "White coaches," says Forrest, "think the answer to everything is money. Arkansas has never been caught, but lots of us got money and cars."

What do you think when you hear Holtz say, "I'm the cleanest coach in the country"?

"You know that's a lie."

Forrest, from Earle, Arkansas, then specifies his accusation: "When Holtz came in '77, Donny Bobo and I stayed the summer in Fayetteville. We told Coach Holtz what we needed, an apartment and stuff. He gave us money. He just handed us the money. There was a lot of that going on. A lot of schools don't get caught, but still there is a lot of that going on. He gave us money to get an apartment and pretty much helped us out that summer. That was the only time he ever really gave us money, but there were things like making sure that our season tickets got sold, making sure we were getting a thousand dollars, at least. At that time it was legal to sell tickets—but only for face value. But when you get a fifteen-dollar ticket and get five hundred dollars for it, you knew that wasn't legal. And they would sell them. We would never have to sell them. The coaches, the trainers, would do it for us.

"A trainer always fixed us up and sold our tickets, and if you needed a car, they would get you a car. My first car I got from Moore Ford out here [in Little Rock] and I never paid anything for it. I threatened to leave school and I said, 'I can't get home. I'm sick of this. I need a car.' One of the coaches [whom Forrest named in his interview] said, 'Well, let me see what I can do.' A few days later, (the coach) told me, 'Go by the Ford company. They are going to have you a car.' They gave me a white Ford, a '75 or whatever.

"But Fayetteville had a way of covering up their little deals. So, ask Coach Holtz, when it comes to the do-right rule, was it do-right to give us three hundred or four hundred dollars that summer? We knew it wasn't right. He knew it wasn't right. But the do-right rule only came in effect when the problem was with the players, not him. It's do-right. Sure it is. He was doing right and we were still wrong because we asked for the money. If he didn't give it to us, he might say he laid it there on the table, and when he came back in the office, it was missing. I mean, you have to realize how Lou Holtz thinks. He's always going to cover himself."

Forrest says he "laughs out loud" when he reads quotes from Holtz about how he's never cheated. "I wonder if he really remembers all that was going on back then," Forrest says.

One of the entries in the very thick book on Holtz is that however much ability he has—which is a lot—he is inordinately poor at taking the blame for his own mistakes. Dr. Miller, the former Board of Trustees chairman, agrees and says, "That's not a desirable trait, that's not a desirable characteristic. That's a person who is lacking in something. Whatever that is, I don't know. I'm accustomed to people who are in charge accepting both the credit and the blame, and that's what usually happens. Isn't that the way you come down? If I'm going to be in charge, why would I blame an assistant for losing a game?"

Hampton understands better than most what Miller is talking about. Prior to the 1978 season, there was a feeling afoot in the land that Arkansas might end up national champs. Then, in that fifth game, the Hogs got beat by Texas, 28–21. "It has been so long ago," says Hampton, "and so many things have happened—too many blows to the head, too—but I remember the next day running the bleachers, cussing, being real sarcastic about the fact that Holtz blamed me because I got a roughing-the-passer call on a third down on which we had stopped them. They went on to convert and get a touchdown. He pointed the finger right at me and said, 'You're the reason we lost.' I had a real big problem about it for a real long time."

. . .

Rumors started circulating as the 1983 season opened that Holtz was in trouble. Even Holtz started to sense that the end might be near.

Kevin Scanlon says, "I did the color work for Arkansas football telecasts with a local sportscaster here, so I was around the team again and Coach Holtz. He and I visited that summer before, and he had done a great job with [the '82] team. He was doing well but he was kind of frustrated at his recruiting. He was frustrated by that. But he told me that there was a problem brewing, and he sensed a problem between him and [AD] Broyles. He said that there was tension there. He didn't go into it with me. He just let me know that there was a problem. He said, 'I'm not sure he wants me here anymore.' But he said, 'I'm just gonna do my best to win this year.' He said that a friend of his, a coach, had called him and said that Broyles had called him and asked, 'Would you ever be interested in the Arkansas job?' "

Hampton, too, heard the rumors that his former coach was on thin ice. He says he believes that Holtz had simply worn out his welcome. "It's like when you visit your relatives for a couple of weeks, you just get tired of them," Hampton says. "It's like the guy that talks and jokes and is the life of the party, then the next day he's no fun to have around, you know what I mean? The guy who always has to be in the middle of something? After a while, that gets old, and Lou always has his one-liners, his witticisms. It was cute at first, but then it started getting a little tired and old, and when the wins didn't come, it got real old quick. I mean, there are no diversions in Arkansas. People love their Razorbacks. Here in Illinois, they've got the Chicago Bears, the Bulls, and the Blackhawks. The Razorbacks are the only thing in Arkansas. You've got six kids and you don't mind if there are a couple of clinkers in the bunch if you have a couple of brain childs, but if you only have one, you bet he better do good. But you've got to give Holtz credit, because he's won everywhere he has been. Lou's problem is, for some reason he seems to burn bridges everywhere."

In December 1983, when the Helms commercials came to light, the last bridge went up in flames. Holtz was fired.

Holtz, according to his closest friends, was shocked. Though Holtz and Broyles issued the obligatory line that Holtz had "resigned," two close friends of Broyles's said the firing occurred this way:

In Holtz's last season, the Razorback defense was dreadful. The team ended the year 6-5, its worst record in Holtz's seven years there. All the magic was gone. The illusionist could no longer distract attention from the man behind the curtain. He had developed a reputation that grew as fast as his bank account: he couldn't recruit. Especially, he couldn't recruit blacks. Even more especially, he was losing the battle to everybody in talent-rich Texas. Others had started to whisper that he couldn't hire and keep quality assistant coaches. After the season, Holtz knew things weren't going well, and following the familiar Holtz MO—Hampton says it was pure Holtz—he fired two defensive assistants, leading his defensive coordinator, Don Lindsey, a popular native son of Arkansas, to resign.

About that time, Broyles hosted a dinner party for major boosters and friends—including Orville Henry, who, as evidence of his special relationship with Broyles, had been given his own office by the AD in Barnhill Field House.

During the dinner, conversation around the table became a symposium on Holtz. It was agreed that Holtz was an excellent coach on the field, but everyone at the table expressed concern about his ability to assemble a first-rate staff, recruit with other conference powers, or win any more than six games in any upcoming season in the then nine-member SWC. As documentation of Holtz's recruiting weakness, several around the table pointed out that Arkansas's top high school quarterback that year, Gene Newberry, had signed with Alabama. Broyles sat back and took it all in.

It should have been a hint to Holtz that the end was near when, twice during the ensuing week, Henry authored columns raising questions about the coach's future. Though he had a seven-year record of 60-21-2, highlighted by six straight bowl appearances before that final season, Holtz was on the ropes. Scanlon remembers that "there was an article about two days before the firing happened that was the most negative article I had ever read about an Arkansas coach written by Orville. I told my wife, 'This is bad. There is something going on here.'"

Oblivious, Holtz set about flying potential assistant coaches in for interviews. On Friday, Broyles called Holtz and said he wanted a Sunday-morning meeting in Broyles's office. Broyles, who would spend that Saturday broadcasting an NCAA Division II playoff football game, flew back to Fayetteville Saturday night.

Sunday morning, December 18, 1983, Broyles waited in his office. Holtz didn't show. Broyles waited some more. Finally, Holtz called Broyles and said he was at the airport, having just dropped off a coaching candidate. He said he was waiting for another coaching prospect to fly in.

"Can this wait until Monday or Tuesday?" Holtz asked.

"No, Lou. We've got to do it today," Broyles said.

"It's that important?"

"It's that important."

"Well, okay," Holtz said with a nervous laugh. "What, am I fired?"

"Yeah, Lou, you are."

Holtz reportedly hung up and called television sportscaster Paul Eells, who was cohost of "The Lou Holtz Show," and blurted out, "I've been fired." Eells told his bosses at KATV, and almost immediately the television station started running a special bulletin across the bottom of the screen:

Lou Holtz has been fired. . . . Lou Holtz has been fired. . . .

Holtz then rushed down to the campus, where he and Broyles worked out the details of his "resignation." Broyles next called Eells and demanded a correction, explaining the "official" position. The station complied.

The next day, Broyles and Holtz held separate press conferences. Holtz, appearing shaken, said his reasons for resigning were "personal," and he asked the press that the resignation be "reported in a positive manner." Holtz was asked if the decision to leave was entirely his. Holtz nonanswered, "I guess that's why I'm here, to announce my resignation." Broyles simply told the world that Holtz had resigned—with four and one-half years left on his contract—because he was "tired and burned-out." Both delivered their lines with straight faces. Broyles failed to mention that the Razorback Scholarship Fund was paying Holtz at least $259,000, according to the *Arkansas Democrat,* for his "resignation." Another estimate of the settlement, made by Houston newspaperman Jack Gallagher to *Sports Illustrated,* was $830,000. Whatever, this sparked one last outrage, since the university had just announced that faculty would have to do without salary increases for a second straight year.

Said Broyles after he had made Holtz walk the plank, "He is as fine a coach and person as I have known."

Holtz had a hard time keeping up the fabrication that he had resigned. Talking of being burned-out, he told a newspaper reporter, "I didn't feel burned-out. Burned up, maybe."

P. A. Hollingsworth says in reviewing Holtz's tenure, "He's a personality that, for some reason, we really thrust beyond his importance. I think that he's a hypocrite; I don't think he tells you how he really feels about issues and I think he says one thing and does another, at least based on the experiences we have had with him at Arkansas. I really didn't think much of him after the incident [in the athletic dorm]. I had a real sour taste in my mouth from what happened, and I knew that he and Frank [Broyles] were going to be on a collision course because this had propelled him into such a national spotlight. I was surprised that he got the Notre Dame job, but obviously this guy is a hell of a salesman. He convinced people that he was the person for the job."

Raymond Miller says, "Lou is not the ordinary kind of person. He is a little eccentric type of individual. He's aloof. I've always felt that Lou wanted to be the superstar of the program."

But Holtz has his defenders, including the Atlanta columnist Furman Bisher, who wrote of that Arkansas situation that "it comes as a shock that their most visible sports figure could be shot down for one political misjudgment." In truth, it was far more than one misjudgment. When Holtz left Arkansas, he said, "Anybody who knows me will realize I've never intentionally offended anybody."

A couple of days later, Orville Henry spoke at a civic club in Rogers, Arkansas, and told the group it shouldn't believe the resignation story. Henry told the group that Holtz was fired because he had let the football program bottom out. Broyles issued the last word on the Holtz firing in a press release four months later: "I am confident that any loyal and dedicated Razorback fan, given all the circumstances, would feel comfortable with the manner in which Coach Holtz's resignation was handled."

But long before this statement, Holtz had had a miraculous recovery from fatigue and burnout, in the unlikely location of Minneapolis, Minnesota.

CHAPTER 9

Minnesota:
Winning Has
Its Price

Four days after resigning because of burnout at Arkansas, Lou Holtz recovered and took over at demoralized Minnesota. Under deposed coach Joe Salem, the Golden Gopher program had nearly disintegrated, losing seventeen of its last eighteen games. Player revolts, especially along racial lines, had become common.

"The players thought Joe's program had become racist," says Minnesota civil rights activist Ron Edwards, who worked closely with UM athletes. "You had things breaking down along black-white lines. There was an undercurrent because the black kids were still not getting the good summer jobs. They weren't working at Pillsbury and General Mills as interns and walking around with a suit on and going to play golf at the country club. The black kids, sure, they had a job, but they were working out here on the highway construction or in some box factory or [in envelope-company owner] Harvey Mackay's shop."

Star tailback Tony Hunter agreed that the job situation became an escalating point of conflict during the Salem years. "It was sending out a couple of messages to us," Hunter says. "For one, coming from a black man's perspective, it showed there was still that plantation mentality. It's that Darwinism, natural-selection thing that black folks are built just to do manual labor. On the other hand, the message that he sent out to me was that 'white players were getting prepared for life after football.' No one really gives a shit about the black athletes after football is done and over with."

Adds Luther Darville, the former minority-office director at Minnesota and a man whose name still sends shivers down the spine of UM boosters, "My observation of the problem was one of a racial nature, and the coaches were reinforcing that. The coaches were doing nothing to compliment or to encourage the black players in particular. And white players were feeling similarly humiliated. But if white players were bad-mouthed, it was probably because of their lack of talent or lack of speed. But when [they] dealt with the black players, it was 'nigger.' Use of that word was not uncommon at the time Salem was there."

In one way Minnesota took very good care of its black athletes: the Gophers had a system in place to pay many of their players and pay them well. How well has never been fully revealed, but parts of the pay-for-play program did become known when the NCAA completed a second investigation of the Gophers in 1988—two years after Holtz had left for Notre Dame.

The level of payments was stunning—as we shall see.

But even money doesn't solve every problem, and as Salem's last season, 1983, progressed toward its rotten 1-10 climax, the situation got worse. Before the year's final game, with Iowa, Salem avoided being fired by stepping down. The Gophers lost 61–10, having lost 58–10 to Michigan the week before.

Minnesota athletic director Paul Giel had called Holtz during the season to ask if he'd be interested in trying to dig the Gophers out of their hole. Holtz, then confident that Razorback fans loved him, practically laughed. But two months later, things had changed drastically. Holtz's surprise firing in Fayetteville gave him a new perspective on the job market. Since nothing else was available—or, at the least, was being offered to Holtz—the prospect of life in Minneapolis abruptly took on new warmth for the cold-hating magic man. Giel was in the hospital for a quadruple heart-bypass operation when two leading Gopher boosters decided to take charge of the effort to hire a new coach.

It has always been disconcerting around UM, but the fact—ridiculous as it is—is that Bill Maddux, another rich and prominent booster, and Harvey Mackay hired Lou Holtz. Giel was notified of the selection.

"We needed someone from the upper Midwest that was rah-rah, go for it, get people interested, fill the stadium, because you're not gonna change the football program overnight with talent," says Maddux. "You need a commitment from the people. These people here are wonderful people, but they don't get excited too quick. They're tire kickers. Holtz was the only guy that I knew with a rah-rah [attitude] that could do something like that. So out of the blue Harvey says, 'I'll bet you that I can get [then University of Maryland coach Bobby] Ross.' I said, 'I'll tell you what. I don't want Ross. I want to try to get Lou Holtz.' Harvey says, 'You're full of shit. There is no way in this world you can get Lou Holtz.'

"This is a Friday. Holtz gets fired on a Sunday morning. I hear about it over the news. Harvey and I are two different people; we get along, but we have nothing in common. But I like the competition. So I called Lou Holtz on a Sunday. I called the athletic department, and the athletic department forwards my name and telephone number. Holtz claims that, as he tells me later, he returned my call because he thought it was from an assistant football coach at the University of Mississippi or Mississippi State. So Holtz says he didn't know who he was calling back. The area code would have told you that couldn't be true, but anyway, Lou calls me back.

"I said, 'Lou, I've got three questions for you. If I get past the first question, then we'll get to the second. First, I understand that you're not at Arkansas now and I have an opportunity for you. It's an opportunity that you can't appreciate until I can look you in the eye and tell you about it.' I would ask him so many questions, and then if he said yes, then I would go to the next series. I would go through three series.

"After the third series, I said, 'You get on a plane and come out here because I guarantee it will be worth your while. I'm not telling you to come up here overnight, because I know you don't like the weather. But I will make a commitment to you personally. I'm interested in doing something for the university. Paul Giel is in the hospital, we need help, and I want to talk to you.'

"So what happens is Lou says, 'Gosh, if I come, I want to bring my wife,' or something, and I said, 'Hell, you can bring your whole family. Just tell me when you want to come and I'll send you a ticket. I'll do whatever you want.' He calls me back and says, 'I can't get any reservations. The planes are booked.' I said, 'Call back again, Lou. I'll send a chartered plane down if I have to.' He said, 'Let me try again.' He calls back and says, 'Four people canceled and I have reservations for four.' I said, 'Okay.' Now he's coming. He said, 'I'm gonna come with my wife, myself, my daughter, my son.' I said, 'Fine. I'll meet you at the plane.' I hadn't told a soul. I hadn't told Giel. I hadn't told Harvey.

"So the story goes that he gets in the car and they have to drive to Tulsa to fly up here. On the way, they run into a storm and he says, 'You know what, let's don't go to Minnesota.' And his daughter and his wife say, 'No, we're going because it will get you away from the press who's all over you right now and we want some time with you. And nobody in Minnesota will know you from anything.'

"He flies up here. I'm going to meet him at the airplane. Harvey still does not know anything. Neither does Giel. Now I'm on the spot, because here I've got a guy coming into town, this is Bill Maddux, and I've got to go tell Harvey and Giel. So I run out and I say, 'Gee, Harvey, I'm sorry, but Holtz is coming into town.' And Harvey says, 'What?' I said, 'I told you. I've got him coming into town.' Harvey says, 'What are you gonna do?'

"I call the Amfac Hotel, it's the Marriott now, and I put Lou's room under the name Robert Wood, which is a kid that I played football with in high school and we used to use each other's names. So I go to the hospital and I say, 'Paul, I'm sorry I don't have your permission. I've done something maybe out of line, but there's nothing to lose. I've got Holtz in town.'

"He says, 'What?'

" 'I've got Holtz in town and I think I can close the deal.' Harvey is a kind of take-over kind of guy and wants all the credit. I don't care if anybody knows who I am or what I am. I just want to get the deal done for Paul. Paul says, 'Okay.' I said, 'I'll tell you what. Leave me alone with this thing and let me see what I can do.' So Harvey immediately gets on the phone and calls the president of the university and starts talking.

"On Monday, I pick Holtz up at the airport, I put a cap over his head so you couldn't tell who he was, I threw an overcoat on him, and put him in my car. It's snowing like crazy, colder than a bitch. It was just terrible. Thirty below or something. I took him down to the hotel and I put him in a room and Harvey says, 'I want to cut the deal with him, I want to talk to him.' I said, 'All right, I tell you what. You take care of him and I'll take care of the family.' So we met with him off and on, and Harvey started talking the business side and I took his wife and kids around and showed them the community, the schools. By the next night, it was basically done. We were going to have a news conference right then, but it was about ten-thirty at night, so that wouldn't work. So they had a news conference the next morning. Harvey went up and told everybody that he got Lou Holtz, and that's when I dropped out of the picture. I'd done what I needed to do."

Mackay, according to UM sports information director Bob Peterson, was deeply involved in the scandal-ridden tenure of basketball coach Bill Musselman at the university. As a result of the NCAA investigation, the university announced it would "formally sever its relationship" with Mackay in order to prevent him from having any contact with the university athletic program (with the NCAA's approval, the university resumed relations with Mackay in the early 1980s). Mackay declined comment. In Minneapolis, Harvey Mackay was Lou Holtz's best friend.

The university's search committee, charged with finding a new football coach, had been turned down time and again by coaches all over the country for an embarrassing two months. It, in fact, had contacted Holtz.

But Holtz never really dealt with the Minnesota search committee. By the time his name was made public, the committee was nothing but a rubber stamp.

Giel breaks out in a smile when he recalls the phone call he got late at night from Holtz. "It was December twenty-first, at about ten-thirty at night, when I get the call. Harvey Mackay says, 'Lou Holtz has something to say to you.' Lou gets on the phone and says something to the effect of, 'Whether you like it or not, I'm your new coach.' But it was almost like a fluke. He was not gonna call back Minnesota. If he knew it was Minnesota, he wasn't gonna . . . well, he wasn't down on Minnesota. It's just cold. He came up here and I guess maybe we caught him on the rebound."

Holtz's arrival in Minneapolis was trumpeted as the greatest moment in recent Gopher football history—maybe in Gopher history, depending on what significance one gives Bronko Nagurski. "When I hung up the telephone," Giel says, recalling Holtz's call to accept the Gopher job, "I turned to my daughter, Gerilyn, and I said, 'I don't think anybody has any idea what the impact of this is going to be on the school, on the state, and around the country. It's going to be fantastic.' "

The words sounded familiar. They had been said by Frank Broyles at Arkansas, and would later be said by Gene Corrigan at Notre Dame— and will be said at Holtz's next stop. Book it.

When Holtz took the job, he won the hearts of Gopher fans by telling them that he grew up listening to his grandfather tell tales of Francis "Pug" Lund, a Minnesota all-American halfback in 1934. UM fans can't be blamed for falling for that line, but that same grandfather, Holtz would say two years later, "was a big Notre Dame fan and always had their games on the radio." Holtz's grandfather clearly had a lot of time to spend beside the wireless.

The hiring was of such proportions that one magazine even declared that Holtz had now replaced Garrison Keillor, the legendary radio story-teller, as the state's spiritual folk hero. Possibly. However, Keillor's fictional tales of the goings-on in the town of Lake Wobegone often have more truth in them than Holtz's versions of the goings-on in Lake Fayetteville, Lake Minneapolis, and Lake South Bend.

Time was when the Gophers were proud and feared. Four times they were national champs—1936, 1940, 1941, and 1960. They have won seven Big Ten championships outright and shared nine more—but none since 1967. The last time Minnesota ended up in the nation's Top 10 was in 1962; the Gophers were tenth.

Holtz recognized the desperation. And he knew how to feed the hungry. He made promises: "In two years—you can write this down—there are going to be 62,500 season tickets sold in [the Hubert H. Humphrey Metrodome] for our games." He'd follow that with, "Nobody's gonna make Lou Holtz and the Minnesota Gophers feel inferior without our permission."

UM photographer Wendell Vandersluis recalls Holtz's first staff meeting: "He said, 'Nobody's job in this room is safe. But I'm the last coach you'll ever have. I'll be here forever, so get used to it.' "

He did the one thing Bill Maddux said was most important: he got people to believe. They believed so much that they catered to his every whim and wish—building him a topflight, $5-million indoor practice facility and buying season tickets as if they were on the endangered-species list.

Holtz, however, repeated at least one of the mistakes he made at Arkansas: he insulted the local community and degraded his team. To some, of course, his jokes were funny because they are funny. To many others, they were not funny because of their own sensitivities:

—"The body and soul of this football program must come from Minnesota. Of course, the arms and legs will have to come from somewhere else."

—"I took a gamble," Holtz once said when asked why he took the

Minnesota job, "that the people of Minnesota are very proud and have a lot of pride in their state. I knew they were tough every time I watched that Die Hard battery commercial."

—"When I'd be on my knees thanking God for what He'd done for me, I'd always thank Him for not sending me to Minnesota."

—"I'm worried about the numbers here," Holtz said the day after he accepted the job. "I don't know how many colleges play eight-man football. And I'm not real good at coaching that, either."

—"I like the idea of living where they have four seasons. Too bad they're not a little more equal."

—He described Minnesota weather as "bitterly cold, unbearably cold, and unbelievably cold." He even purchased a heated office chair. Asked where he planned to live in Minneapolis, Holtz said, "Definitely indoors."

—"We do have some problems with talent, obviously. We're playing with the same guys who got beat an average of forty-seven to sixteen [per game] last year, and we lost three of our best players."

—Holtz said he was told to move his car one day because he had parked in a spot reserved for handicapped drivers. He replied: "Who could be more handicapped than the football coach at the University of Minnesota?"

Holtz also repeated lines he's thrown at every gullible booster who would listen in every town in which he's made a whistle-stop: "I think that coming to Minnesota was one of the wisest choices I've made, and I plan on being at Minnesota for the rest of my life. I think Minnesota is one of the best-kept secrets in the world."

Further, as Holtz always does, he began explaining how impossible the task ahead would be. "Most of the kids on our team," he said gravely, "would not make the third team at Arkansas. This is the worst group of athletes I've had, including William and Mary, top to bottom."

The people of Minnesota, however, were so desirous of a winner that they laughed at his jokes and fell for each Holtz promise. Almost overnight, Gopher fans were brimming with optimism. This was before Holtz had coached a game. Consider:

—More season tickets were sold (nearly 24,000) than had ever been sold before. This was even more than when the Gophers made back-to-back trips to the Rose Bowl in 1961 and 1962.

—Boosters instantly arranged funding for the indoor football-practice facility, which was completed early in Holtz's first season.

Previous Gopher coaches had requested such a building, only to be ignored.

—More than 43,000 tickets were sold to the spring intrasquad football game, and more than 25,000 fans showed up.

—More than seven hundred high school coaches attended the Gophers' annual coaching clinic, nearly five times as many as had attended when Joe Salem was coach.

Never mind that the cold, hard truth is that Holtz didn't do all that well at Minnesota. His two-year record was 10-12. Holtz was 4-7 his first year, 6-5 his second. Big deal. Joe Salem was 3-8 in 1982, 6-5 in '81, 5-6 in '80, 4-6 in '79. Not a lot of difference, particularly when you compare their first two years. Holtz's single biggest achievement was in his second year in Minneapolis when the Gophers narrowly lost, 13-7, to eventual national champion Oklahoma. Still, when your biggest achievement is a defeat, you shouldn't get too carried away with yourself.

"One thing that has to be kept in mind is that people in the state want the Gophers to do well," Gopher ticket manager Ken Buell told the *Minneapolis Star-Tribune*. "They've gotten demoralized a lot because it seems like we've never really turned the corner and kept things going. But the fans want to have that glow. Our fans want to be on a good ride."

What they would soon learn was that a ride with Holtz usually meant a roller coaster.

Before his first season, Holtz told an interviewer, "It's not easy to win in big-time football without breaking the rules, but we'll do it. This has to be the most honest state I've seen. People from this state—the Humphreys, the Mondales—all have great, honest reputations. People would be offended if I did anything dishonest. It's not uncommon to see winning programs where cheating is rampant."

The problem with Minnesota, the NCAA would later prove, was that it was a losing program where cheating was rampant. And Holtz, despite all his claims to the contrary, was right in the middle of it. This was a football program that was out of control in ways that only SMU boosters could appreciate.

As NCAA investigators began to circle, it seemed at times as if Holtz had a hard time remembering what he did—or what he said.

In a speech to his team, Holtz once said, "I've been a head football coach for eighteen years and been involved in the game of football as a coach for twenty-eight. In twenty-eight years, I've never done anything illegal to gain an advantage. I have never cheated."

Later, as rules violations began to become apparent, he said, "I have never said that I didn't make a mistake, but I have always contended that my actions were never intended to gain a competitive advantage."

At a news conference after being forced by the NCAA to admit that he had given one player cash, Holtz said, "When I reflect back on my decision [to give the player the money], it was an instantaneous one and one which I should not have made and I'm sorry now that I did make it. By no stretch of the imagination did I attempt to gain a competitive edge by this action."

In a subsequent *Chicago Tribune* story, Holtz issued a prepared statement: "I sincerely tried at all times to run the football program within the framework of the NCAA and never intentionally broke a rule."

And finally, as word spread that more than a dozen of his Gopher players were receiving illegal payments, Holtz moaned, "The thing that bothers me is why I didn't know about it. A coach should know it. . . . I've looked back and thought, why didn't I know? Usually, where there's smoke, there's fire. Never once did I ever hear it."

Dang, it's a slippery slope.

One of Minnesota's best recent players was a quarterback from Waterloo, South Carolina, Rickey Foggie. He is rhapsodic over his experience playing for Holtz: "He was the best thing that could have happened to me. He really teaches you the facts of life. He has changed my mentality as a football player. He was my savior in football. He made me realize it's only a game. He told me once, 'Rickey, you're very fortunate to be able to play the game, so just have fun doin' it.' "

Foggie was in the Canadian Football League in 1992, with Toronto. Thinking back to those Minneapolis days while having lunch in a local bar, The Draft Pick, Foggie is asked if he thinks Holtz knew about the illegal payments being made to players. "I don't know, man. I just don't know. He's involved in so much stuff. And he always seems to be involved in everything."

So if Holtz is so involved, doesn't it seem likely he knew?

Foggie shrugs, says nothing. Foggie, one of the players who received illegal money (about $8,600), realizes he's about to step in deep stuff. To buy Holtz's argument that he knew nothing means you have to accept the premise that a coach who insisted on knowing absolutely everything going on with his program, down to the most minute detail, somehow didn't know about this one major aspect.

For his part, Foggie says his crooked walk started when he was strolling across campus with another player, Mike Barber, shortly after he arrived. A man who turned out to be Luther Darville, the financial Santa Claus, said, "You guys football players?"

"Yeah," said Foggie.

"Good. Want a ride?"

It was that simple. Explains Foggie, "We was poor. So I asked him for fifty dollars, something like that. Then I kept asking. One hundred dollars. The most I ever asked for was two hundred dollars."

Are you embarrassed you took the money?

"I don't know if you'd say I was embarrassed. I think that in hindsight, I wouldn't have done it."

Did you know it was illegal to get money?

"I didn't know that. I thought Luther was just doin' it out of the kindness of his heart. He was a nice, sincere person. Frankly, I never even worried about taking it. He did give me money. There's no denying that. It was unfortunate, wasn't it? Luther is the good guy. The bad guy? I guess they're still lookin' for him. Nobody seems to know."

Could it be Holtz?

"I don't know, man."

Despite Holtz's ever-changing answer to the simple question—"Were you cheating at Minnesota?"—Notre Dame athletic director Dick Rosenthal praised Holtz for the "forthright way" he responded to the charges. Holtz's answers, though, weren't forthright enough for NCAA investigators, who charged him with three rules violations:

1. In the spring of '85, Holtz handed star recruit Roselle Richardson two $100 bills after he was told the recruit had lost his wallet during an official—and legal—visit to Minnesota in January of that year. Holtz said it was an emotional decision and he said it was two $10 bills, not $100 bills. But former assistant coach Pete Cordelli, who was there at the time of the transaction, said it was $200. Holtz sniffed of Cordelli, "His story changed the same month I named Jim Strong offensive coordinator." Strong got the job in 1989. Cordelli, now the head coach at Kent State, refused to be interviewed on the subject. In declining to talk for this book, Cordelli wrote on November 19, 1992, "I believe that

Lou Holtz's record speaks for itself. He has done an excellent job not only at Notre Dame but everywhere he has coached. There is no other comment needed." To the NCAA, it didn't matter if the figure was $20 or $200. It was still a violation.

Roselle Richardson was considered one of the nation's top running backs coming out of high school. His coach was sure he was destined for a big-time school, probably Ohio State. Suddenly, Richardson decided he wanted to play for one of the nation's worst football programs. His decision was made just weeks after he sat in the backseat of a rental car and was handed cash by Lou Holtz.

Richardson says there was no doubt what Lou Holtz was doing when he slipped the two $100 bills into his hand. He said there was no doubt about the denomination, either. "I was on my recruiting trip to Minnesota and Jason Bruce (a flanker from Eagan, Minnesota) was my chaperon," Richardson says in a tape-recorded interview. "So he showed me around and I lost my wallet. I had twenty dollars in there, I think, and a credit card, phone card, and some other stuff. So when I mentioned it to Coach Holtz when he came to my house (in Warren, Ohio) later on that week, he gave me two one-hundred-dollar bills and he just slid them to me like that, and he said that should take care of all the expenses that you lost in your wallet. So I never thought anything else about it."

It was definitely two $100 bills?

"It was. It was two one-hundred-dollar bills. Absolutely no question about it, because I know the difference. I was sitting in the backseat. It was Coach Holtz on the passenger side and Coach Cordelli was driving. Coach Holtz just slid the money back nice and easy, kind of sly. But Coach Cordelli can't talk either, because he gave me five hundred dollars one time. I went to the prom in May. He gave me five hundred dollars before the prom for my tux and stuff. I went out to this hotel on Youngstown Road, we call it The Strips, and he gave it to me there. I had to sign an IOU, but you know how that is. I never saw that IOU again. He tore it up, I think. Me, myself, personally, if you lost twenty dollars, right, I would reimburse you your twenty dollars. I wouldn't give you two hundred dollars, you know, because that's gonna make me think."

Richardson, then seventeen, admits of the tainted Minnesota money, "That [was part of what] made me go there. I was like, this ain't right, but I just took it and put it in my pocket, like any teenager would do. Coaches shouldn't be giving money, it should be wrong, but it isn't.

When I got home, I told my mother. She got upset for a minute. She said I should give it back, but there ain't no way I was going to give it back. Why should I give it back? I mean, you know."

2. In the summer of '85, Holtz gave $250 to linebacker Jerry Keeble from St. Louis to pay for a marketing course being offered by the Continuing Education Department. It was a correspondence course that Keeble, who was penciled in as a starter, needed in order to reenroll at the university. Paying for the course, the NCAA said, allowed Keeble to remain in school and retain one more year of eligibility. The NCAA report said that "the young man did receive athletically related aid during the 1985–86 academic year." In an interview, Keeble laughed about the incident. He said the somewhat obscured point here is that his athletic scholarship covered payment for all courses, including correspondence courses, so the $250 wasn't needed. It was, simply, a hands-down gift. An illegal gift. Holtz acknowledged the payment, but said he did it for "humanitarian" reasons.

Keeble said there wasn't anything surprising about Holtz's handing him $250. Money was flowing through the Gopher football program like water over a dam. Keeble says he was more surprised by the subsequent outrage: "The two hundred and fifty dollars that he gave me, he basically just gave me because I asked him. I told him I needed it. Me and LeRoy Gardner. We approached him. I approached him."

3. Holtz gave former Minnesota academic adviser LeRoy Gardner $500 to pass on to Keeble. In an interview with the *St. Paul Pioneer Press*, Gardner contended Holtz had given him the money with instructions that it be used "if a player had a financial need." Gardner said he was shocked, and that he felt uncomfortable after he did it. Holtz denies this one, saying the $500 was money that he personally loaned to Gardner and he never intended that it be paid to athletes. Holtz said he loaned Gardner money three times for personal needs: "Why he said that one of the checks was to be given to athletes, I do not know." Gardner later recanted.

Keeble, however, confirmed getting the money from Gardner and backed up Gardner's original story that Holtz knew where the money was going. "Yeah, LeRoy Gardner gave me five hundred dollars," says Keeble. "I needed the money because I wanted to stay in school. I was married and the scholarship doesn't really support you when you're not on campus. So I did need the money. Basically, it was for several specific bills."

How did Holtz come to know that you needed that $500?

"I told him."

You told him? You said, "Coach Holtz, I'm having a hard time?"

"Right."

Although Keeble's version substantiates Gardner's, Holtz vigorously denied Gardner's claim. In the book *Champions*, Bill Bilinski writes that Gardner "alleged Holtz was aware of an illegal distribution of funds. Holtz denied the charges. 'What can I say, other than I didn't do anything? But it makes me a little upset when it's made to look like I'm not being honest and truthful, when I am. I do not lie.' "

But the greatest violation Holtz committed may never have been caught by the NCAA. According to both Richardson and Keeble, Holtz called them when the NCAA started bearing down on him for his part in Minnesota's rampant rules-breaking. Both players said they received late-night phone calls from Holtz warning the players that the NCAA was on his trail. In both instances, the players say that Holtz encouraged them to match their stories to the version that he had given the NCAA.

Says Richardson, "He called me at home and we were talking on the phone, and he told me that the NCAA was going to come and talk to me about that incident. And he told me that he had told them he gave me two ten-dollar bills and he told me what to tell them—that he had given me two ten-dollar bills to compensate me for what I had lost. And I told him, 'Coach Holtz, I couldn't do that. I can't lie. I mean, you know.' And then he said, well, how did he put it? He made some type of statement. He said something and then we got off the telephone."

He said what?

"I don't even recall. But I think he tried to make me feel bad."

For not lying?

"Yeah. Then another night when I was at home, I got a phone call from Coach Cordelli, and he let me know that they [the NCAA] were going to ask questions about it. He told me that they had came and asked him questions and he had told them what happened. He said he told them the truth. I told him that I was gonna tell the truth, too. And I just told him the truth. Coach Holtz taught me if you always believe in yourself, be truthful to yourself, you can do whatever you want to do. One thing I didn't understand was that he always tried to teach us to tell the truth, be truthful, and then you're asked to lie."

Asked why Holtz would want him to change his story, Richardson answered without hesitation, "Being at Notre Dame, I feel if anything ever happened that would jeopardize the type of person that Lou Holtz is, like if they find out that he is illegally recruiting people, I mean they would fire him."

Jerry Keeble's story is eerily similar:

"They [the NCAA] didn't know that the two hundred and fifty dollars was for a correspondence class. Lou Holtz called me [one night at home in 1988] and said, 'This is why I gave you this money.' "

So the money wasn't really for a course, like you told the NCAA?

"No. He [Holtz] told me I should remember when he paid for the class. Several times he said that. Then I agreed to say that. He said, 'Jerry, you hold my career in your hands. My career is at stake with this investigation.' I can tell you this much, Lou Holtz lied. The reason he knew he could continue to lie was because he knew I wouldn't tell."

Keeble said that in addition to receiving two calls at his home from Holtz, he also took a call, while he was working late one night at a downtown St. Louis hotel, from one of Holtz's lawyers.

Richardson and Keeble aren't the only people who remember Holtz's telling them he planned to shade the truth with the NCAA. Says LeRoy Gardner, "Lou Holtz was the only person who told me the truth at Minnesota. He said when the NCAA asked him questions, he was going to lie."

Luther Darville, such an important player in this charade being strutted on the Minnesota stage that he merits his own chapter (see Chapter 13), says, "Well, Lou Holtz told me that whatever he did, if anything were said about it, he would deny it. It was probably in the same setting as LeRoy. LeRoy and I met together with him on a few occasions, and it was basically the same context. He knew that certain players had to get extra help, things to deal with financial assistance. He knew they needed it and he said, 'If anybody asks about this or about giving players financial assistance, I will deny it.' Lou Holtz would deny anything that would jeopardize his career."

The NCAA shouldn't be offended that Holtz chose not to tell the truth. He didn't tell it to Notre Dame, either. Notre Dame vice president William Beauchamp said in August 1990 that he thought Holtz would be "exonerated" on all charges. Beauchamp also said the alleged violations were "rather minor" and "technical." That was later disputed by Alan Williams, then chairman of the NCAA's infractions committee, who said, "The committee believed the sum total of those constituted a major violation."

After the NCAA's final report was issued with Holtz admitting to two charges, the coach finally did acknowledge, "I realize now that this was wrong and I should not have done it. I made two errors of judgment."

At least one of those errors caught Beauchamp and other Notre Dame administrators by surprise. When asked about Holtz's admitting giving $20 to a player, Beauchamp said, "He never told me that." But still trying to defend his coach, Beauchamp said he "absolutely" would still have hired Holtz if he knew the coach had committed NCAA violations. This is an extraordinary admission from Beauchamp, one that gives a good insight into how far Notre Dame has sunk.

Beauchamp insisted that the infractions were ones that "under similar circumstances, without thinking, you and I would probably do the same thing." Ultimately, Beauchamp did refer to the mess as "unfortunate."

Although other college coaches have since been banished by the NCAA for committing far more "humanitarian" violations, Holtz was saved because he could be punished only if his violations took place after an NCAA rule change on September 1, 1985. All the violations involving Holtz at Minnesota took place before then.

Roselle Richardson said he could have told the NCAA even more, had investigators asked:

"Coach Holtz did rent me a couple of cars when I was a freshman to come home," Richardson says matter-of-factly. "I went in there to his office. It was in the winter, and I told Coach Holtz that I needed to get me a job or something like that because I wanted to go home. And he asked me when I wanted to go home, and I told him this weekend, and he told me don't worry about it. So anyway, Friday he called me into his office. I thought I was in trouble. But he told me that he had gotten me a rental car and the only thing I had to do was go to the car-rental place. It was Budget and I went there and picked up a car, and it was already in my name and everything, and then he gave a hundred dollars to me to come home. Right out of his pocket, twice. He took it out of his pocket like this and he gave it to me on the desk."

Did the NCAA ask you about this?

"No, they didn't. They dealt primarily with me being recruited. They never asked me about what happened there. There was a lot of things I could have told them. But they didn't ask me, so I didn't bring it up."

Holtz's claim that he didn't know that rules were being broken in his program is almost as incredible as his statements that none of his players were living a lifestyle that should have tipped him off. All Holtz had to do, Luther Darville says, was take a look in the stadium parking lot. "I know Tony Hunter was one of those people during his last year who was thinking of transferring. Tony Hunter suddenly got a car from somebody and he had to make payments, well, token payments, really, but he had a car to drive and he had an apartment to live in that was furnished. I helped him make payments on that car through indirect money. I wrote checks for payments on that car."

There weren't many defenders of Lou Holtz by the time the NCAA came nosing around. But in Minnesota, if you have to have a defender, you want it to be Minneapolis newspaperman Sid Hartman, one of the nation's last true old-style sportswriters. He remains a "homer" years after that went out of style in favor of far more objective journalism. To this day, he maintains Lou did nothing wrong.

Holtz may have thought he had a second ace in the hole when he found out that the NCAA's investigation was being spearheaded by former Notre Dame football player turned NCAA supersnoop Bob Minnix. Holtz promptly hired as his attorney Larry DiNardo, who was a Fighting Irish offensive lineman in the late 1960s—and one of Minnix's teammates. But Minnix remained unswayed. To this day, his pursuit of violations by Holtz has strained his relations with many in the Notre Dame athletic department, Holtz included.

"Notre Dame was so hot," says Ron Edwards, who became one of Minnix's best sources and confidants, "that Bob told me someone, either Holtz's lawyer or a lawyer from the university, came down to Kansas City and lit into him, trying to get him to back off." Asked about the story, Minnix paused, then said, "No comment." Subsequently, Minnix said, "Let's just say Lou and I had a disagreement over how we saw the facts."

So dogged was Minnix's pursuit that Sid Hartman even authored several columns calling on him to back off. "There is no doubt in my mind that Minnix and his buddies were out to get Holtz," Hartman wrote. "It would have been a big score if they could have discovered that the famous Notre Dame football coach was caught cheating."

As the NCAA investigation continued to leave Holtz twisting in the wind, many began to wonder what Holtz's Minnesota legacy would be. The legacy as far as Paul Giel is concerned is this: "Even though he was only here for two years and his record was 4-7 and 6-5, just about the time an athletic director is getting pretty discouraged about Minnesota's ability to compete favorably at the Division I, Big Ten level, he made me believe. He showed me that under the right kind of leadership and motivation and the expertise as far as the coaching profession [goes] that Minnesota might not be 11-0, might not ever be national champions, but he would have you 10-1 and 9-2 and 8-3, going to major bowls, and somewhere along the line, like a Hayden Fry at Iowa, going to a Rose Bowl."

But as it did at William and Mary, North Carolina State, the New York Jets, Arkansas—and is doing today at Notre Dame—Holtz's show began to wear thin in the Twin Cities. "You get a little tired of Lou after about three years," says Gopher booster Bill Maddux. "Same stories over and over again. The ripping up of the paper and all the magic tricks. But if that's what it takes to win football games, well, God bless him. It works pretty well with the players because after three years, they're tired of it, they go into their fourth year, but there's a new crew around to listen to all the same old stories and same old tricks."

As his second season wound to a close, Holtz continuously faced rumors that he was headed somewhere else. At one time or another during that year, word among boosters had Holtz leaving for the University of Pittsburgh, the University of South Carolina, Ohio State, and the head coach and AD's job at North Carolina State. "There have always been rumors with Lou Holtz," he said at a hastily called press conference on November 24, 1985. "I never gave substance to them by making any comment about them. But there have been so many lately that I want to make some comments now."

Holtz said he called the press conference after hearing an ESPN commentator say he was headed to Pittsburgh. "Then my in-laws call and say they've heard I'm going to Southern California," Holtz told reporters. "I'm going here, I'm going there. I'm not looking to go anywhere. I wouldn't go to another Big Ten school. The best job in the Big Ten is at Minnesota. I wouldn't take a job in the Southwest Conference. I wouldn't take a job in the Southeastern Conference. I've never entertained any thoughts of going anyplace else. I'm not interested in leaving Minnesota. I'm not planning to leave Minnesota. I'm perfectly content being at Minnesota. If that doesn't answer the questions, then I don't know what else I can say."

Three days later, Holtz resigned at Minnesota to replace Gerry Faust at Notre Dame.

Holtz forgot all of his promises. But his players didn't. "We've heard him say he wouldn't leave here until we won the Rose Bowl," linebacker Pete Najarian said bitterly. When a reporter reminded Holtz of his promise to Najarian and the players that he wouldn't leave Minnesota unless he "died or went to the Rose Bowl," Holtz said, "I don't recall everything I said along that line."

CHAPTER 10

Notre Dame: The Big Change

When Holtz arrived in South Bend, it no longer mattered what he had previously said. That was Minneapolis, this was South Bend. Big difference. Holtz kept right on talking, people kept right on hanging on his every word, and not a soul was confused as to the compass reading. Nobody was saying nay—especially the players.

"It really became a lot tighter ship," says Aaron Robb. "You got the message real quick that you'd better adhere to his policies and rules, or you weren't going to be around too long." Brandy Wells, a strong safety from Montclair, New Jersey, says of Holtz, "You looked at some of the things he did and some of the things he said and you just kind of went, 'No, no, I don't believe this guy.' But there's a saying that when the student's ready, the teacher will appear."

The teacher appeared with the now-infamous winter workouts.

Talk about emotional. They were just plain atrocious. But now when players gather, it's often the first thing they bring up—and laugh about. Frank Stams says, "When Coach Holtz came here, we were a team begging for direction." They got it. Stams could not have been more impressed. "He was so directive," Stams says, "and so goal-oriented and had such a plan. We were fired up, but at the same time we were nervous, because that first year we had those winter workouts. We had to get up at 5 A.M., and it's dark out, and we go through our workouts and when we leave, it's still dark. You go back and go to bed for an hour or so and wake up, and think you've had the worst nightmare of your life. These guys were puking during the workouts and you know that was good, because it showed us that we had a long way to go to get to where we wanted to be. We never doubted Coach Holtz because he was a winner. Everywhere he went he would win. So if this was what we had to do to win, everybody kind of hung with it and stuck with it."

Chris Kvochak, the walk-on free safety, says that Holtz "tried immediately to get us to suffer together in the winter workouts. So you appreciated more the guys you were out on the field with every day, by going through some kind of hell—and it was." John Carney says that "the players were hungry. He used that formula that has always worked for him—which is to find out how hungry you are. That's what those 6 A.M. workouts did. Those were tough times, and what he knew would happen is guys would either quit or become closer."

Remembers Jim Baugus, "Those workouts were an incredibly good idea, because we were getting up in the middle of blizzards and everyone was just killing themselves. Everyone was going to town and it really brought the team together, because you're looking around and these other guys are throwing up and doing everything just like you are. They had these big fifty-five-gallon barrels all over the place to throw up in. Those were pretty intense workouts. It was a great thing because everyone was saying, 'We're going to do it now.' "

Matt Dingens describes the workouts as "breaking the colts. He was implementing his expectations in the minds of us." But such a strenuous workout, followed by a shower and a huge breakfast, mainly put the players back in bed for the rest of the morning. Since a lot of college courses are in the mornings—especially for football players, who have to keep their afternoons free for practice—this didn't do wonders for the athletes' educational pursuits. Dingens says that the team grade-point average dropped from 2.7 to 2.5. Notre Dame refuses to confirm or deny Dingens's statement. Regardless, Holtz had the winter workouts just this one season, and Dingens says he believes that "those workouts were the turning point for the Holtz era."

Jeff Kunz is asked about the workouts.

"The first one I got sick," he says.

They called them the puke fests?

"Yeah, that's what I did. You do wind sprints, agility drills, just about anything. You go from one station to another. I remember going and saying there's no way I can go to class. I'd come back and I was dead. I missed class. It was good, but it was hard."

Arriving at the morning workouts, Holtz would be there, clapping his hands, chattering, "This is a great day to be alive and to go to work. Come on, it's noon in London." And then the throwing up would begin.

How excited were Domers? At Holtz's first intrasquad game in the spring of 1986, 32,017 fans showed up.

The change from Faust to Holtz was earthshaking for the players who experienced both. "Suddenly," says Tom Byrne, "you have someone who says, 'Business is business, and my time here is to teach you how to play football and to teach you how to be the best football player and get you into the NFL and make Notre Dame football the best football program in the country.' And he's not putting his arm around you and he's not saying, 'Hey, how are you doing? How's your family? How's your girlfriend?' It's more like, 'Get your ass moving and your technique was wrong on this.'"

That first season under Holtz was "so strange" in Pat Terrell's mind. "You knew there was a lot of talent," he says, "because Notre Dame was gonna attract the best players from around the country, but it was a scary feeling. We knew we had great football players, great high school players that we had signed, but it was still, 'Who are we?' I still remember Holtz brought us together and showed us his plan and program, and he definitely knows how to gain respect of a new signee. And so it was exciting. The atmosphere was that something big was about to happen at Notre Dame, because you just knew from the intensity that he brought to the program." One of the first things Terrell remembers Holtz telling the team was, "We will not succeed until you decide you don't want to be average. To be average means you're the best of the worst, or the top of the bottom. So the question should not be who wants to win, since all players want to win, but who cannot live with losing."

It was clear, from that first home game against Michigan on September 13, 1986, that Holtz had horsewhipped the Irish into being much better. The players sensed it. Says Mike Harazin, "The best memory I have is that Michigan game. We lost by one point [24–23]. John Carney missed a field goal with a few seconds left. That whole feeling is just amazing because even though we lost, the whole crowd stood up and gave the team a standing ovation." There was the distinct feeling that things were a lot better, and that victories would soon begin to flow again.

. . .

What became obvious immediately and dramatically that first year was Holtz's motivational ability. Indeed, the coach's talent to motivate was a crucial ingredient. Players who had begun thinking maybe they weren't very good suddenly were working their tails off to demonstrate to Holtz that maybe they were after all.

Says Father Joyce, "He's one of the great motivators in the country."

"Lou knew how to deal with collegiate athletes," says Pat Terrell, "because he could get you to sit up on the edge of your seat one minute and scared to blink, and then the next minute he'll start doing some magic tricks and you make fun of the way he looks or something. He knew how to keep you kind of loose, but at the same time focused." That is not a bad definition of motivation.

Bryan Flannery says he remembers "the first time we played Colorado in the Orange Bowl [in 1990]. We were at halftime, a 0-0 tie, and he came out and put it bluntly and said, 'For many of you, it's your last game. We have thirty minutes to play, a lifetime to remember. What you do now, how you react now, is going to determine how you are going to be the rest of your lives, whether you're successful or not. If you can answer this adversity and rise above it and come out victoriously, you can set the path for your life.' I thought it was very nice the way he put it." Of course, this is a perfect example of how motivation works—that is to say, it only works if the players let it. In truth, whether Notre Dame beat Colorado—it did—was not going to determine the rest of a player's life.

At the core of his motivational expertise is Holtz's ability to take simple themes, and expand upon them. Tom Freeman says, "My favorite motivational lesson from Holtz is that there are only two ways you can do anything or something: either with great enthusiasm or in self-pity. It worked great when I was working on my MBA. I would sit there studying and say, 'I wish I wasn't doing this. I'm having a terrible time doing this.' Or I could say, 'I'm improving myself.'

"If you ask yourself these questions and you realize you never want to have self-pity, you stop and find something to get excited about. Every day when I'm feeling like shit and I don't want to do my job, I find something to be enthusiastic about. That was a great line, and I'll take that with me forever.

"Another one I learned from Coach Holtz is that whenever you do something, you can either be better at it or worse at it. I mean, it can't stay the same. So whenever I'm doing something, I'm always asking myself, 'Am I getting better at it, or am I wasting my time?' Those are probably his two lines that I'll take to my grave. He has a lot of great lines. However, I don't know if he's such a great original thinker. I've seen clips of Woody Hayes and heard a lot about Hayes, and I think he's exactly what Woody Hayes was."

Nobody appreciates Holtz's motivational abilities more than Tim Grunhard: "Lou knew that I was an overachiever, and he knew that if he gave me any kind of compliments, I may become a little bit lax. In fact, before our senior year we had a meeting in which Holtz was making a list of all the guys he thought would get drafted in the NFL —Anthony Johnson, Jeff Alm, Dean Brown. And then it came to me and he said, 'Well, I'm not really sure about this guy yet. I'm half-thinking he might get it, but it depends on how he plays this year.' I was an all-American going into my senior year and he says this in front of the whole team and I was like, 'Wow.' He kind of knocked me down a peg. But I came to realize I worked extra hard that season just because of that, and I think that helped me get drafted in the second round [by Houston]. Just to spite him.

"He knew that I needed somebody to really get me agitated so that I would play better. He knows your psyche. He knows what buttons to push. He knows how you'll react to certain situations. And even though he's only five-eight and one hundred and thirty pounds when he's soaking wet, he also knows exactly what it takes to make you feel inadequate or make you feel like you're not doing your best or make you feel like you really did something well. Even when I see him now, I feel kind of uneasy around him—still."

When it comes to motivation, as it always does in college football, insiders generally agree that Holtz's shiningest moment came immediately following the 35–10 Cotton Bowl loss to Texas A&M on January 1, 1988. Kevin McShane was on that team and he recalls, "Coach Holtz is the biggest competitor I've ever met, and it tears his guts out to lose. You can just feel it. We walked into the locker room and you could just see the pain he was going through because he lost. You thought he was gonna fall over and have a heart attack. He stepped up on a chair. This is not verbatim, but what he said was, 'This is what it's like to lose. You'll never experience this feeling again. This is the first day of next year. We are gonna start today.' He set the tone right then and there for things to come in the future. Instead of coming in and saying, 'Oh, we had a good game, too bad we lost,' he started over. 'We're gonna change some things in the program,' he said. 'We're not gonna go backwards. We're gonna go forwards with the players that will do it and get the job done and these losing days are over.' I thought that was instrumental in us turning the corner right then. He demanded perfection from that day on, and then the next game, the next year, we beat Michigan twenty-six to seven. So I think he was so positive, looking into the future, demanding perfection, that that just carried over to his players. Instead of all the players sulking after the loss, he got us fired up that day for things to come." The next season the Irish won the national championship.

Former coach Ara Parseghian, a motivational genius himself, says of Holtz, "He just has a knack for saying the right thing at the right time to his team. He knows when to pat 'em on the back and when to kick 'em in the ass. A lot of coaches are kicking when they should be patting and patting when they should be kicking."

Then there are times when Holtz, who never uses fifty words when fifty thousand will do, can motivate by shutting up. Matt Dingens remembers the halftime of a game—exactly which one is foggy in his mind—in which "we were losing and playing absolutely miserably, just very, very flat. Coach Holtz came in fuming. He used his favorite line —'You gotta be kidding me'—and slaps a chalk board and walks away." The Irish returned for the second half, played great, and won.

Former quarterback Steve Belles from Phoenix, not one of the Irish's major stars, still recalls the time "I threw a touchdown against Purdue, and I came back on the next play on the kickoff team and made a tackle." As he came off the field, Holtz came up to him and shouted, "You're a helluva competitor." Nothing can be sweeter music to the ears of any athlete than that. And, of course, Belles certainly was one motivated player at that point. Holtz had the same effect on Brandy Wells. Says Wells, "Lou Holtz has this saying. He said it to me and he probably said it to four hundred other people: 'Brandy, I'd love to own just ten percent of your future.' "

John Carney remembers a time he had just missed an extra point, "which, of course, wasn't my fault," and while moping around, he didn't get into the huddle prior to the ensuing Irish kickoff. Recalls Carney, "Holtz grabbed me by my face mask and pulled me into the huddle and screamed at me, 'Have you given up?' It was humiliating. It really was. But I remember looking at him and thinking, Is Lou Holtz gonna climb inside this face mask with me?' " But Holtz was making a strong point. After something has been screwed up in football—in this case the point after—then you can't do anything to unscrew it. So what's most important is not to foul up whatever comes next—in this case the kickoff. That is not a bad lesson for life.

Mike Crounse says he soon determined what he saw as the cornerstone of the Holtz motivational attack: "Every week it was a different crisis. We always had a crisis. Every week something was wrong. Our offense was no good. Our defense was no good. Every week it was something different."

Holtz wasted no time shifting into high motivational gear when he got to South Bend. Knowing that a coaching change is especially hard on older players, even though they have been suffering from all the losing, Holtz knew he needed to get the best he could out of the veterans. So, says Tom McHugh, Holtz told the older players on the team, "I'm looking at you guys to give us leadership and set the tone for my first year. Whatever we do next year, which would be kind of a reflection of what we did this year, if we go to a bowl, win a national championship, or whatever, I will buy you guys the ring or the watch, whatever the main thing is." And the next year, when the Irish went to the '88 Cotton Bowl, he sent each of the seniors from the previous year's 5-6 team a Cotton Bowl watch just like the ones given to each of the current members. "That," says McHugh, "was my only firsthand experience with Holtz, so I kind of appreciated that follow-through, number one, and number two, he obviously appreciated what we did that last year, which is somewhat fulfilling to me."

One player who was not helped by Holtz's efforts was quarterback Tony Rice. Their relationship was difficult at best, several players said. A few were blunter.

"Holtz ruined Tony Rice," said Dan Quinn. "Rice was one of the best athletic quarterbacks I've ever seen. I don't just mean he could run. He could pass. I remember when I was back up there for summer school and he was throwing eighty yards to Todd Lyght [cornerback from Flint, Michigan, who was drafted by the Rams] and Lyght was reaching out with one hand like, boom, catching it. . . . Tony didn't have that great touch, but I'm talking ball on the money, one hundred and eighty miles an hour. It might have hurt the receiver's hands, but it was right there, and he had all the confidence in the world. Coach Holtz busted him down in practice relentlessly. He treated him like shit. In front of people, that's where you've got to be most careful. . . . With quarterbacks in general, they have to be the ones with all the confidence. Holtz just tore him down."

George Marshall echoes Quinn's thoughts: "Tony was a really good quarterback. He had a hell of an arm, but Holtz never let him throw it. Even during practice, Holtz wouldn't let him throw it. For the life of us we couldn't understand why. Tony could stand at the thirty and throw it in the other end zone. And if he would just have let Tony practice it more and then actually let him throw it in the game, we could have won a lot more. I just think he did Tony a great disservice by keeping him stifled."

To Rice's credit, he did possess one of the few personalities strong enough to stand up to Holtz. Kurt Zackrison recalls a time in practice when "Lou was upset because the offense wasn't clicking, something wasn't going right. Tony was calling out cadence and Lou was screaming at him for something, and Tony was underneath the center and he turned around and looked over his shoulder and said, 'Chill, Coach, I've got everything under control.' Nobody, I mean nobody, talked to Holtz like that. He got away with it; he ran the play and everything was cool."

Rice, despite leading Notre Dame through an undefeated season to a national championship in 1988, was not drafted by the NFL. He has had a few brief trials in the Canadian Football League, but he has not become the great pro quarterback many thought he would when he arrived in South Bend.

When the point would come when Holtz would have no more time to prepare his players' bodies, he would shift his attention to their minds. This meant a different kind of motivation. He'd gather his team in a large room, have everyone lie down on the floor, and, recalls Marc Dobbins, a safety from Chicago, "tell us to relax. We'd start out relaxing our feet, our right leg, our left leg, and let our back sink into the carpet. He'd tell us to let our minds be totally at ease, let your head sink, and just visualize what was gonna happen in the game from the time you warmed up to the time of the opening kickoff, and visualize the first play and just being successful. Don't have negative thoughts in your mind, and envision our success on the field. We come in at halftime and we're gonna talk about the things we did or the things we didn't do well, and we're gonna go out and win the third quarter and then just think about the end of the game, four, three, two, one, and the gun sounds and we win. And it's over with and we're gonna salute the crowd with the helmets. We always do that at our home games, and just think about the great times we had out there. When you visualize doing it, you actually believe it's going to come true on game day."

The benefit of the pregame relaxation period, says John Foley, is that "a lot of us are really intense and flying here and flying there and off the wall. He just wants you to relax and concentrate on what you've got to do. Psychology is really important. If you want to get an A on a test, you want to focus on that. Really work on it. The guys on the team would be like, 'I can do this, I can do this, I can do this.' You do your best when you're relaxed and your head is clear and you're focused. Sometimes the guys wouldn't be focused."

George Marshall recalls another motivational technique Holtz would use: "He said for us to picture somebody that you want to win this game for, and he'd have you just close your eyes and you would actually go through it, and you would picture your mother, your parents, whatever. Then, subconsciously I guess, it gives you motivation to do it for them and not yourself, and it's not for Coach Holtz—so that way, if he pisses you off that week, it doesn't matter; you're still going to perform your best because you're really doing it for somebody else."

Kicker John Carney from Centerville, Ohio, remembers benefiting greatly from Holtz's motivational efforts. Before the USC game in 1986, after some shaky kicks during the year—he blew kicks against Michigan and Pitt that would have won both games—Holtz told the team, "I hope the game comes down to John Carney, so he can finish his career with the winning kick." Carney laughs at the memory: "I thought, 'I've had enough attention this year. Let's just win the game fourteen to seven with me kicking two extra points.' What he said scared the shit out of me."

Notre Dame trailed by 17 points with just 12:26 remaining in the game. In fact, at a crucial point, Lou's son, Skip, roughed the punter. Holtz prefers to describe the offending player as "my wife's son." Holtz said he was so furious that as soon as Skip got close enough, he screamed, "What happened?" Responded Skip, "Didn't you see it?"

But, somehow, that error ignited the Irish.

In a storybook, fantasyland finish, Carney—who had already kicked two field goals during the game—kicked a 19-yarder with two seconds remaining to give the Irish a 38–37 win at the L.A. Memorial Coliseum before a stunned Trojan crowd of 70,614.

And that win turned around Lou Holtz's career at Notre Dame.

The reason this win was so important was that a loss would have meant a 4-7 season, worse than anything Gerry Faust had done. And it would have meant a dismal season in which Notre Dame hadn't beaten a single team ranked in the Top 20; USC was ranked seventeenth.

Four-and-seven would have put the whole of Notre Dame in a depressing winter funk. Four-and-seven would have made it extremely difficult for the players to believe they were being coached by a genius. However, 5-6—but with a win over USC—allowed the Irish to look at their losses to Michigan, Michigan State, Purdue, Alabama, Pittsburgh, Penn State, and LSU, as very correctable flaws.

Chris Kvochak says, "The previous years under Faust, and even the first few games under Holtz, we lost so many close games, it was like, we can never win the close games anymore. Finally, we realized, 'Hey, we can do this again.' "

For all of the euphoria, plenty of people were not certain Holtz was the ideal choice; they were not swept away by the adulation. When Holtz arrived, John Askin says, "He took the position, 'I'm authority.' We needed that, but we didn't need an abuser, basically. We needed someone who would take the team under his wing and carry it and nurse it and bring it back to life and new belief. We didn't need all the tricks and the mind games and everything else that came along with it. We didn't need what that does to some of these younger players. Some of these younger players are going to be antitrusting of people through-out the rest of their lives and in all of their relationships with other people—and I don't think they needed that."

Because of what Holtz did?

"Yeah."

Plus, for all of Holtz's motivational genius, there are storm clouds in South Bend because his motivational act wears poorly. It's a great one-nighter; it's not a long-running relationship. Joe Allen says, "The players felt like, 'Okay, I heard that one before. Give me something new.' I just think all the players get bored with him quickly. He has that great personality right off the top for the first couple of years, but it gets old." Scott Kowalkowski says of the Holtz motivational act, "It's a joke with the players. How many times are you gonna hear his 'what it takes to be successful here at Notre Dame'?" Then he falls into the litany ingrained in his brain: "Love, trust, and commitment. You have to love each other like you'd want somebody to love you. You have to be committed to what you're doing and to this common goal, and you have to be able to trust each other."

PART
IV

A Soul
Is Sold

CHAPTER

11

Special Treatment

"We had to have someone [as head football coach] of impeccable integrity and character. They have to live without redshirting and athletic dorms and special treatment from the admissions office."
—Father Edmund Joyce, quoted in
The Sporting News, November 28, 1988

No part of the Notre Dame image is more cherished, more critical to its efforts to distinguish itself from the grubby football factories with which it must compete, than the notion that its football coach will receive no special favors from the university to help him along. Let the Oklahomas of the world sully their schools by bringing in unqualified students who can run and block and tackle; Notre Dame proves that you can maintain high academic standards and still put a championship team on the field. Let the Nebraskas automatically redshirt the freshman class to let them grow bigger and stronger; Notre Dame reminds the world that college is a four-year experience, and that treating it otherwise severs the connection between school and team that lies at the heart of college sports.

Former assistant coach Kurt Schottenheimer says that the school will not stand for anybody who does anything "that is going to compromise the integrity of the university, and if you can put together a great football program, they're all for it. If you put together a great basketball team, do it. But don't compromise the excellence that this university stands for. Once you know what you're there for and what you've got to live up to, it's easy to live up to."

"My image of Notre Dame prior to going there," says Tom Riley, who played there from 1984 to '86 and now works in Democratic Party politics in California, "was it was a school that was a complete success and it did it the right way. Everybody bought into the Notre Dame image. It was the Golden Dome and all that. Now, Notre Dame football falls into that category of so many other big-time football schools. It traded part of its image for a few wins. They had the years of Faust and found out they didn't like losing. What separates Notre Dame now from any other school? Absolutely nothing. The things that drew me to Notre Dame as a senior in high school aren't there anymore."

One of the first standards to fall—despite Joyce's public pronouncement to the contrary—was the refusal to redshirt. Redshirting is a common—and legal—occurrence in college football. If a player is redshirted for a season, it means he cannot play in any games and thus does not use up one of his four years of eligibility; NCAA rules give a student-athlete five years from the time he enters college to use his four seasons of sports. However, he can still go to practice and fully participate—and keep receiving his scholarship, which pays all school expenses.

Redshirting can accomplish several things. It can give a young player time to grow bigger. Or it can give him time to learn more complicated college football schemes. It can let him recover from an injury without costing him a competitive year. It can allow the coach to hold him out while another, usually better, player at the same position uses his remaining eligibility.

The point to understand is that redshirting, while legal and ethical in the eyes of the NCAA, has everything to do with football excellence and nothing to do with academic life. The official Notre Dame position is that it doesn't do it unless a player has been injured or has received his undergraduate degree and has been accepted into graduate school. Holtz writes in his book that "there's no redshirting." That's the official position.

The truth is that Notre Dame redshirts. But that's not in tune with the image.

Mark Nigro doesn't even try to pretend otherwise: "From the first day [in 1986], there were a bunch of us who knew we were going to be redshirted, and that's okay. There were lots of seniors ahead of us."

Explains Scott Kowalkowski, "They say they don't redshirt, but they do and there's always that option."

Linc Coleman hates the redshirt charade. "I remember my buddies Pierre Martin and Bobby Carpenter. First they were told by their position coach, 'Coach Holtz is going to redshirt you guys, and next year after you put on a little muscle and get a little faster, you'll be able to contribute to the team.' Then Coach Holtz brought them into his office and told them the same thing."

The understanding that Notre Dame doesn't redshirt, says Coleman, is "the one thing that got me to go to Notre Dame. Then when I got up there, I thought, 'I've got to work because I don't want to be one of those guys that's gonna be redshirted.'"

Is that like false advertising?

"False advertising, bait and switch. They get you up there thinking you're gonna be able to go and see all these nice places. I don't know why they have to false-advertise to get quality players. They have a quality program, they have history. I don't know why they say, 'We don't redshirt. Don't worry about it. You're gonna come up here and you're gonna contribute to the team and you're gonna be a big part of this big scheme and you're gonna be everything.' Then you get up there and they go and you have to sit here at home while they're playing Michigan or whatever. I don't know why they still do it, but they really don't have to. I really can't figure that out."

The answer is that other schools admit they redshirt, and since Notre Dame has created the myth it doesn't, that gives the Irish a recruiting advantage.

Philosophically, Holtz likes redshirting. He liked it at North Carolina State, he liked it at Arkansas, he liked it at Minnesota. It's just that he is forced to sneak around the image to preserve what Notre Dame professes is its more honorable way.

Nobody works harder at preserving the illusion of no redshirting at Notre Dame than Lou Holtz. When David Rosenberg first got to South Bend, he says that "Coach Holtz said, 'David, we might put you on a developmental squad to get you bigger, stronger, so that we don't redshirt you.' "

Did he use that term—*developmental squad?*

"Yeah. [Then,] after a couple of linebackers got hurt he said, 'David, you're gonna have to play. We're not gonna be able to redshirt you.' I said, 'Okay,' and then I broke my leg and so he didn't really have too much of a decision."

Clearly, Holtz was going to redshirt Rosenberg; the "developmental squad" dodge was an effort to dress up the decision in convoluted English.

Bob Dahl, a defensive lineman from Chagrin Falls, Ohio, recalls being told not to go out on the playing field during one season.

Somebody said that to you?

"Yeah, one of the coaches. I haven't thought about that in a long time."

That means they wanted to redshirt you?

"Yeah, they wouldn't let me out there on the field, even if they said, 'Fifth-teamers go in,' yeah, so . . . I accepted it because at the same time they had a lot of good players ahead of me and I was physically not ready to play. I was only 225 or 230 pounds."

Because the redshirting issue is so awkward, Holtz often has a hard time facing up to it. Rob Carpenter says that right at the end of summer training camp, he incurred a bruised shoulder and "at that time Lou Holtz decided he wanted to redshirt me, but he didn't tell me." A bruised shoulder, obviously, is an extremely minor injury.

Carpenter knew Holtz wanted to redshirt him "because the last day of practice, you come in and there's a list of players to have their pictures taken who are gonna be on the official roster. It's for TV stations and so forth. I wasn't on it. There were different freshmen on it, but I wasn't. I kind of got the hint from that. Then, three weeks later, Holtz came to me and told me he wasn't gonna play me this year. He was gonna just let me travel and get the experience and things like that."

Sounds suspiciously like redshirting, doesn't it?

Rob Carpenter was so furious over the deceit—Holtz, he says, told him during recruiting that Notre Dame doesn't redshirt—that he transferred to Syracuse. "They say," he grouses repeatedly, "that they don't redshirt players, but they do."

Isn't that kind of hypocritical?

"Oh, yeah, it is. I think that a lot of guys that left took it that way. I know I wasn't the only one that left that year. Guys just felt that there was so much talent in that class, and then they decide to redshirt some of us. Saying you don't redshirt and then doing it is something a lot of guys don't take too lightly."

Did Holtz lie to you?

"I guess you could call it lying. . . . You're told it doesn't happen but you know it does happen. You've just got to figure out that that's what goes on. Supposedly around the country, Notre Dame has that aura that it's such a nice university that those things don't go on and everything's done correct there. It's kind of funny because once you get in on the inside, you see things a little differently. You're not so blind to that."

As the years go by, redshirting has increasingly become a way of life at Notre Dame. Mike Crounse says that especially as the Irish improved their record under Holtz, the entering freshmen "didn't really have the potential to play and were pretty much settling" for being redshirted.

The redshirting began in earnest during the Faust years. Jim Baugus, a Faust recruit, says, "When I was there, almost the entire freshman class was redshirted. It was the unspoken thing. You weren't allowed to say it. My freshman year, we played some team and we killed them. The coaches were going up and down the sidelines saying, 'Is there anybody who hasn't played yet?' I said, 'I haven't, Coach,' and they said, 'Anybody but you?' I was one of the few freshmen on the sidelines. Another player came up and said, 'Jim, you've just been redshirted.' The way they redshirt is they just don't put you in any games. At the end of your fourth year, you would go back and they would say, 'By golly, you didn't play your freshman year.' And the player would say, 'Gee, I guess not.'"

Cedric Figaro, who currently plays in the NFL for Cleveland, says that when he was a freshman, he had a conversation with Faust in which Figaro said he thought that "I should be playing a lot more than I was, and his answer was that if it was up to him, no freshmen would play. They would all redshirt. And I said, 'Well, I wish you would have told me this when you were recruiting me, because there was no way I would have come all this way up here to sit on a bench.'"

Kurt Zackrison says that late one season, one coach, Bishop Harris, who was on the staff in '84 and '85, told him he could either go in for his first action against USC and play the rest of the season " 'or you can sit out and get an extra year if you want.' I said, 'I'll take an extra year.'"

Jim Dadiotis is another truth teller. "In 1986," he says, "I was redshirted, but I'm not supposed to say that." Dadiotis says the Irish tried to act as if it were a medical redshirt, as a result of a shoulder separation, but that injury is routine, not serious, and quickly played with. Dadiotis says, "Notre Dame wants to act like it doesn't redshirt, but it does. Let's be honest. The reason I was redshirted is there were seniors ahead of me."

Even *Blue & Gold Illustrated,* in August 1987, said, "The reality of the situation is this: If Notre Dame hadn't made a move to allow more athletes to compete during their fifth year, Lou Holtz would have an unbelievable rebuilding project on his hands this fall. Instead of returning four starters on the offensive line, only two would be back." Concluded the publication, "In the long run, a school just cannot expect to remain competitive when other schools have players on the roster for a 20 percent longer period of time."

If Notre Dame were willing to admit that remaining competitive was all that mattered, it could drop the charade and redshirt openly. It's not the doing it but the lying about it that rankles. Holtz is quoted in Bilinski's book as saying of redshirting, "It doesn't blend in with Notre Dame's philosophy or its purpose." A salient defense of redshirting can be made, but the administration in South Bend is happier preserving its image through blatant hypocrisy.

While there are still no athletic dorms, the university has been willing to provide Lou Holtz with what he says he needs. Former coach Dan Devine notes that Notre Dame "is the last place I thought an indoor practice facility for the football team would be built. It just goes against their philosophy. They don't want to be labeled a football factory. But that's Lou. He just has the ability to get things that are necessary to win."

But when that includes athletes who are patently unqualified by Notre Dame's academic standards, Domers must start to ask themselves if the wins that follow are worth the cost.

Tom Freeman, who started at guard in 1987 under Holtz but who was recruited by Faust in 1984, definitely doesn't like the path academics at Notre Dame are taking. "I don't know what the academic standards were before, but I know they were much higher under Coach Faust than they were when Lou Holtz came in," says Freeman.

What Freeman says worries him is that it seems Notre Dame is in the business these days of academic rule-bending on behalf of football players, Father Joyce's protestations to the contrary. Freeman, whose grandfather, three uncles, and five cousins attended Notre Dame, continues, "I think what the school did was say, 'Let's get all the alumni off our back and we will lower our standards and try to get the best athletes rather than the best academic athletes,' and they did that. When Lou Holtz came in, they lowered it quite a bit. All of a sudden you saw the Tony Rices show up. Tony Rice is a great guy, but to get a seven hundred on your SAT [the minimum NCAA requirement to play football; Rice failed to achieve that] you have to be able to spell your name right and that's about it. Then there was that Foley or whatever his name was."

John Foley?

"Yeah. He was another Prop 48 guy [a player who did not meet the NCAA's minimum standards of 700 SAT and a 2.0 average in high school; such players can enter a school, but can't practice or play for a year while they improve their academic qualifications]. For me, I went there because I didn't want to play with those kinds of people and I didn't want Notre Dame to have that type of person, but . . ."

John Foley, who coming out of high school was named National Defensive Player of the Year by USA Today, probably didn't qualify to go to anyone's university, much less Notre Dame. Still, everybody wanted him. Admits Foley, "I had a very bad high school experience with academics. I did really bad. I took football too serious. I had serious academic problems. What happened is, I went in for my interview, and I think it was [Kevin] Rooney, the Notre Dame admissions officer I talked to, and he felt that I could make it at Notre Dame. He knew I had academic problems but he said, 'I don't know but there's something about you.' That was the reason they gave me a chance."

What was your SAT?

"Six eighty. I did terrible. I was like, 'Oh, well.' "

How did you feel being a Prop 48 player?

"Embarrassed. I felt I embarrassed my family."

Do you sometimes wish you had gone somewhere where being a Prop 48 wasn't a big deal?

"Oh, yeah, but I never knew I had this fire inside of me to do well in school. I figured if I was gonna be around smart people, I might get smart. That was my attitude. I can maybe learn something from these people. I may not get my degree, but I'll learn something."

How did the students react to you?

"At first they were upset that they accepted me and Tony [Rice]."

A lot of alumni were, too?

"Oh, yeah. A lot of people thought I was an idiot, which I was at the time."

How did you feel about Holtz taking so much criticism for taking you and Rice?

"I felt bad for Holtz. But that was one reason I wanted to do so well, because I wanted to show everybody that Holtz knew what he was talking about when he decided to take me."

Entering Notre Dame freshman these days have an average math score on the SAT of 670; 82 percent score above 600. That's just half the test; the other part is the verbal section. Foley scored 680 on the entire test.

Foley eventually graduated in 1990, thanks to the support of a lot of people who wanted him to make it. Foley tells of a science professor who talked to him about becoming a dentist. Said Foley, " 'Do you know who I am? I'm an idiot.' He said, 'I'm serious. I'll tutor you all four years at Notre Dame.' I said, 'Do you realize I'm not very bright?' He said, 'Listen, I'll tutor you, I'll work with you all four years. I promise you'll be a dentist when you graduate.' I said, 'No, I really don't want to be in the medical profession because my sisters are.' "

Certainly, it can be argued that the fact that John Foley made it academically shows that Prop 48 does what it was designed to do: it allows talented athletes time to learn academic skills without the pressures of competing on the field. But it's hard to imagine a nonathlete being given the same chance at Notre Dame. If that's not "special treatment from the admissions office," what is?

Admissions director Rooney refuses to say what either the average SAT score of entering regular freshmen students is, or what the same score is for entering scholarship football players. *Barron's Profile of American Colleges* says, however, that regular students average 1250 on the standardized test, out of a possible 1600. One Notre Dame insider with intimate knowledge says his "best guess" is the football players average less than 900. Some people think it could be much less. Not long ago, in an interview with *The Washington Post,* Rooney confessed that when it comes to the academic abilities of the football players, Notre Dame admits, "We're about halfway to where I'd like us to be."

To its credit, Notre Dame quickly reversed its policy of admitting Prop 48s after Foley and Rice and announced it would not do such a thing again. But it still, as the numbers show, is letting football players into school who are far below Notre Dame standards.

James Bobb had three years with Faust and one with Holtz. He says that when Holtz arrived, "The one thing I did notice is that he was bringing in athletes that were below the Notre Dame [academic] standards." Bobb, like everyone else, quickly points to Rice as Textbook Example A of nonconformity. Mention the admission of Tony Rice to Linc Coleman and he hits the ceiling: "Oh, man, Tony Rice, I'm telling you, he may have learned to read before he left Notre Dame, but he did not know how to read the year I was there."

Rice laughs at the accusation and says, "Tell him if he wants, I'll read him a bedtime story." Rice says his high school grade average coming out of South Carolina was a 2.3, giant steps behind all regular students accepted in South Bend, for whom a 3.5 is marginal qualification. Understand that in 1990, for example, 36 percent of Notre Dame's entering freshmen ranked no lower than fifth in their high school graduating classes, and 84 percent were in the top 10 percent of their classes.

It was the admission of Tony Rice in 1986, in Holtz's first recruiting class, that put Notre Dame's football team back on top. After the '86 team went 5-6, Rice was the quarterback in 1987 as the Irish were 8-4 (including a Cotton Bowl loss to Texas A&M), and again in 1988, on the 12-0 national championship team that beat West Virginia in the Fiesta Bowl. Without Rice, the odds are very good that Notre Dame was going to continue floundering. That's what made Rice worthy of attending Notre Dame.

Former assistant coach Schottenheimer tries to rationalize taking football players who, if they weren't players, would in no way qualify for admission: "I believe [that] just because some people don't have the test score or the GPA and that sort of thing and so may not look like they exactly qualify, still there are certain guys that you know would bust their ass, a Tony Rice type of player. I mean, it's important for those guys to go to Notre Dame. They want to be at Notre Dame. If they didn't have the academic success in high school that many of the student body have at Notre Dame, but they wanted to be there bad enough and they wanted to work at it, and they would do anything that was asked of them in order to be a part of that program, then let them. And that means going to class, going to study hall, and busting their ass. It never came easy for them, I'm sure. But those guys were the kind of guys that if they had the right character and right type of background that made Coach Holtz think they would work extra hard and it was that important for them to be there, and that you knew would go the extra step in order to be successful academically, then Lou would consider that type of a player." Notice that Schottenheimer refers to that type of "player," not "student"; the academically motivated with two left feet need not apply, no matter how hardworking.

There is a saying around Notre Dame admissions: "The thicker the applicant, the thicker the file."

But Father Joyce, the former second-in-command, says, "If we think that a player can make it at Notre Dame with tutorial help, we'll take a flier on two or three—if everything else is very positive, and if they are blue, blue chip athletes." However, Holtz's first recruiting class, in addition to Rice and Foley, included such academic suspects as Jeff Pearson, John Zaleski, and Jason Cegielski. The latter three were kicked out of Notre Dame for a variety of infractions—hardly suggesting everything else was "very, very positive."

Joyce argues that the conventional college board scores are not indicative of what a black athlete in particular can accomplish, which is one reason he thinks some of the football players should be cut some slack. Still, in an interview for this book, he admitted that "there is preferential treatment for football players. They don't have to come up with the board scores. If they were ordinary students, we wouldn't take them."

So why take them?

"Because a football player contributes a great deal to the University of Notre Dame. We have nothing to be ashamed of."

Tom McHugh, a Faust recruit who scored 1150 on his SAT, says he and his good friends detected an increase in academic sleight of hand in South Bend once Holtz arrived. "We got the impression," he says, "that the administration and the [Holtz] coaching staff, either formally or informally, had come to kind of an agreement that 'let's go after the top athletes that are going to make the immediate impact to get us back on a winning program as soon as possible.' That meant they'd have to look the other way on some of the other qualifications that someone might ordinarily need when they are being recruited, more so than in the past. That's just the overall impression that I had."

Leave it to Dan Devine to best explain the admissions policy under Holtz: "Lou gets more average kids in than anyone can imagine." Devine insists that during his five years as coach, he was only allowed to take in one football player who didn't meet Notre Dame's academic standards; star running back Jerome Heavens. Not even the most fanatically image-conscious alumnus will complain about the occasional bending of academic standards for a great athlete. The problems come when such bending becomes standard policy.

Shawn Smith, George Williams, and Chris Zorich are just a few of the players who told the authors that their academic credentials fell short of those usually required for admission. Smith and Erik Simien, rather than being the hardworking, motivated students that Schottenheimer and Joyce portray as valid exceptions, skipped classes frequently, trading their free books (paid for under their scholarships) for class notes from roommates who would attend in their stead. Zorich did ultimately graduate, though the school's alumni directory curiously reports that it doesn't know what in.

One former player, asking for anonymity because he fears retribution from Holtz, says, "The truth is, the type of player Holtz recruited while I was there *usually* [emphasis added] wasn't good enough to get into Notre Dame. The academic caliber of the football players is not what people think when they think of Notre Dame."

Ted FitzGerald is another player who admits that if he weren't a football player, he wouldn't have gotten in. He says in high school he made Bs, and "Bs are not going to make it at Notre Dame for a non–football player. In the history of my high school, six kids got into Notre Dame—five valedictorians and me. That'll give you an idea."

Jeff Kunz says, "When I came into Notre Dame, all I was thinking about was playing football. I didn't really know anything about a degree." Of the recent penchant for lowering standards for football players, Kunz adds, "I think the board of directors or the president or whoever runs the school will put a stop to it sooner or later. I don't know if it will take new people in there or what, but this can't last. Finally, alumni and everybody are gonna say, 'Hey, this is ridiculous putting football before academics.' Now it seems like we have football with academics way below."

Not long ago in a speech in Denver, Lou Holtz looked his audience dead in its collective eye and said, "Notre Dame is not gonna lower the standard for anybody."

What is objectionable is not so much that Notre Dame does it, but that it pretends it doesn't. (In that same talk, Holtz said he doesn't use any profanity on the sidelines during games, which strikes everyone who has been on the Irish sidelines as a total untruth.) In 1992, there were 912,845 high school boys playing football. There are only about nine thousand scholarship players at the major football-competing universities. Surely—surely—there are twenty each year who are both smart and good whom Notre Dame could convince to come play at the most famous university in the country, with Notre Dame paying for everything. Many former Notre Dame players—including John Askin, Tom Riley, and Tom Freeman—support this theory; they are certain it shouldn't be as hard for the Irish to find both brains and brawn in a single body as it was for Diogenes to find an honest man.

Each year, the Collegiate Sports Information Directors of America, along with GTE, select an Academic All-America football team. The program was started in 1952, and the Irish have had twenty-eight different players named—but nobody since 1987, when punter Vince Phelan and kicker Ted Gradel made it. In other words, Lou Holtz has not recruited a single top scholar, while the Irish averaged nearly one a year before his arrival. The National Football Foundation and the Hall of Fame annually select scholar-athletes to receive $3,000 scholarships for postgraduate study. Since this program was started in 1966, Notre Dame has had thirteen of its football players chosen, more than any other school. The last one was defensive tackle Greg Dingens in 1985; again, no Holtz recruits.

Notre Dame won both the national championship and the College Football Association (CFA) award for highest graduation rate of its scholarship football players in 1988. Holtz said the CFA award was more important than the national championship. But it is important to note that it was Gerry Faust who recruited the players who won the CFA award.

Mark Nigro is not amused by what has gone on in the transition between Faust and Holtz: "I think the obvious difference was, all of a sudden we were looked at as a school trying to get players in as opposed to a school trying to get students in. Everyone could see lower SAT scores and you started to ask, 'Do we want to lower standards to win football games?' The answer obviously was yes. Those were the things that bothered me. I was there because I belonged. But taking these others cheapened being a Notre Dame football player.

"The recruits Holtz brought in were less polished. That's a decent way of putting it. Maybe Coach Faust only went after the high school all-Americans he knew he wouldn't have problems with succeeding academically. It surprised me a little that the administration put up with [Holtz's recruits]. There have been players suspended and released from school. There may also have been incidents where they've turned their heads."

One of Notre Dame's greatest all-time players agrees. Says offensive lineman Tom Thayer, "It does seem they're more willing now than ever to let people in who wouldn't have gotten in in the past just to play football. If they're sacrificing academics for winning some ball games, that's not right."

One reason for the high graduation rate is that Notre Dame is amazingly easy to stay in. It's almost as if academic failure violates campus rules. Even Holtz notes that to get a diploma in the hands of a student, the school "will work to the nth degree to help you." For example, Holtz claims in his book that academically troubled Tony Rice solved his problems one summer when he "worked fourteen hours a day with a tutor."

As we've seen elsewhere, such statements from Holtz should not be treated as if uttered under truth serum. Can you imagine Tony Rice, tutor at his side, poring over philosophy books from nine A.M. to eleven P.M., seven days a week? And such intense bolstering is another thing that bothers Notre Dame purists; a student worthy of admission should not require such extensive tutoring, and particularly shouldn't need it to overcome deficiencies in basic skills of reading and writing. Rice did ultimately receive a degree in psychology, a fact that may help underscore the sentiments expressed by other players, that "you almost have to want to flunk out" (Dan Tanczos) and "they make sure you pass" (Shawn Smith).

Joe Allen says that "academically, I wasn't impressed once I got there. It wasn't that tough. I think I maybe opened a book under twenty hours to study in four years. I didn't have the greatest grades, a two point four. That's with never studying."

In fact, says Matt Dingens, "you have to work hard not to graduate from Notre Dame. You have to lie, you have to make excuses. Unless you go in and just try to fail everything, you'll make it. They've been doing that forever, way before I ever got there. If you go to class and take tests, you're gonna pass and you're gonna get through. There's no basket weaving or anything like that, but there is Greek classics and translation and a couple of courses you know from upperclassmen and dormmates to take if you need a good grade."

For all of Notre Dame's palaver about there being no scuba-diving classes, no physical education majors, and no place to hide the athletes where they will be safe from troublesome intellectual challenges, the no-brainer in place for the football players is American studies. Says David Rosenberg, "I'm not here to knock it, but eighty percent of the football players were in American studies. Maybe they like America a whole lot."

The fact is, a football player mostly wants to play football. When a player gets to be eighteen, the preferred place to play is at a university. What gets difficult for the institution is trying to somehow dress up a football player so that he looks like a student. American studies may not be an appropriate costume.

Another means of progressing toward a degree, several players said, was cheating. Jason Cegielski says, "Academic-wise, it was a joke how we used to cheat our asses off. We used to have rows of like twenty to twenty-five people in a big auditorium. Everybody used to sit together. Everybody looked over shoulders. We had it all set up. Something happened where a TA [teaching assistant] got a hold of mine and another person's paper. They were exactly word for word. They called me in. I think their rule was they were supposed to expel anyone who did that. I didn't get expelled for that. But they gave me an F. There were so many people cheating it was ridiculous. I never seen anybody get expelled for cheating while I was there."

Cegielski also says it's a "very big misnomer" that outsiders somehow think of athletes at Notre Dame being more sound academically than athletes elsewhere: "They're not. Playing football and academics is hard. They'll get around it just like any other school."

Did football players know where to go if they wanted to cheat on a class?

"Oh, sure. Especially if somebody knew someone who was good in that subject, they'd set something up, like seating arrangements. That was no big deal. I remember times when we used to be taking a test and we'd be talking out loud. Just yelling. Some of the teachers knew. It's just a normal university with a very hypocritical image. Things like this just tell you how hypocritical they are."

Dan Quinn says, "I swear to God there was rampant cheating. I'm not talking about with just the football players. I'm talking about on true-false tests [where different color-coded tests were given to adjacent students to prevent copying], people switching tests so they get the same color next to each other. It was ridiculous. I finally got out of that. I don't want to cheat my way through school and then go into business."

The problem that Notre Dame—and every other football power—faces is that academics are always going to be an impediment to college football. Gone forever are the days when a bright young student enrolls and says, "I want to learn all I can about molecular biology, and as an extracurricular activity I want to play football." Increasingly, football on campus is a full-time pursuit. So, ideally, is education.

Dan Hampton states the academics vs. football dilemma well: "[Lou] Holtz has got to be too much to too many people. But if you want to try to keep the curriculum high and the academics up, then you have to go get players who can pass the courses, but who can be six and five every year?" In other words, it sounds good to say academics are ahead of football, and most right-thinking people want desperately to think that. But the reality is different.

Andre Jones notes that the emphasis Holtz puts on academics, especially during recruiting time, contains a catch-22 when it lines up across from football. For openers, Holtz has a rule that if a player doesn't practice, he doesn't play. Jones says he approached Holtz before the 1990 Orange Bowl game against Colorado and told him that because he was taking both Japanese and Russian, he needed time off from practice to study. Holtz reminded Jones of the rule.

"I wanted to play," says Jones, who was a starter for two years at linebacker, "but I had to make that decision. My mom has been an educator for the last twenty-six years, so it wasn't really a [tough] decision. I had to pass those exams. For a lot of people, I think they would have opted to have gone the other way, to have practiced and played the game and just dealt with whatever grade they got.

"I didn't understand why I had to basically choose between the two, but I understood in the long run that he was just going by his rules. After the first day, it didn't bother me anymore. Plus, Holtz said I could go down there [to Miami], but I just wouldn't be able to play. That was to me enough, just to be down there supporting the team."

Norm Balentine also recalls an exception to the academics first and always and forever philosophy. He says he asked Holtz "if I could skip practice because I had a class. He said, 'Okay, but don't let it happen again, though.'" By any yardstick, that is not a ringing endorsement of the importance of academics in South Bend.

. . .

Although Notre Dame isn't thrilled, Holtz has in recent years taken to saying he thinks the best way to handle the academics vs. football partnership, which really is an adversarial relationship, is to create national sports academies funded by professional sports teams. At these academies, suggests Holtz, the athletes would learn about picking agents, handling finances, doing media interviews, and would devote themselves to physical training and playing football.

Upon hearing this, Mel Durslag wrote in the *Los Angeles Times* that since Holtz was only in his mid-fifties, "we don't like to disillusion him at an age so tender. But he must be informed that we already have pro academies in this land. They are called Notre Dame, USC, Ohio State, Nebraska, Oklahoma, Clemson, Miami, and the like."

And sometimes, academics just don't add up. Rodney Culver, a back from Detroit who was once the starting Irish fullback but subsequently switched to tailback, gives the perfect illustration when he says, "I'm twenty-five, and the average life expectancy is seventy to seventy-five, and you've got one-third of your life over with and then there's this other half." Read it again, and weep.

Gerry Faust is asked if Notre Dame tries to act as if it's purer academically than it is. There is a pause, followed by a longer pause. He shifts uneasily. He acts as if he wishes the question had never been asked or, at the least, would just go away. Silence.

Finally, Faust says, "I'm not gonna answer that question. I love Notre Dame."

The truth is, Faust says, "plenty of football players at Notre Dame wouldn't get in if they weren't football players. And that's true at any university."

So Notre Dame does bend its allegedly straight-arrow admission requirements into whatever shape it takes to allow whatever player it wants into school? Sure, says Faust, "I think it's fair. Every university in the country does it. And why not? Universities hire noted scholars who don't teach in order to enhance the university and make it prominent in education. We take musicians who are poor at math but who will enhance the school. So why shouldn't Notre Dame take in football players who don't happen to meet the standards?"

The answer, of course, is because the Irish always belittle others who do exactly the same thing. Once, when a high-ranking Notre Dame official was asked why the Irish defensive backs were so slow, he said, "Because we aren't like Pittsburgh or Southern California or Oklahoma, where they will take anybody. They can't get in school here. That's our problem." Yet, the fact that Notre Dame does allow obviously nonqualified student-football players in is not as shocking as how often the school does it. Says Faust, "It would probably be at least fifty percent." That was when he was coach and academic standards—as we've heard —were much higher. Faust says that the average Notre Dame SAT score when he was there was 1,150 with a 3.5 high school grade point average; his football players, he says, scored around 950 average on the SATs and had a 2.3 in high school.

Then, realizing he may have deprecated his true love, Faust says, "I don't think that all of our future leaders come from brilliant backgrounds. Some are street-smart people. There's not a real true formula. It's not all grades. I've seen people with fourteen hundred SAT scores and three point nine high school grade averages flunk out. And I've seen guys with 700 on their SAT and two point ohs in high school make it." He's right. But it is rare. And if the only such students you admit are the athletically gifted, then your real interest is what they'll do for you and not vice versa.

Faust, who can't help himself when it comes to truth, says, "When it comes right down to it, administrators have a double standard. They say they want you to graduate kids, but if you don't win, you're gone." Faust says that of one hundred or so of his recruits, only eight failed to graduate—but he lost games and he's gone. Holtz had that many academic failures in his first two recruiting classes—four from the 1986 group, five more from the 1987 class—but he wins and he stays. You figure it out.

Nobody ever said it better than veteran Chicago newspaper columnist Bob Verdi, writing in *The Sporting News*: "Honor is of the utmost importance, which does not mean that defeat with honor is an acceptable alternative."

So Notre Dame not only persists in playing football, but has—its pious protestations notwithstanding—made it the top priority. There is absolutely no question that what Notre Dame is best known for is its football. Hesburgh always talked about the chemistry department, but how many people, when asked about Notre Dame, say, "Well, first off, it has a terrific chemistry department"? Notre Dame gets its identity from football. The legendary Subway Alumni exist solely because of football. Does anybody think the Subway Alums ever become vocal over shortcomings in psychology instruction?

Cedric Figaro says of Irish players, "Anytime anybody goes in and says, 'Well, football is secondary to education,' he's not giving you the full truth, because actually football is his life. I know he puts more time in football than he does anything else."

All of this is not to say that Notre Dame is an academic sham in its entirety. It's not. "This may sound corny to you," says Tim Brown, "but the reason I went to Notre Dame had nothing really to do with football. I went to Notre Dame because of the education I thought I could get and what it would do for me after I was done with football."

Brown's statement notwithstanding, when it comes to its football players, Notre Dame's academic standards are a shadow of their former self. But, as any photographer knows, shadows can be removed with proper lighting. Holtz's pronouncements on the subject are just one more way the master illusionist makes us try to doubt what we've seen with our own eyes.

CHAPTER 12

A Different Kind
of Recruit

"When Gerry Faust recruited players, it was about their families, their values. When Holtz recruited, it was about football. Clearly Holtz and Notre Dame have taken kids who were socially maladjusted. Holtz went for a different kind of kid, and Notre Dame suffered. They won games, but so has Miami. And who wants the image of Miami?"
—Tom Riley,
former Irish offensive lineman

The pressure to win at Notre Dame clearly is enormous. To win at the level Notre Dame expects to win—national championship or bust —the Irish need to recruit great players. Sometimes the pressure can blur one's vision.

Dan Hampton, who benefits from a lot of years playing for and then observing Holtz, says, "You have to put yourself in his place. They're on NBC and there is such an emphasis on winning." All the focus on winning, Hampton says, forces Holtz "to go out and get some of these outlaw players every once in a while because you've got to have those guys to win. Look at the teams that don't have them, they don't win."

When it is suggested to Shawn Smith that Holtz did get some renegades in the interest of winning, Smith agrees: "Sure, look at the people he had. He had some characters—Tony Brooks, Ricky Watters, Todd Lyght, Chris Zorich, me, Erik Simien, a bunch of others, from all different areas of the country. We were just different. We weren't Catholic, we didn't care too much about the mystique, and we were always into trouble."

There's no question that the quality of the recruits, especially as it relates to character and academics, has hit the skids in many instances since Holtz arrived. Even insiders and Holtz confidants are telling the boss he has to put much more emphasis on getting better human beings into the program.

But the impression should not be left that Faust recruited nothing but choirboys. Faust may not have known what he was getting when he got Dan Quinn and Marty Lippincott, but he got them, and they are his. And they are Notre Dame's.

For some, it is difficult to admit the school may be lowering the quality in its football recruiting. Fullback Pernell Taylor says, "Knowing other people that have gone to other places, how their programs work, I believe Notre Dame is far better than the other schools. They have bad apples that come in and run astray, but they try to weed them out and try to get them out of there."

But weren't you surprised at some of the bad apples they took?

"Yeah, I was kind of surprised." He was particularly surprised, Taylor says, at all the messing around Notre Dame did with Tony Brooks— including sending him off to a junior college to try to get him propped up enough academically after he flunked out of Notre Dame so he could come back and play football.

Would Faust have done any of that kind of stuff?

"I don't think so. I don't think so."

Blue & Gold Illustrated, which relies on the goodwill of the coaches, players, and administrators, said that in Faust's first year, he signed thirteen *Parade* magazine all-Americans. It was one of several star-spangled recruiting classes under Faust. But Anthony Johnson wonders if "maybe the players there were just too vanilla, so to speak. They didn't have that wrinkle that a lot of great players need."

John Askin says of the Faust recruits, "They were good, quality people. They were caring guys, they were good students, and they had other activities, other than football. They were gentlemen. When Holtz came in, it seemed like some of his guys were gangsters. I remember sitting there in my fifth year and seeing some of these guys and wondering where in the hell they came from. I had never seen Notre Dame guys wear an earring until Holtz came in."

Steve Huffman says he could tell Holtz recruited different kinds of players than Faust because "Faust's kids read, Holtz's can't." Nor does Anthony Johnson have any trouble seeing the difference in the new breed of recruit at Notre Dame: "They had wild people come in."

In Chicago, veteran guard Tom Thayer (through 1992, he had started eighty straight games for the Bears) thinks back to his days in South Bend and what continues to go on and says, "I have to say, Holtz definitely has got a different kind of guy getting in there now. When I go over there, I can't believe the kind of cars players are driving. I went to a pep rally and couldn't believe that, either. It wasn't the old 'win one for the school' type of pep rally. It was more like an 'Arsenio Hall' show. He definitely has some guys there who are trying to outshine the Golden Dome. Derek Brown walked out first and he was wearing a UNLV jacket. He should be wearing a Notre Dame jacket. There's just, obviously, a different emphasis than before."

"Before our class," explains Faust recruit Dan Quinn, "Faust was getting a reputation with these nice guys off the football field, blah, blah, but they couldn't do it on the football field. Then came our recruiting class. There were some guys I didn't like, but there weren't really guys I wouldn't trust in my room at a party. There was some badasses on the team that no one would mess with, and they were real good football players. But then Holtz's guys came in, and they were street kids. There were a few who came in like Jeff Alm [a defensive lineman from Orland Park, Illinois], who was a goody-goody; he wasn't like those guys. When Jason Cegielski and those guys were on a trip to Illinois, Cegielski knocked Alm out in one of the bars."

In fairness, understand that Dan Quinn had a stormy career in South Bend. He was kicked out of school and he subsequently sued the institution for breach of contract. University officials said they expelled him after a female student at nearby Saint Mary's College said he attempted to have sex with her against her will. Quinn filed a second suit, this one against the woman for slander. Both suits were dropped because, according to Quinn's mother, Joan, the legal fees were too expensive.

Mike Crounse says he believes "they've obviously lowered the standards of the people they accept as far as athletes. Obviously they're trying to stay competitive, so obviously you have to lower the standards.

I'll mention people—Tony Brooks. I don't feel he felt he fit into the program that well. He was always on his own doing things he wanted to do, and he didn't live by the guidelines."

Crounse wonders if the Irish are worried about "being left behind if they don't react [by bringing in academically marginal athletes]. The competition is constant, day in and day out. Maybe they're afraid of the program becoming outdated. I think basically it's trying to keep up with everybody else—the Miamis, the Washingtons, the Colorados, the West Virginias. Notre Dame likes to preach that what they're doing is like it was in the 1930s. Football is such a different game now. There are certain variables that you have to have. One of them is recruiting. You have to recruit the best players. If you don't, you're not gonna be competitive."

It's Jeff Kunz's feeling that "when Holtz's recruits started coming, it just wasn't the same. It was a different kind of person than what Faust was recruiting. I can't pinpoint what it was or anything. I remember people were saying, 'What's going on? They're bringing in these guys who could barely pass SAT tests.' I remember thinking, 'It's just not Notre Dame anymore.' The Holtz guys weren't going to class. They don't care about graduating. It makes you think that they don't care about going to school and all they do care about is football. I sort of believe that when Holtz came in, it was all football and who cares about the other stuff. He says otherwise, but I always felt there was something behind that."

Why does the university continue to let it happen?

"Probably because they're winning. I don't know why else."

"Faust's problem," says Ted FitzGerald, "was he recruited from the heart, not from ability. He looked at me as an Irish Catholic kid. He came and sat in my living room. My mother's very religious. They hit it off and they talked more than we talked about football. They talked more about life, how are things going, what kind of background I came from. That was the important thing for Faust. He always wanted the Notre Dame kid to come in who had the ability to play and who also was the good kid. I think that's what Faust tried to do. We had talent and we had all-Americans, but the difference in speed is unbelievable. That's the bottom line in my eyes. What changed with Holtz is the speed." An axiom in college football is that speed on the football field and speed in the classroom are almost always in an inverse relationship.

Jim Baugus, a Faust recruit, agrees that the Holtz recruits are decidedly different, and he explains, "They were the guys that were there because we were gonna win. I'm not saying they were thugs or anything. But they were probably a little rougher than we were."

However, John Carney, a devout Notre Dame defender, says he can explain the growing Notre Dame practice of taking in players who do not measure up academically or in some other way: "The hope is to turn a young man's life in the right direction, take a guy in the gray area and do something." Naturally, that's what every renegade school in the country says. Jerry Tarkanian said it at UNLV. Barry Switzer said it at Oklahoma. Similarly, John Foley says proudly, "Coach Holtz gives everybody an opportunity to come in and play Notre Dame football." But those are words that make many formerly proud Notre Damers cringe.

Foley says that "it's true that Faust did recruit the kids from real good families. Rich kids. They had everything. They were really nice, good kids. They didn't have the mentality of a street fighter or let's go out and kick some butt. I don't think Faust went into the really bad neighborhoods. And where are you going to get the great athletes? They're gonna be kids who didn't have a bike and ran to school. Holtz goes after good athletes."

When Cedric Figaro is asked about bringing in players like Jeff Pearson, Jason Cegielski, and John Zaleski—all of whom were in Holtz's first recruiting class—he says, "Well, like the guys you just named, I mean, Faust probably never would have touched those guys." Bryan Flannery feels similarly about the new breed of Holtz recruit—and especially these three; says Flannery, "You have your image of Notre Dame, and I don't think they were the most gifted intellectually."

"If I go back," says Bob Dahl, "and I think of the guys, like Jeff Pearson . . . they all seem more cockeyed."

Ned Bolcar, a linebacker from Philipsburg, Pennsylvania, who now plays for Miami in the NFL, suggests that "maybe Holtz had to take some guys he wouldn't otherwise take so he could get it back on track. I think they realize some of the recruiting mistakes. . . . I've complained about it and so have others. The coaches have been criticized for it."

Drawing a comparison of a Faust recruit and a Holtz recruit, Pernell Taylor says that "a Faust guy that came in was more family oriented. He'd do a lot of things with the team and for the team. The Holtz guys that came were selfish. They're in it for themselves. They wanted all the glory right now. You could see that." The mixing of the two different kinds of recruits caused big problems. Taylor says that the offensive line, recruited by Faust, "hated blocking for the Holtz running backs because the Holtz back would take the glory upon himself. They wouldn't give the line any credit. They loved to block for Mark Green, me, Tom Monohan, and Alonzo Jefferson, because we would get up and say, 'Great job, line, great job.' "

Tom Byrne says Faust was always strong on getting "a Notre Dame man. What the hell is a Notre Dame man? I don't know. He said to me, 'I wasn't gonna offer you a scholarship until I met your family.' I was like, 'Shit, what the hell does that mean? You like my parents, my brothers, my sister? Great, but that doesn't make me a better football player.' I had enough talent to be there, but it was real important to him that I fit into the Notre Dame mold. I'm glad he decided to take me on because I got a hell of an education out of it and I've done pretty well so far with that.

"But what Holtz did was bring in the premier athlete. Maybe some of the guys he brought in didn't have the proper table etiquette, use the right fork all the time, didn't place their napkin over their lap, and ate with their hands instead of silverware. But it didn't matter, because they were great athletes. [The other stuff] eventually someone will pick up if you're around it enough. You need to have manners and talk to people properly and maintain a conversation at some sort of proper level and talk about something interesting outside of 'I kicked his ass this week.' But Holtz just went for the premier athlete."

George Marshall says, "It seems like Faust guys were a lot more old school, meaning there were a few that were wild and crazies, but most of them were very intelligent. They were very on top of the game, very personable, presentable young men." Marshall, who was recruited by Holtz, says he thinks Holtz definitely recruited more characters. "Holtz got more talent," says Marshall, "and in getting that, sometimes you had to give up something else, so some of the guys weren't as refined as the Faust guys."

When it comes to characters—and very different kinds of recruits— Marshall points to Ricky Watters and Tony Brooks in his class as prime examples. Marshall says he was "really close to Ricky. Ricky has a really super, super good heart. There were signs he was having a really rough time, and a lot of it was because he was all mouth. He came in and he was really cocky, just because he was really flamboyant, but what he failed to remember was [that] guys at Notre Dame are all good. It just depends on whether you talk about it or not. Guys actually hated him, but I was one that took him to the side and we just talked, one-on-one, and he really is a great guy. But when you get him in a crowd or when he has an audience, he's one of the characters. The same thing with Tony Brooks, a great guy. He would do anything for you if you were his friend, but when he has an audience, he feels he needs to be the stand-up guy."

With the "different kind of recruit" came an avalanche of screwing up. Bar fights, drinking and driving, drugs, theft, starting fights on the field, and inappropriate behavior—to be charitable—with women. Such incidents are the public manifestations of the tarnish on the Golden Dome.

The two players mentioned most as illustrative of the changing Notre Dame character are running backs Tony Brooks (now with the Eagles) and Ricky Watters (with the 49ers). Both were trouble from the get-go off the field, and both were starry prospects on it. Both *The Sporting News* and *Football News* said the two players were among the top one hundred high school players heading for college in 1987. Brooks, from Tulsa, was named national player of the year by Gatorade; Watters, from Harrisburg, Pennsylvania, was so good that as a high school freshman, he accounted for all his team's touchdowns (10 rushing, 1 passing), and in his senior year, one opponent passed on every fourth down rather than risk punting to him. Nobody, however, bragged on their character. It was phrased differently by George Marshall: "Both these guys are characters."

Ted FitzGerald describes Brooks and Watters as "like Frick and Frack." He says both had numerous disciplinary problems—none of which were ever disclosed to the team. "All I know," says FitzGerald, "is those guys had discipline problems. Again, they don't disclose Tony Brooks did this. They're not gonna tell you. All I know is I remember was Tony got tested positive for smoking dope."

Asked point-blank about his drug use, Brooks says, "You have drug users all over the country. And Notre Dame brings guys in from all over the country. But at the same time, you don't know everybody's personal life. Of course, I'm sure there was marijuana and those types of things used with different guys on the team. Different guys tested positive for drugs."

He is told that one assistant coach said that, without being racial about it, a number of black players were using marijuana and other things. Did he?

"From my knowledge, there were more white people doing it than black, to be honest."

Did you ever test positive for it?

"No. For drugs?"

Yeah.

"No. I never tested positive for any kind of drugs ever in my life. I've tried a drug before but I've never tested positive for anything. Especially not during season. I've always thought that was really stupid. Maybe some guys can't stop or whatever and that's a different situation. I heard a lot of that stuff is physical. Where it's like a physical problem for a lot of people."

The addicted part?

"Yeah. But at the same time, for other guys that don't have that problem, it would just be stupid to take drugs during season. Performance-wise for one, and you've got to know that they're gonna test."

Linc Coleman remembers things differently. Says Coleman, "When we were freshmen, Tony was busted for dope. He would come to my room and say, 'Hey, man, how do you get that stuff out of your system? Some people say you've got to drink vinegar or whatever.' Or he would ask someone to take the urine test for him."

He was asking you to do that for him?

"Yeah. He would ask me to do that because he couldn't ask any of the guys he was smoking with. All those guys were like, 'Oh, man, I've got to take the test,' and start panicking."

How do you know he got busted?

"He told me."

Did they do anything to him when he got busted?

"At the time he was scared, because he didn't know what they were gonna do. He was like all fading out and going, 'Oh, man, I don't know what they're gonna do.' All they did was call him into the office and say, 'You need to cut that out.' [They] just slapped him on the wrist. They didn't do anything to him, [unlike] some guys [who] couldn't go on the traveling squad or something. They didn't do any of that. He traveled and everything. Even after he got busted it was no big deal."

Did players worry about getting in trouble for it?

"The only person I ever saw worry about getting in trouble was Tony Brooks, and that was because it was his first time getting caught."

So you were pretty tight with Brooks and he talked about getting caught smoking dope?

"Yep."

And he was pretty open about it?

"Oh, yeah."

Did everyone know he was doing it?

"Yes. Brooks told everybody about it."

Why would he tell everybody?

"It was no big deal to him."

Did you see him smoking?

"I've seen Brooks smoke before, and other guys. I never really worried about drugs because I knew I wasn't gonna do them. They would sit there and do them, but they would never try and offer them to me. If you're gonna smoke, you're gonna ask for it."

So everybody on the team knew he was doing it?

"Yeah. Tim Brown came to me one time and said, 'You need to stay away from those guys', because he knew we were really tight. He asked me, 'Are you smoking reefer with these guys?' I was like, 'No, I drink, but I'm not smoking dope with them.' He said, 'You need to stay away from those guys. They're gonna get themselves in trouble and get their butts kicked off the team.' "

So Tim knew?

"Yes."

And the coaches knew?

"Yes. One coach asked me about it one time. He said, 'You tell them guys they need to cool out.' So I would go back to them and say, 'Hey, man . . . ' "

What would Brooks say?

"Brooks would be, like, it's no big deal."

A prominent Notre Dame player on the inside of most things illicit there says that "Tony Brooks told me he got caught positive for smoking dope. He told me about it and told me they didn't suspend him for it. Everyone knew that him and some of our other biggest stars were smoking it. But Lou didn't do a damn thing. What are they going to say on national TV if a starter is benched for smoking marijuana at Notre Dame? That wouldn't go over well at God's school. Instead, Holtz would go public with a suspension if a player was late to a meeting, because that makes him look good. It sure wouldn't make Lou look good if it was drugs."

Holtz was fully tested in his ability to deal with his different breed of player in Los Angeles the week of the 1988 game against the University of Southern California. The Irish were 10-0, hell-bent for a national championship, ranked No. 1 and playing No. 2 USC. It was a game of huge importance.

Brooks was the team's leading rusher, while Watters was the leading pass catcher. Both were sophomores. But the sun and bright lights and beaches and girls and malls and freeways were too big a temptation for the good-time boys from Tulsa and Harrisburg. The two were late for a team meeting on Friday before the Saturday game because—they said —they were unable to locate a car they borrowed for a trip to a mall.

The official reason given by Notre Dame for the suspension of Brooks and Watters was their "repeated irresponsible tardiness for team meetings and functions."

Kevin McShane says that one major problem Brooks and Watters never came to grips with was "LLH time, Leo Louis Holtz time. That means ten minutes before a five o'clock meeting, you've got to be there in your seat, LLH time. They were late to two meetings, and you have nightmares when you're on the team about being late. If you think you're late for a meeting, you wake up sweating. Those players were late for those meetings during the week, and then they were late for the Friday meeting and Saturday's the game. They all of the sudden put Coach Holtz in a bad . . . "

Do you think they were trying to push him?

"I don't know. I wouldn't say that. I just think they lost track of time and they were irresponsible. So all of the sudden Coach Holtz says, 'LLH time applies to everybody.' But since these two guys are the best runners we've got, he had a big decision. He's in a tough position, because this is the biggest game of the year so far. He has two choices: come in to the meeting and say, 'We have two players that are late but they're gonna play tomorrow.' What does that tell the other ninety players? Or, Holtz can say, 'These guys were late and they're not gonna play tomorrow so we're gonna go in without our two best running backs.'

"So he has to walk a fine line. What he does is he comes into the room, gets the seniors together, and he gives the whole scenario, totally honest about what these players did. The two players are in the hallway, and instead of the iron fist saying, 'This is what we're gonna do and everybody will like it,' he says, 'I'm gonna put it to a vote. You guys can discuss it amongst yourselves and you can let me know what your decision is, whether these guys are gonna play tomorrow or not.' I'm not sure if he left the room, but some of the seniors stood up—Andy Heck, Pat Eilers—and said, 'We've lived and died by this rule. These players are late and we shouldn't have them play.' Some players, like Andre Jones, stood up and said, 'This is the biggest game of our lives. We need these two guys. Let's punish them in other ways.'

"Frank Stams was in the back row, slouching back in the chair, and everybody's kind of waiting for Frank to say something. Finally, Frank says, 'I don't know about you guys and I don't give a shit whether they play or not, but I'm gonna kick some fucking ass tomorrow.' And that set the tone. Everybody said, 'Fine, we're not gonna have them play and we're gonna kick ass with the team we have right here.' We finally decided, about ninety percent of the team decided, that night that they have to abide by our rules, send them home. Frank Stams set the tone for the next day, and if you remember, he had an all-America day.

"I think it was a great move on Coach Holtz's part. It was one of his best moves. He put it in the hands of his seniors, and they took the ball and ran with it. So it wasn't his decision—but I think that was the decision he was looking for. So the players took the view, 'Let's bond together and win this football game tomorrow.' " The Irish did, 27–10, which catapulted them to the national title.

Brooks admits that he and Watters had been late the day before, too, and he says, "I think Coach Holtz after a while takes things personally. I was a free-lancing guy. I wasn't really conscious of time. I wasn't really conscious of too many things other than me getting the work done, getting by, making the grade and having fun at the same time."

George Marshall says that as the season had progressed, "a lot" of the players were getting tired of Brooks and Watters. "There was a lot of looking at them," says Marshall, "by guys who were showing up early to meetings or being on time and everything."

LLH time?

"Yeah, so there was a lot of saying, 'Oh, they're getting away with it. What about me? Why can't I?' That's just the whole attitude. I'm not saying I looked at Holtz like a terrific god or the best man in the world or a priest, but he has his own little ways. One thing I do respect is that he'll give you what you give him. I mean, what you put in, he'll give you back. If you respect him, do what he tells you to do, there is no way that he can have a problem with you.

"But they didn't deserve to get sent back that day. It was a critical time, it was USC, and we thought, 'If there is one time you're gonna bend the rules, please bend them now and let them play.' We needed them, because they both were really great players. We needed them, and this was a dumb time to prove a point."

Did the other players say that to Holtz?

"I don't know if they actually said it to him, but it was voiced to the assistant coaches. That was the sentiment of the team, that this is not the time to prove a point. Nobody has to know about them missing a meeting. I think Coach Holtz thought, 'It's time to put my foot down. Let's get things rolling the way they are supposed to. Let's make an example, and this is like a big example. It hurts. So it's kind of like to let you know that we mean business.' But then I can also see that, politically, it was great. That feeds into the mold of Holtz being like a father and not caring about football as much but caring about doing the right things."

Is that really what Holtz is about, though?

"I don't think so. Honestly, I really don't think that. I think there is a little bit of politics to his job. He's great when he talks on TV and says, 'I don't think we're going to do very good this year,' or, 'I don't think we're going to have a chance against Michigan,' or whatever. But when he comes into the locker room, he's telling us all a different story. So I think that's part of it. For the public, he wanted to have himself talked about that weekend, not two of his star players, when we are about to go into a critical game like USC at USC. A lot of guys were bitter. I was bitter. I was thinking about a lot of things he could have let go and a lot of the times he did let things go when he should have tightened up."

"That," says Watters of the USC suspension, "was a situation we all wished wouldn't have happened, and I still to this day don't totally understand him doing that, but he's the coach and he felt that it was right. I don't know what his motive was behind it. I don't particularly go with it. I'm sure Tony didn't agree with it and our parents didn't agree with it and a lot of people behind us didn't."

Including a lot of your teammates?

"A lot of my teammates I'm sure didn't. I don't know what his motive was for it, but what he told us was basically the fact that if you do something wrong like that, you're gonna be punished for it."

In your opinion, was it an overreaction?

"Of course I felt that way, because I wanted to play. I mean, that's a whole game that I missed. A big part of my college career that I missed. That was a big game, big on big, number one against number two out there in California, my first time being out there, and the same for Tony. So it was a big part of our college career that we missed. And we can never get that back."

Heisman winner Tim Brown says, "I love Ricky like a brother. But I think they knew with Ricky what they were getting. I don't know what Ricky's problem was at Notre Dame."

Kevin McShane says it was always a struggle for Watters, in particular, to get with the program, largely because he was a pouter. "Other older players tried to help him," McShane said. "Mark Green once told Watters, 'Hey, Ricky, you better get your act together. We don't need that shit here.' " But McShane says that Watters just couldn't get over the hump and "I was a little distraught at seeing that. Basically, Watters displayed an attitude of superiority that didn't sit well with the rest of the team or the coaches." Brandy Wells says he was a senior when Watters was a freshman, "and I was probably one of the few people, especially as a senior, that even spoke to him. I always talked to him because I believed in him. He was one of the more unique people at Notre Dame. A guy like Ricky Watters, if he thinks that Lou Holtz ruined his career, he should have been there under Faust. He'd be flipping burgers somewhere just because he had his ear pierced."

Many of the other players didn't care much for Watters or Brooks. It was because while the two clearly had enormous talent, their too often ho-hum attitudes were detrimental to the team chemistry. Frick and Frack invariably were disruptive.

Marty Lippincott had run-ins with the two. Lippincott says he suspects they took his things, including sneakers, and most important, "my gold chain, which is what pissed me off. After that I stole one of Tony Brooks's helmets and two of Ricky Watters's helmets. I gave them to some people here who owned bars. I took their shoes. I was gonna take whatever I could. I never stole to steal. I stole to get even."

It would be unfair, however, to pin all disciplinary problems on just Brooks and Watters. For example, Pernell Taylor says he once "walked in on" several other players in the rest room of a bar and they were "doing some other drugs. They shouldn't have been in there in the first place because they were too young." Taylor says that widespread drug usage among football players came in with the recruiting class in '87. Says Taylor, "I never seen any usage until those guys came in. When Holtz first came in and got the class that included Watters and Brooks, when those players came in on their recruiting trips, we all noticed just the way they looked, the way they acted, they weren't the same Notre Dame boy that they usually recruit. I think Tony out of high school had a problem."

When Jason Cegielski is asked about rumors of widespread marijuana use among the players, he says, "There was a lot of that. I know it was prevalent, especially around black players. I'm not saying white players didn't do it. I think it was just kind of a thing that most of them do. They prefer that over drinking."

George Williams, who stayed five years under Holtz, admits that "I had tested positive for marijuana. I did it. So they told me that if it happened again, I would be kicked off the team and that was all. I said, 'Cool, I'm not going to do it again.' So when we came back after summertime, we had a drug test. I knew we were going to have a drug test because we had them every year in the summer. When you get back the first week or two, you're going to have a test. So I get back and we take the test. Fine. About ten days later, I get a message that Coach Holtz wants to see me immediately. We had voted on a captain, so I'm thinking that I'm going to be the captain.

"So I go in his office and I'm sitting there and he comes in and tells me to sit down. He says, 'Do you know why you're in here?' I said, 'No, I have no idea.' He says, 'Do you really not know why you're in here?' And I said, 'I don't have a clue.' He said, 'You tested positive for marijuana.' I was like, 'Are you joking with me?' I mean, it was a feeling that I had never felt before. There was obviously a mistake, and I thought the way he came off to me was he was trying to make me think that I had done it. I'm not fucking crazy. I know what I did and I know what I didn't do. And I didn't do it." Williams, who had been suspended two years earlier for drug use, was suspended again, but his size and talent was so great that he was drafted by Cleveland despite not having played his senior year.

Addressing the drug issue, Williams says that "it wasn't a thing where we blacks were the only ones doing it. Everyone was doing it. You follow what you see being done, and all those guys were partying hard, did all kinds of drugs, and a lot of those guys were like big connections.

You could get mushrooms from them or certain drugs. You could get a whole bunch of stuff from them. For the whites to say that it was us doing it is not right. They were just as bad as we were. And all of us were no different than any other class that was there.

"Guys were just getting high, snorting cocaine, doing everything. I mean everything. I was like, I can't believe you all are doing this, because I was a freshman and these were older guys."

Erik Simien backs up Williams regarding the drug culture among Notre Dame players: "I can tell you straight up that players were using cocaine, acid, hallucinogens, mushrooms. There were guys there into some serious shit. Did I do drugs? Well, first of all, I don't consider marijuana a drug. The university drug-tests. But everyone knew how to beat it. If you got called, you wouldn't show up until your system was cleaned out. Sometimes you had to hide for a day or two. You would disappear, not go to class. Everyone knew how to use goldenseal, a diuretic . . . they'd take eleven or twelve tablets to clean out. That's how you get around the test. I never got caught testing positive for anything."

Simmering under the surface of many of the remarks about drug use is some clear racial tension. Notre Dame likes to portray itself as a place where the only colors that matter are blue and gold. But questions of race and racism have long dogged Holtz, going back at least to his Arkansas days and the Helms endorsement.

P. A. Hollingsworth, the former Arkansas Supreme Court justice, says, "My theory of racism is probably different from what other people would normally consider racism. I really feel that if you exploit people and don't do anything affirmative to help them become the best products in whatever you're doing—and this is directed primarily to the black athletes or African American athletes, whatever term you choose to call them—that's racist. And I believe that Lou was completely insensitive to the plight of black people in general, black athletes in particular, and that he should have been more attuned to it. But he didn't give a damn then and he doesn't care now. There's going to be a movement eventually that we eradicate Lou Holtz, because Lou has a tremendous impact on the population in this country."

With this in the background, it's troubling that there is the growing concern about racial friction at Notre Dame. Admits Dan Devine, "The racial issue at Notre Dame runs pretty deep. There are, sadly, a lot of people who feel that Notre Dame has way too many blacks." When confronted with race questions, Holtz invariably falls back on his well-traveled explanation: "Yes, I am prejudiced. I am prejudiced towards people who can block and tackle."

But in a more serious moment, Holtz openly acknowledged the problem. Walk-on Tom Galloway says that at one team meeting, Holtz said bluntly to the players, "There's a problem of racism on this team." Everybody agreed, says Galloway, but nobody knew what to do about it.

George Marshall says it was "great" for Holtz to acknowledge the problem, but he took no responsiblity for the situation. Marshall says that he believes Holtz doesn't have much respect for blacks as people, though he knows they can help him win football games. Says Marshall, "He made comments about the Rocket [Ismail, the gifted and speedy flanker], saying, 'Look at the monkey run.' He said that in front of the team, and I really don't think he was just saying it."

What did the other players say?

"A lot of us, not only the black players, but the white players, everybody was like 'That's fucked up,' but all of that talking between the players was done in the locker room or off the field, or among ourselves. We didn't actually appoint somebody to go up to Holtz and say, 'We think that was a bad comment to say, "Look at that monkey run," when Rocket was running.' "

This was during practice?

"Yeah. And it was just kind of like, 'Well, what can you do? Oh, well, what's the next play, Coach? Let's play ball,' When it comes to a head coach, you can't really say anything."

A different kind of recruit obviously has created a different kind of Notre Dame, and different has not necessarily meant an improvement. How could it be, with players—as we have seen in this chapter—admitting that the new recruits include outlaw players, selfish players, the academically inept, and many with a fondness for dope and steroids of all stripes?

Then thrown into the mix are racial problems. Says Mirko Jurkovic, "Racial friction [at Notre Dame] just happens to be a fact." Be it real at times or imagined at others, it's always there and it's an increasing problem.

What's most unsettling is that Notre Dame is supposed to be above and beyond all this, an academic and athletic utopia. Americans have always thought that in a sea of ugliness in college football, at least they could believe in the lagoon of beauty at Notre Dame. Time was, they could. Now, they can't.

CHAPTER 13

Haunted by the Past

The Fighting Irish were defending national champions and were enroute to a 12-1 season in Lou Holtz's fourth year as head coach when his Minnesota past revisited him and haunted him in dramatic fashion. Indeed, the stakes were huge all around when Hennepin County district judge Patrick Fitzgerald gaveled open *The State of Minnesota vs. Luther Darville* in November 1989. Officially, it appeared that Darville, a former University of Minnesota administrator on trial for swindling $186,000 in school funds, had the most to lose.

Not so.

For the university, if Darville was truthful in his contention that he had passed along most of the money to Gopher football and basketball players, testimony from the trial could have led the NCAA to hand down the "death penalty." That's the harshest of all college sports sanctions; it is ordered only in extreme cases to teams that just can't stop breaking the rules. It decrees that the school may not participate in a sport at all for a given time. SMU got the death penalty in football. After the time is served, the institution can, if it wants to, start all over. If ordered in Minneapolis, it would have dictated the suspension of Gopher football and, possibly, UM basketball. University officials, who could calculate the financial loss the athletic department would suffer if the death penalty was imposed, sweated as each witness stepped to the stand.

"They were very concerned about the death penalty," said Darville in the summer of 1992 in Nassau, where he granted Don Yaeger the only interview he has given since being deported. "That athletic program generates ten million dollars a year. They told me they couldn't afford to lose thirty million dollars. [UM figured the loss over a possible three-year banishment to collegiate athletic hell.] How important was this to them? The boosters packed the courtroom at my trial. I looked at some of them and just saw in their faces them pleading with me, for the good of the university, not to destroy the athletic department. It's all about economics. I was dispensable. A little black boy from a third-world country. Get rid of this nigger. I wasn't even a pawn. Pawns usually get to take somebody off the board."

And, while the weather was cold in his new hometown of South Bend, the man who may have been sweating the most was former Gopher coach Holtz. He knew he could easily become the one Darville would take off the board. Holtz had plenty to be worried about, because, although the docket said Luther Darville was the man on trial, the media was looking for a piece of Lou Holtz.

Darville's attorney, James Lawton, says, "The attention centered mostly on Lou Holtz, because he becomes the figure that everybody would like to take a shot at. He left here a few years earlier under bad circumstances. The trial starts on Halloween. The football team is in the jar again. It's a mess, and you want to blame all the troubles on the departed hero whose [new] team is doing great."

For eighteen days, the Darville trial dragged on. One by one, former Minnesota basketball and football stars stepped forward and testified that Darville had given them cash, bought them meals, and outfitted them with clothes.

Tailback Tony Hunter said he received $15,000 from Darville, and another $200 to $500 a week from assistant coach Robert Rankin. Quarterback Rickey Foggie said he received about $8,600 from Darville, including payments made on his Nissan 280ZX. Donovan Small, a free safety from Wheeling, Illinois, said he received $1,000 in aid from Darville, including visits to a health club, lunches, and dinners. Andre Gilbert, a strong safety from Chicago who later quit the team over racial tension, didn't leave before getting $1,000 from Darville. By the time the parade ended, twenty players admitted taking money from Darville.

Still, AD Paul Giel says of Darville, "My guess is he kept most of it himself."

However, defense attorney Lawton insists, "Luther's one of the most decent and honest men I've ever known. He would not consciously steal things and he would not consciously hurt anybody. Basically, what he did was he saw a wrong and he tried to right it. Maybe he didn't use the right means, but maybe somebody should have told him to do something different. Yes, he reached into the till to get his mom some money to do some other things, but by and large, the rest, seventy-five to eighty percent of the money, went to students."

Whatever, Darville also said he spent some of the money helping entertain Holtz and Salem recruits: "I would schedule the cheerleaders for help in recruiting. One on the right arm, one on the left, and the fellas were walking into, they thought, pure heaven in Minnesota. And we take them and put them in the finest hotels, and they would eat until, I mean, I've seen some guys eat so much in some of the fine restaurants, but that was part of the recruitment trip. The young ladies and myself would take them up to the nightclubs and show them the best of times, and with that came the other fun things like the pleasures of the flesh, and they were excited about the place. They thought, 'This is where I need to be.' That was the pleasurable side of it.

"But when it came to serious business to make their decision, one-on-one with the boosters, the boosters would meet with them and want to chat with them individually, making promises to them that 'we will take care of you, and if you need anything, just let us know.' Players were promised packages. One player that was so good was promised that his mother would get a house and he would have a car to drive. This was at the end of Lou Holtz's reign. The player told me about it. I was interviewing him for academics and he was asking me if these people are real and did I think they are going to keep their word?"

But all the details of who received the money was just the preseason. The real games began when Darville took the stand in his own defense to tell the world who ordered him to make the payments.

Luther Darville, a 5-8, slightly pudgy, well-educated, well-spoken native of the Bahamas, hardly seems the type who would become central to a major-college athletic scandal. Darville came to the University of Minnesota to help keep fellow countryman and basketball superstar Mychal Thompson comfortable. After Thompson left, Darville stayed and rose through the ranks in the university administration, mostly because he had proven to be an effective troubleshooter when UM's athletes found themselves in trouble.

Eventually Darville was promoted to director of the Office of Minority and Special Student Affairs, which gave him great influence in the university, located in a liberal state with few minorities in attendance. In its zeal to keep its minority population happy, Darville said the university had told him his office had almost limitless authority to spend money.

As Coach Joe Salem's tumultuous tenure neared its end, Darville was also assigned the task of analyzing why the black athletes were so often near revolt. It was no mystery to Tony Hunter. "Some of Salem's staff members were always making racial jokes and discrediting remarks," says Hunter. "The flavor was just not professional or humanitarian, and I did not come up here a thousand miles away from home and leave everybody I love to have some white man make racial jokes at me. It just didn't sit well with me. I talked to Salem about it numerous times. I said, 'Salem, I'm not gonna tolerate this.' Nothing was ever done. They talked about it amongst themselves behind closed doors. It was like, 'Tony, you're being an asshole. You're just bitching for no reason at all.' It continued to happen and I just said, 'Fuck it.'

"My personal opinion, yeah, I think Holtz [also] is a racist. I think he still has the slave mentality. It's his attitude. He don't give a shit about nobody but himself. Anybody that hides behind religion to try and get people to move I don't think is a very nice person. I know for a fact that he didn't take care of his black players like he did his white players."

You're talking about the summer jobs?

"Summer jobs, just how he talked to people, talked to black players versus the white players."

If you had a black player who was a friend here in Minneapolis who got recruited by Notre Dame, what would you tell them?

"Don't go."

In view of this kind of criticism, Darville says, "My mission was to go into the athletic department, assess the problem, and be sure we developed some solutions. And when we found those solutions, I was to be sure they were implemented. Part of those solutions that I brought back to Wilderson [Frank B., former vice president for student affairs] was that these kids were from poor families, they don't have money to go home at Thanksgiving or Christmas. Or, if their grandmother dies and they need to go home and they don't have any money, we need to help them."

Darville said he reported to Wilderson that these black athletes, who often felt alone on the overwhelmingly white Minnesota campus, had come to the university believing booster promises of cars, cash, and women. Upon arrival they found that the cars were used, the cash wasn't as much as was expected, and the women were less compliant than advertised. Darville also told university officials that the players coming in from the South didn't have the clothes for the long winters to which Minnesotans were accustomed. He reported that they had been promised trips home to see their families, and sometimes those promises went unfulfilled. Solving these problems, he said in a nutshell, would require some serious cash.

And, says Darville, Wilderson replied, "Go ahead. Let's do it."

Wilderson has steadfastly denied any knowledge of Darville's activities.

In his testimony, Darville, the man whom players called "Money," explained his scheme. It was simple.

Each summer, the university's Office of Minority and Special Student Affairs sponsored an orientation program that allowed minority students to get acquainted with the campus and college life by taking a few courses before the rest of the student body arrived. Each student was given a check to pay for his tuition and room and board. For several years, though, a number of students had paid only the tuition, then kept the cash that was supposed to be paid for room and board. Word had gotten around that the university, eager to keep its minority students happy, would still allow the students to move into the dorms and eat at the cafeteria, even if they hadn't paid their housing costs. The net result was that the bill was never paid.

In 1983, Darville put a stop to that by setting up a card table across from the window where students cashed their checks. As soon as they turned from the window, cash in hand, Darville nabbed them and collected for food and housing. This eliminated the possibility that they would simply walk away from their financial obligations.

There was one problem: although he had stopped students from their trickery, the cash accounting procedures used by Darville would give any accountant tremors. Darville took the cash—estimated at $30,000 to $40,000 each summer—and locked it in a drawer in his desk. He now had the means by which to solve the greater problem—keeping black athletes at the university happy.

For nearly six years, everything went along fine from Darville's perspective. This scheme was so perfectly concealed that NCAA investigators, who spent a good portion of the 1980s on the University of

Minnesota campus investigating major violations of one sort or another, were left completely in the dark.

The only time, in fact, that the NCAA investigators even interviewed Darville was to discuss his hiring of Don Evans, a longtime assistant to Gopher basketball coach Clem Haskins, who had just taken the UM job. When Haskins was hired in 1986, he was saddled with sanctions levied against previous coach Jim Dutcher. One of those sanctions was a limit on the number of assistant coaches he could have on his staff, so Haskins got Evans a job in Darville's office even though, as Darville said, Evans had no duties, responsibilities, or office hours other than to be an assistant basketball coach. In finding a way around the sanctions levied for previous wrongdoing, Minnesota and Haskins had violated the rules again.

Darville's decision not to cover for Evans put him on a collision course with Haskins, who began openly questioning Darville's "loyalty." At the same time, Nobuya Tsuchida and Santos Martinez, employees in Darville's office who were responsible for dealing with Asian and Hispanic students, became disgruntled over the cash they saw Darville pull from his desk drawer and hand to star black football and basketball players. Darville claims Tsuchida and Martinez leaked the story to local reporters. Suddenly, Darville was facing charges from above that he was disloyal to Haskins, and charges from below that he was dishonest. He quickly became a liability.

Asked if it was possible that Darville could have done all this without people above him knowing, Jim Lawton says, "No. Unless it's the most stupid, archaic, incompetent system you could ever find, it would not be possible for that to happen. The university, in fact, is a sophisticated system. The method Luther had to get the money was the most homespun method you could believe. He literally put the money in a suitcase and walked across the campus with it at twilight and put it in his desk and locked it up. Nobody ever said, 'Where are you going with the money?' "

Civil rights leader Henrietta Adams Faulconer says she confronted Darville about his payments to the players: "I was trying to get control of it and pull it to the curb. I said, 'Luther, if you don't stop spending all this money on these guys, I'm gonna go and tell Dr. Wilderson.' Luther says, 'Don't bother. Dr. Wilderson knows what I'm doing.' "

It was no surprise, then, that during his trial Darville swore that his superiors knew of his actions. He explained that it would be impossible for a midlevel administrator to have pulled this off. "Vice President Wilderson knew what I was doing," Darville says. "Every year we had a budget approved and Wilderson would have to sign off on it. I would meet with him and bring him up to date on my budget every three months, basically. Anytime there was a problem with funds, I would go to him, and it would be taken care of. No problem, they would tell me. Wilderson used to send students to me, okay? Does that answer your question? Wilderson used to send students to me to get money."

So students would walk in and say, "Dr. Wilderson sent me here"?

"No, Wilderson would call me and tell me he was sending the students. And I know Wilderson informed Lou Holtz, because he told me that 'I've spoken with Lou Holtz and I told Lou Holtz to get in touch with you to help in any way with players, anything that athletes need to keep them happy.'"

Although Darville's fund was established pre-Holtz, the new coach also needed it to help keep black players in harmony with white Minneapolis because his arrival was greeted with suspicion amongst blacks. The Jesse Helms commercials were still fresh news.

Holtz's anxiety level must have climbed several notches when he heard that Darville, on the witness stand, had said basketball coach Haskins was aware of his player payments. But Attorney Lawton said later that Darville looked at Holtz and Haskins as separate issues. While Holtz was always kind to Darville, Haskins took the stand and said he and Darville had only met on a couple of occasions and that he viewed Darville as a rogue. That offended Darville. "It was ludicrous for Clem to say he hardly knew Luther," Lawton said. "Haskins and I met probably six or seven times after basketball games. Luther would go down and talk to the players and I'd see him [Luther], and we'd shake hands and Luther introduced me to Haskins a bunch of times."

None of it mattered to Pete Conner, the assistant county's attorney who prosecuted the case. Conner says he and his staff obtained Darville's financial records—bank records, credit cards, and so on—"and we just retraced where most of the money went. Most of the money went for . . . a BMW, he flew his family from the Bahamas up here fairly often. He had fairly expensive taste. For instance, he would buy fifty-dollar bottles, not just wine but more than fifty dollars of cologne. . . . This was over a three-, four-year period of time. Five-year period. That's about thirty thousand dollars extra a year. That sounds like a lot of money, but things are expensive these days and it didn't take him long to piss the money away. He also, in my opinion, wanted to impress people. Especially athletes. He would take the athletes out for expensive dinners and things like that. What I thought after I got into the case was [that] Darville stole this money and used it to enhance his living style. The money he gave to athletes was to make himself appear to be a big man, an important man. I think in a lot of ways Darville was a fairly despicable individual. Darville was an embezzlement case. It was nothing less, nothing more."

As the trial wore on, all the stories of big-time cheating started to run together. But everyone, including Holtz, was waiting to see how seriously the trial would wound the coach of the one school that wears its clean reputation on its sleeve. So how worried was Lou Holtz?

Kathy Woxland, a University of Minnesota graduate who works for the county attorney's office scheduling witnesses for trial, dreaded the day she was assigned to call Holtz. "I have to say I was mad when he left as coach, so I really didn't want to talk to him," Woxland said. "But when I got him on the phone and told him why I was calling, he was my instant best friend. It became a joke around the office when 'my good friend Lou' called. He was real concerned about the media. He was, I don't want to say reluctant to testify, but he wasn't looking forward to it, and so we just kept in touch every few days or so about what was going on in the trial. His level of concern was great. He was very attentive. I would imagine that anybody, any old Joe who tried to call him, could never get through to him. When I called, I talked to him immediately. I told his secretary who I was and he was right on the line. If he was at practice, he'd call me back within ten or twenty minutes. At the time, it was surprising that he seemed so concerned, because he always said he didn't do anything wrong.

"Actually, it turned out that we were only gonna use him for rebuttal testimony. So we were gonna use him in case Darville got on the stand and said Lou Holtz knew about this or something like that. Then we were gonna bring Lou Holtz in to tell what his story was. Of course, everybody knew who he was and everybody was mad at him when he left. It was like people either loved him or they hated him, but no matter who it was, they had strong feelings about him. So I think he was a little nervous to come up here and have to face the press and have to face the scrutiny of maybe somebody saying he actually knew about what Darville was doing. I think he was overly kind to me in hopes that I would be overly kind to him in that I wouldn't force him to come to Minnesota to testify. It was getting a lot of attention here and the news media was just crazed with it."

Holtz was especially overly kind when the trial ended and he wasn't called to testify. In thanks, he sent Woxland a copy of his book about Notre Dame's 1988 national championship team. Inside the cover, Holtz wrote: "To Kathy Waxland [*sic*], Thanks for being so nice and helpful. Hope you and your family have the luck of the Irish as Notre Dame had in 1988. Hope you will come see us at Notre Dame. Lou Holtz."

Defense attorney Lawton also had listed Holtz as a potential witness, prompting Holtz to call him several times, too. Asked if Holtz sounded concerned about testifying, Lawton says, "Big time. He was very concerned. I think he really loves that job there. I felt as a person to another person that I owed him to tell him prior to the trial that I was not gonna call him as a witness and his name would not come up in the case. If a person is scared that much, I think it's better to tell him. My almost exact words to him were, 'I want you to know that I'm not gonna call you in this case and your name is not gonna come up in this case.' The only way he would have helped us was if he would come forward and say, 'Yes, I did know and I told Luther to do that.' There was no way he was gonna do that. I did talk to his wife one time, who is a very nice lady, and she said, 'We're really good people and Lou's been so scared about all this, and it was nice of you to call him.' I talked to her one night just by coincidence when I got her instead of him. I said, 'Well, his name is not gonna come up,' and I reiterated it and she said again, 'He's been so worried about this and we're good people. We've prayed about it.'"

Lawton was rewarded after the trial with a promise from Holtz that he could be the coach's guest at the Notre Dame game of his choice.

Neither defense attorney Lawton nor Kathy Woxland's boss in the county attorney's office called the name Leo Louis Holtz.

The sigh of relief in South Bend could be heard all the way to Minneapolis.

In addition to repeatedly asking attorneys from both sides not to call him as a witness, Holtz got word to Luther that he hoped Luther would leave him out of his testimony, Darville says. "Lou had said that he would do whatever he could to help me to get back on my feet again once this was all over," Darville recalled over dinner in Nassau. "He sent the message through my lawyer. It would have been a critical time for him and it might have cost him his job. I had mentioned [in the trial] Clem Haskins, President Kenneth Keller, and others. They all suffered consequences internally in the university, and I'm sure he would have likewise."

So you had information that, had you not held back, could have affected him and maybe his employment?

"Information like we are talking about now, I didn't talk about during the trial," Darville says. "About the fact that students were receiving money, he [Holtz] would send students to me, that kind of information I didn't. The man did nothing to hurt me and he promised to help. I didn't see it necessary to ruin his career by mentioning things that did not have to be mentioned. It wasn't going to help my case at the time. All they [the people in Minnesota] wanted to do was pull him down, but since he promised to help me, I saw no need to make matters worse for him because he was actually going through a lot of pressure.

"He told me when he first came to Minnesota after I had done certain things for the players, he would do anything I needed. He promised me a trip to Pasadena to the Rose Bowl. He said, 'If we go to the Rose Bowl, I'm taking you with my family.' He did things like that."

Lawton confirmed Holtz's promise to stand by Luther if he would avoid getting into what Holtz did or did not know. It was a good trade, Lawton said, "because it really didn't matter in the eyes of the court if Lou Holtz knew."

Darville went to prison believing that Holtz would arrange a job for him when he was released. But when the time came for Holtz to help Darville find work, the coach came through with far less than Darville expected. On November 18, 1991, Darville wrote a warm, friendly letter to Holtz, a copy of which was provided to the authors. Wrote Darville, "I am now seeking employment in Nassau, Bahamas, and I would be most grateful if you would support my candidacy for employment in whatever business establishment that you can."

On December 5, Holtz replied, "I will be happy to provide you with a letter of recommendation, Luther, or speak with someone on the telephone, if you can provide me with the names of people you wish contacted." Darville thought he'd be getting a job; all Holtz would provide was a letter. Darville remains unemployed.

The jury deliberated only ninety minutes before agreeing that, indeed, it didn't matter who knew of Darville's actions. He did take the money, and that merited conviction on three counts. Darville was sentenced to eighteen months in state prison, plus six more in the county workhouse for contempt of court, a penalty levied because Darville refused court orders to name all of the players who had received money. In the end, Darville served a total of seventeen months before being deported to his native Bahamas.

Dr. Rob Hunter doesn't equivocate on whether Holtz knew: "The players were driving 280Zs, Mercedes, BMWs. Where did they get the money? What was happening is the players were measuring their value in dollars and cents. They were measuring their worth. A lot of it was black kids who didn't have two nickels to rub together. Look, Holtz knew absolutely everything. He knew everything down to the pennies. So for him to say he didn't is completely ridiculous. He demanded total control."

Holtz, after the trial concluded, claimed he had been exonerated. He said it had proven that he had no knowledge of the Darville banking system. About that time, Holtz even held a team meeting at Notre Dame to discuss the trial. Says former Irish player Mike Crounse, "He told us all [the allegations of his involvement] weren't true, pretty much just to put our minds at ease and that it never happened."

Explaining himself to the *Chicago Sun-Times,* Holtz said, "I think the reason I didn't sense anything is that those [players] who weren't involved didn't know somebody else was. I believe it was totally secret. You cannot run a disciplined program if you're running a dishonest program. If someone is getting illegal inducements, he's usually the first one to tell others. I had absolutely no idea. The players went to great extremes to keep it confidential without exception. The ones I asked about it had no idea."

The players, however, say that was completely untrue—that Darville's handouts were one of the worst-kept secrets in the locker room. "Coach Holtz knew what Luther was doing," says Roselle Richardson. "I remember once me and [fellow player] Michael Baker was in there talking to Coach Holtz because I wanted to come home because I had problems in my family for one weekend. And Michael had financial problems, so Coach Holtz referred us to go to Luther Darville."

He said that straight out, go to Luther?

"Yeah; he said, go to Luther."

Tony Hunter has his own reasons for believing that Holtz was fully aware of Darville's actions: "If you're the head coach of any team, you should be concerned about what's going on with your players and who they associate with. I know Holtz knew."

How do you know?

"I talked to Holtz at one point. There was a rumor going around camp that I was going to be redshirted. I said, 'No way.' At that point I think I was rated like third in the nation as a running back. I was a hot commodity coming out. I'm not gonna stay another year. The four years that I stayed there wasn't pleasant. You can't keep me there for another year. But Holtz was looking on down the road as far as not having any running backs coming for the following year, and it just would have been a good situation for him. So I discussed it with Holtz and told him, 'No, I'm not gonna be redshirted.' He basically copped an attitude. So I called down to the [USFL's] Memphis Showboats and talked to my former coach, Chuck Dickerson, about possibly getting on with him. He said he could probably make some arrangements and look at who had my rights and things like that. Holtz heard about it. So Holtz okayed me to stay out after curfew to go have dinner with Luther. Something had to happen. Obviously, Holtz knew that I was pissed off. Luther knew I was pissed off. Whoever initiated it, I don't know. Luther delivered the message to me saying, 'Let's go to dinner.' "

And you said, "I've got curfew"?

"Yeah. He said, don't worry about that. It'll be okay. So we stayed out and we talked. That conversation between me and Luther got took back to Holtz and things got squared away. I know that for a fact that Lou Holtz knew."

Did Luther ever tell you that Lou knew?

"Oh, yeah."

What would he say?

"Me and Luther was real tight. Luther expressed that everything that he did had to be okayed. You cannot keep people out after curfew without the coach's permission. Holtz was the type of person that rules are rules and no rules are broken for any cause, and for him to let me out on curfew, I found very strange. Lou Holtz and his whole staff knew about Darville. For him to sit up there and say he knew nothing was a crock of shit. It's funny just knowing the history of Holtz, because I got recruited by him at Arkansas out of high school. And he gave me this big spiel about how he wouldn't give anybody a roll of toilet paper to wipe their ass because of fear of going on probation. When I walked around the campus and saw all new cars, all the players had new cars,

I knew it was a crock of shit. But you can never catch Lou Holtz with his hand in the cookie jar. Everybody knew, including the white players."

Darville remembers the dinner vividly: "Let me put it this way. Had Tony agreed to be redshirted, he would have been taken care of because the system was in place to take care of him."

Were you told to make that clear to Tony?

"I was told to tell Tony that his needs would be met during the year. Whatever he needed would be there for him."

Was that one of those examples of your being able to say I know Holtz knew because . . . ?

"That's right. When I'm given a direct mandate, I was following directions. I was an administrator carrying out the policies, practices, or wishes of my superiors. If you sent somebody to me with a financial problem and you find out later that everything is fine, I mean, it doesn't take a lot of deduction to get that figured out. He sent them to me. He knew that they were being taken care of."

Said Attorney Lawton, "Did Luther know Lou Holtz? Yes. Did Luther go to the practices and watch the practices? Yes. Is Luther involved with the students that were athletes? Yes. All those things are yeses. If someone in that position [head coach] did not know that Luther was giving them money, he was either a fool or didn't care."

Others believe Holtz knew everything Darville was doing because they simply know Holtz. Says Dan Devine, "I would say that if you asked people if Holtz cheated, one hundred percent would say yes. In fact, the reason I think—and everybody thinks—he cheated is because Holtz has total control of every situation he is in. He insists on it. He knows everything that is going on. So to believe him when he says he didn't know requires us to believe that in this one case, he for some reason didn't know what was going on. Of course he knew. Either way, he is guilty. If he didn't know what was going on, then he's guilty of being an extremely bad coach. And if he did, then he's guilty of cheating and he's a hypocrite—just like almost all other coaches think."

Whether it mattered in court or not, the one thing players said repeatedly in interviews was that Darville was acting on direction from the coaching staff—including Holtz's staff.

Said Tony Hunter, "We did get direction to go see Luther."

To do what?

"Financially."

They were that blunt?

"Yeah. Go see your boy, Luther. He'll tighten you up."

According to activists in Minneapolis's black community, Holtz and others did more than reassure Darville that they'd help him get resettled after the trial. Word among those activists is that another of Luther's closest friends, Henrietta Adams Faulconer, encouraged Darville to keep Holtz out of the trial.

"You're talking about significant betrayal here," says Ron Edwards, a civil rights activist who knows Faulconer well. "Holtz was very dependent upon Henrietta to make sure that Luther never testified negatively about Lou at the trial. She was the person Luther had the utmost respect and belief in, even more so than me, because he had known her longer. Henrietta advised him not to do that. Her recommendation to him was that it would serve no purpose and that Lou had been a good man and had been good to Luther."

Faulconer was one of the first black leaders in Minneapolis whom Holtz met, and she says the two of them hit it off famously: "That day I met Holtz, he said, 'I heard that you're a lady that looks after these kids and I want to thank you very much for what you've done. It's a terrible shame when kids come into a community and they don't have relatives or friends. It's nice to know that somebody like you exists.' We talked about one or two other things, nothing real specific, but my main message to him was that I knew he inherited some misfits. We had the dregs of society, almost because that's what the program had been reduced to. That was all the more reason why Luther was so important to his system."

Faulconer's relationship with Holtz grew closer about the time Darville's trial was to begin. Edwards said that Holtz asked for Faulconer's help in convincing Darville not to mention Holtz's name. Then, after the trial ended and Darville went off to prison, Faulconer went looking for money to support a charity in Minneapolis for the black community; among her first contributors, Faulconer told friends, was one Leo Louis Holtz.

Holtz chipped in $10,000. And he got his friend, Harvey Mackay, to throw in another $10,000.

Edwards says that Henrietta told him that Holtz called her "just out of the clear blue sky and said, 'I'm hearing a lot about that program you're putting together up there in Minneapolis, and I'd really like to do

something. Why don't you send me an outline of what you're doing?' "
Edwards says Faulconer told him that she "sent this outline to Lou in
South Bend, and Lou said, 'Henrietta, it's a wonderful idea,' and sent
her a check for ten thousand dollars and said, 'I'm so strongly behind
it that I'm gonna get my good friend Harvey Mackay to give you another
check.' "

Henrietta told you about this?

"Yeah. She told me the check that she was gonna get next was from
Harvey and she got it. In fact, she tells me the story that Harvey was at
the airport getting ready to fly out and called her to tell her the second
check was on its way."

Faulconer has a hard time answering the question about whether
she took any money from Holtz. She doesn't have a hard time, though,
being plainspoken about the charity's failure. "The church," she says,
"kept getting broken into and vandalized and all kinds of stuff, so I've
not had anything to do with that place in quite a while."

Asked if she took money from Holtz, Faulconer at first said, "No. If
you can catch up with Harvey Mackay or Lou Holtz, I'd like to talk to
them. If they're gonna help me, they haven't done it. Years ago, before
Lou Holtz even left town, he knew of my work in the community and
he had said to me, 'Henrietta, I respect what you're doing, and if I can
ever be of any help, let me know.' "

When asked why friends would say she bragged of getting Holtz's
check, she snapped, "They are lying as far as me telling them anything.
I know when I talked with Gwen [the late activist Gwen Jones Davis],
and she's the woman I was working with, I had mentioned to her I was
putting together a wish list of people I wanted to ask for help, and she
had that list with her. I can pretty much tell you that Lou Holtz's name
was on there. Same with Harvey Mackay's."

Pressed again on whether she ever received checks from those two,
Faulconer started to get increasingly defensive: "I think that if I did or
didn't, that's something I won't answer because I feel that that's not
really your business or anybody else's business. But I can truthfully tell
you that I would not make any phone calls or solicitations to any
of those people on that list that I put together and that's the bottom
line."

Could you see that if you did take a check from Holtz that it could
look kind of awkward?

"I don't know. I couldn't care less what it looked like because if anybody knows my reputation, they know that I don't play those kind of games. I have no need to."

So why would people say you told them that Holtz gave you a $10,000 check?

"I don't know. I don't believe, whether they will lie or won't lie, that those are questions that I will answer any further as far as who gave me what and who didn't give me what because I think that's something in a person's private life."

Despite her waffling claims to the contrary, two friends support Edwards' account that she boasted of Holtz's sizable "contribution."

"I was very disappointed with her actions," said Pat Robinson, a friend and fellow activist, when asked what she thought when Faulconer told her about the check.

Russell Krueger, an investigator in the county public defender's office, heard Faulconer tell the story, too. Though Krueger is a crusty old white guy, he's well known and well respected in the black community because of his work defending poor blacks in court. As a result, he is close to Faulconer. "When Henrietta started her little charity," he says, "I was working with her and I said, 'Why not call Lou? You saved his job.'" Krueger sits in his office, adorned by autographed pictures of himself with Gopher basketball and football players, as well as one with John Gutekunst, who followed Holtz as coach, and continues, "She said, 'I already did and he sent me ten thousand dollars.' I never saw the check, but she told a lot of people, including me, about it. I heard it all over town."

Ron Edwards, the former Urban League official who still keeps in regular contact with Darville, was especially outraged that Faulconer didn't share any of the proceeds with Darville: "I forced Henrietta to tell me that she received the money. She said she received it in two installments. Lou Holtz sent her a check for ten thousand dollars, and a few months later Harvey Mackay gave her a second check for ten thousand dollars. I couldn't believe it when I heard it. I had to ask her. And she didn't see any problem. Everyone else did."

Both Holtz and Mackay declined to be interviewed.

In the end, Holtz got the job of a lifetime at Notre Dame. Darville is unemployed in the Bahamas. Says Darville, "I believe that he would rather me not bother him, I know that. He would rather me disappear. I've survived it. I'm forty and I feel like starting over will be an invigorating experience. I'll be back, but it's going to be a hard road. It will surprise a lot of people when I make it. I'm back into helping young people again, working with high school dropouts. But I'm living proof that after you've given your best to an institution, when you become a liability to the institution, they can get rid of you very quickly, very viciously.

"Lou's a strategist. He's a winner. He won big on this one."

CHAPTER
14

Fallen Idols

With Lou Holtz's last skeletons from his Minnesota days safely locked away, he could again turn his focus to the transformation of The Fighting Irish from nickname to literal description.

While Notre Dame perseveres in trying to act as if it is far superior to all others—routinely making behind-the-back snide comments about the likes of Miami, Oklahoma, USC, Texas A&M—its players continue acting like, well, players from Miami, Oklahoma, USC, Texas A&M. When a scuffle once broke out on the Notre Dame practice field, a high-level Irish official laughed admiringly and said, "My goodness, looks a lot like Miami at its best, doesn't it?"

Through the second half of the eighties—which is to say since Holtz arrived as coach—Notre Dame players have been involved in numerous episodes of unacceptable behavior. John Foley explains, "We weren't loose cannons on the field and we weren't loose cannons in the classroom. That's because we were always watched, we were always disciplined. We couldn't do nothing wrong. We had to be perfect.

"You went to college. You tell me you went to class all the time? How many times did you sleep in? You did it. We couldn't do that. Holtz had it that we all had to get up at six-thirty to go to breakfast just to make sure we go to class. That means every day, boom, get up and go to breakfast. Who in the hell do you think you are, Coach Holtz? There were times I hated Holtz. A lot of times I was questioning what he was doing and what he was thinking. But right out of school, I learned that everything he did, he did for a reason.

"But the problem was it just got to a point where a lot of us had to blow off steam. I did a lot of that. I was a wild man, especially when I came home. If I had done half the stuff in South Bend that I did in Chicago, I would have been in the paper and all over the place.

"I went to bars and I got wild and did stupid things. I didn't drink and drive. As I grew up, we had a problem of that in my family. I know you just don't do that because you kill people. That's one thing, there were a lot of incidents like that [drinking and driving, fights in bars] and they are still like that. Because we are always watched so closely, when we get away from everybody, it's just like, *'Yeah! I'm away! Good! I'm going to go off the wall!'* "

Tony Brooks, who struggled academically and behaviorally, thinks the football players deserve more breaks than they got. Says Brooks, "They made it really difficult only because they didn't want to treat the players any different from the regular students. But the players are different. They have different schedules, and you have to work with them, especially with the revenue we're bringing in to the school. Of course, it's a privilege to play and all that good stuff, but at the same time you have to have a tension release. Guys have to have some relaxation time. Guys have to do different things. In the dormitory they wouldn't allow you to play music at a certain hour. There was so many restrictions. That was fine for the students because they had time to do different things, but when it came to athletes, the schedules were different. We had to practice late, everything."

Marty Lippincott, who certainly had a bad-boy reputation at Notre Dame, says, "I never had a problem with discipline. Academic probation three times, but that's just with schoolwork. Not for screwing around, not for fucking around or doing something wrong." It takes a quantum leap in logic to buy Lippincott's theory that he had no problem with discipline. It would be far more accurate to say that all of Lippincott's problems stemmed from problems with discipline. And when it came to Lippincott, as it often did, he thinks Holtz enforced all rules; when it came to Brooks and Watters and plenty of others, Lippincott thinks Holtz did not.

Pernell Taylor admits that Holtz brought—and brings—in a lot of players who are on society's fringe. Naturally, that leads to discipline problems. "I think," says Taylor, "they let out a lot of steam off the field because they couldn't on the field, where everything is so disciplined under Holtz. So this affected their social lives."

George Williams admits, "You could call us free spirits. The thing that irked them [the coaches] the most is that we didn't give a shit what they told us to do. We were going to do what we wanted to do. That was our whole thing. We're not gonna let anyone punk us. We're gonna do what we want to do, and if it comes down to blows, then we'll just have to fight."

In defense of the athletes, Foley contends that in South Bend, football players repeatedly are the subject of provoking actions. "Do you know," asks Foley, "how many times we'll walk in somewhere and kids would say, 'Come on, you great football player, kick my ass'? Do you know how often that happens? Too often. Do you know how many bars we go to and people start fights with us just because we're Notre Dame? It's just because they know they can start a fight and get us in a fight and we're kicked out of school. Then they're on TV, in the newspaper. You don't realize it because you don't go to the bars with the guys. I lived it. We've got a townie that loves to start fights with football players. You know why? Because he's in the paper. He's famous. They say everyone's famous for ten or fifteen seconds. He's famous.

"We can only take so much. We're human. Then again, we are high-profile athletes. We are heroes. We are what we are. It gets out of hand sometimes. It's kind of rough. I could have gotten into a thousand fights when I went to Notre Dame. Where I grew up, if someone like Rocket came into the neighborhood, they'd kill him. They'd shoot him. Why? Because they'd be famous."

It's difficult to quantify the perceived increase in undesirable incidents involving Notre Dame players because such incidents are more vigorously reported these days and many may have been covered up in the past. Regardless, the perception is strong that Notre Dame players have been compiling police files at least as long as their media-guide bios. A few examples:

—Defensive tackle Troy Ridgley from Baden, Pennsylvania, was arrested at three A.M. in a lounge on charges of public intoxication, disorderly conduct, and resisting law enforcement. The problem started when Ridgley was accused of throwing popcorn on another patron. He eventually pled guilty.

—Michael Stonebreaker was charged with DUI, then violated his probation by driving on campus and was suspended from the team.

Stonebreaker had a .157 blood-alcohol level at the time of his arrest; the legal limit in Indiana is .10.

"What happened to me," explains Stonebreaker, who says the person in history he'd most like to meet is Jesus Christ, "is when I started my junior year, I got disciplined for some actions, so my driving privileges on campus were suspended. At Notre Dame that's a big thing, and then they caught me driving on campus, which I wasn't supposed to be doing. So the only next step they could take was to put me on disciplinary probation, which means you can't represent the university in any way."

Did you think that was too harsh?

"Looking back on it, that's the rule. It's in black and white and that's what they go by and I broke it, so it's my fault. It's not their fault. . . . I thought it was too harsh." Stonebreaker makes a vague attempt at trying to somehow explain what he did, but there really is no explanation and no justification. Concludes Stonebreaker, "It was my fault and I should never have put myself in that situation, so you have to pay the consequences."

—Then there was the much-troubled Tony Brooks, involved in all manner of wrongdoing, including leaving the scene of an accident, driving with a suspended license—in addition to the USC suspension, drugs, and so on. He withdrew from school for a while.

—Quarterback Rick Mirer was arrested in 1991 for public intoxication and disorderly conduct, but he was not formally charged.

Mike Crounse says there "definitely was an increase in the number of off-field incidents in the time between when we came back from the national championship year in January [1989] and the beginning of winter workouts in mid-February. It got bad enough that Holtz had a team meeting and asked everyone what was up. He asked why everyone was going wild." No answers were provided.

Dan Quinn remembers walking into a bar in South Bend, Chip's (now out of business), "and everybody's standing around in this big circle and standing on chairs. It was like a human wall and this place was jumping. I figured someone was dancing in there. It was Pearson kicking the shit out of somebody. Zaleski got into a fight with some guy who's about six-four and two-forty, big guy, beating the shit out of him and Zaleski didn't need any help. But Pearson comes up in these boots, and Pearson's a mean, mean fucker. He steps on this guy on the side of his face. He didn't hurt him. He just pinned him and he says,

'Hey, if I were you, I'd cut this bullshit out because you're gonna go down.' I can't remember word for word, but it was something like, 'Quit struggling. You're gonna get fucked up really badly. You better just get out of here if you know what's good for you.' Chip's was a football-controlled bar. It was a biker bar until the football players went down there, and then the students would feel safe and we'd get free beer to go in there because the place would be jam-packed with Notre Dame students. When we were there, everybody felt secure."

So football players got free beer at Chip's?

"I don't think I ever paid for a beer there."

Dining out was also no problem for football players. Linc Coleman says he was "able to go places and eat free."

In South Bend?

"Yeah, in South Bend."

Where could you go and eat free?

"Sometimes a lot of the older guys would go to this certain restaurant at the hotel and eat free. There's a hotel right by the school where they would keep all the recruits when they'd come up for a visit. I could go anywhere, like to a Burger King if I just want fast food, and they'd say, 'Oh, you play for Notre Dame,' or if they'd seen me on TV, 'Here, have a burger, fries, whatever.'"

Where else did you go?

"It was a spaghetti place that I went to one time with my girlfriend. We were just sitting there talking. And the waiter came over and said, 'You're Linc Coleman? I read about you. I saw you against Alabama.' It just started like that. By the time I was ready to take care of the check, he said, 'Don't worry about it. It's already taken care of.'"

Mike Crounse says a favorite football-player haunt was a local spaghetti restaurant. "People would take care of you," he says. "No harm intended."

At NCAA headquarters in Shawnee Mission, Kansas, investigator Bob Minnix says that NCAA Bylaw 16.02.3, commonly known as the extra-benefit rule, prohibits any university employee or booster from providing anything to a student-athlete that is not generally available to the normal student. Minnix says free meals clearly qualify as a violation of NCAA rules. It's difficult to enforce this bylaw, says Minnix, because "we find that some restaurant owners/boosters do it as a way of showing their support. That doesn't make it right, though."

. . .

Marty Lippincott, a Faust recruit, is living proof that not all of Notre Dame's loose cannons can be laid at Holtz's doorstep. He will forever be a Notre Dame legend—not like Gipp and Rockne and the Four Horsemen, you understand, but a legend among almost every player who has a wacky bent, which covers almost every player.

That's because shortly after Holtz arrived, he had a team meeting on discipline and . . .

"I mooned him," adds Lippincott helpfully.

What happened?

"Did you see that on a Trivial Pursuit card? There's a card and it says, 'What did Notre Dame footballer Marty Lippincott do to Coach Lou Holtz after a discipline-and-decorum meeting?' Flip it over: 'He mooned him.' How they got [that story], I have no idea. But what it was was, we're in a meeting and we just got done talking about discipline—"

What prompted the meeting?

"Who knows. It could have been fighting in the locker room. It could have been anything. There was always something that Holtz was having meetings for. If we had a free hour, he'd hold a meeting. God forbid he gives you that hour of free time. He always did it. Always did it. You were his little toy is what it came to. If you let him, he could take your personality, he could take your whole life away for that four years."

About the mooning?

"I didn't actually moon him."

What did you do?

"We came out of the meeting, which was in the upstairs Monogram Room. Holtz had made a big speech about discipline, staying in line, don't get out of line. When the meeting ended, we were walking down the hallway and we were rushing to get somewhere, and Pete Graham or someone just kept bugging me—'Hey, your shorts are queer looking' or something—just bullshitting, and the whole team was coming along and I was up front. Somebody said something about my fairy shorts or something, so I pulled my pants down. A couple of the coaches were standing there, and that got back to Holtz and he freaked. Bam, suspended."

That got you suspended?

"Oh, yeah, I got kicked off the team for that."

Was that the first time, third time, what?

"I don't know."

There were plenty of Lippincott low-lights. Another time he was suspended because of a dispute involving Tom Rehder. Says Lippincott, "Tom was starting ahead of me and I was second team and it was like back and forth. . . . He came out and told Holtz that 'Marty Lippincott was drunk and he tried to hit me.' " Lippincott was driving one car, Rehder another. Lippincott explains that he was driving "down the road and you know when you see something and you swerve and you swerve back? But Rehder knew I was at a party earlier, so he comes out and says, 'You were drunk and you tried to hit me.' Get the fuck out of here, Tom. Why would I do that? I'm funny and stupid but I'm not that stupid."

Another gloomy moment—and another suspension—came when Holtz again landed on Lippincott with all fours about his lack of leadership. "He was," says Lippincott, "talking and hollering and making me feel so fucking bad, and I remember sitting there and always in the back of my mind was my parents. I don't want to embarrass my parents and I never have. I'm sitting there and I'm so frustrated and so angry, and you know you just can't get up and shove that playbook right up his ass. It's funny telling it now, but I could see myself doing a hit of acid and going in and just killing him for the hell of it. You hate him. You grow to hate him."

Player misbehavior at Notre Dame takes all forms.

For his part, Erik Simien doesn't like to think of it as misbehavior. Rather, he says, "we got caught trying to make it more interesting, things like taking all the sodas out of the vending machines and turning the machine upside down. But I think the big thing for me was getting caught with the illegal use of the calling card. Someone obtained the number from a coach. Having that saved me my freshman year since I was all homesick. It went on from like August to January. All these guys were using it every night. It could have lasted longer, too, but too many guys had it. Fifteen people got caught. Some of us got suspended. We had to pay it back, but when they told me mine was four hundred something dollars, I laughed. That was nowhere near as much as I spent."

Shawn Smith says he also was in on the calling-card gravy train. Says Smith, "I started calling, and there was another number and another number, and I started calling, and this went on for six months and I started thinking, it's not causing any problems, somebody's paying for it. I heard that a lot of people on the team had it. I guess the people that used it really used it. Some people that had it used it once in a while. The university didn't care except about the outrageous number of calls that were being made."

How many did you have?

"It was like a hundred and fifty dollars' worth."

Oh, that's all?

"Yeah, because I knew that we were going to be caught sooner or later. I think we'd have gotten in more trouble if some big stars hadn't been in on it, too. How could you suspend your leading guys, you know?"

This is all evidence, says Smith, of "what's really going on inside and out. Doing the drugs, people cheating on tests and stuff like that, how they promise their alumni will help the players out. It was understood that people were getting helped."

How?

"People get letters in the mail, maybe money in it. There wasn't no names on it, so you couldn't place that on nobody. It's just money. It could be from your parents. It's free money."

Did you see that happen? Or did you just hear about it?

"I'd hear about it."

Was it just guys talking or was it for real?

"For real. They ain't got to lie. I mean, you'd see people driving good cars and stuff, a Cadillac or a Lexus or something like that. We'd go, 'What? Did your mom buy that for you?' "

The familiar refrain when it comes to college football is that "everybody's cheating." That's no excuse, clearly; still, Notre Dame most certainly is not the only one. It's just the one we wish most desperately weren't debasing itself so.

Lippincott knows firsthand about the ways things are done around Notre Dame that have, to be kind, a slight aroma to them. "I sold an autographed football for a thousand dollars," he says. "I've given someone a helmet and they turned around and gave me three hundred dollars, four hundred dollars. I give someone spikes and they take twenty [of our] guys out to dinner. My uncle—he's not really my uncle but I call him my uncle—he used to come out and bring me a case of pepperoni, ten cases of Tastykakes, a case of cheese steaks, and twenty cases of Schmidt's beer." Then, to make double sure the point is clear, Lippincott says, with a wink, again, "He's not really my uncle."

He's not your uncle?
"He's not my uncle."

Not all players had "uncles." Some just had great employers. John McDermott, a 1966 Notre Dame graduate with an undergraduate degree in finance who lives in Laguna Beach, California, is a partner in a prestigious Newport Beach law firm, McDermott & Trayner. What Mc-Dermott provides, according to some of the Irish football players who have worked there, including Quinn and Lippincott, are the classic kind of high-paying jobs for football players that require minimal work. McDermott vigorously denies the accusation.

"We give them responsibilities and they generally, you know, are no problem at all," says McDermott. "It's like everything else. Every once in a while you have a problem. I don't supervise them personally, but, you know, they are around doing their job, taking their instructions, and performing their work."

McDermott contends that the players—he says there have been ten to fifteen Notre Dame football players who have worked there over the last fourteen years, including Troy Ridgley, George Poorman, Derek Brown, and Todd Norman—"basically file, messenger, Xerox, you know, move furniture when we need them to, basically take care of the massive paperwork that we have in here and assist the staff with the paperwork." He insists that the players "were paid on an hourly basis, and we have had throughout the years situations where players would work less than a full forty-hour week and they are paid for less than a forty-hour week, and that's been typical all the way through this thing. But the players that are working full-time for the period that they are working, you know, will work that. If not, they are paid less. Typically over the last few years we've had it more typical where the players are not working full forty-hour weeks [so they are] not getting paid a full forty-hour week."

What hours do they work?

"Well, it varies, but I would say a typical day would be eight-thirty or nine to five to five-thirty. Sometimes they will be in earlier if there is something going on, or later if something is happening."

McDermott insists he only paid Dan Quinn—and everybody else—for the hours they said they worked, and that the employees submitted those hours on signed time sheets. McDermott provided the authors with a sample of two of Quinn's time sheets for an August time period, indicating the player said he worked and was therefore paid for forty hours each week.

To hear Dan Quinn describe it, however, the "work" was considerably less grueling than, say, football practice.

Joan Quinn says her son Dan "got eleven dollars an hour for eight hours of work. He didn't need to get there until ten-thirty to avoid the traffic. He got to leave at three-thirty and he played basketball at lunch. He got paid extra for making deliveries."

Dan Quinn—who says that he "like[s] McDermott very much"— says he learned of McDermott when he was being recruited by Notre Dame. Says Quinn, a Golden Gloves boxing champ, "I got a big manila envelope that said from McDermott & Trayner or whatever, and [inside it said] that if you come to the University of Notre Dame, you'll be making thirteen dollars an hour in the summertime. . . . Our job was [to] go to the University Athletic Club and play basketball and lift weights and hit the punching bag and do shit and get paid."

Joan: "You did some filing, didn't you?"

Dan: "Every once in a while."

Joan: For thirteen dollars an hour that's pretty—

Dan: "Well, actually it was eleven dollars, but then we got club privileges. John was real smart. That was where the extra two dollars an hour came in. Because, you got to understand, we went to the club after I'd get up to the job at eleven or eleven-thirty A.M. I lived in San Diego, which was an hour away, and Mark Green lived in Riverside, which was an hour away. So we got an hour allowance to get in there. We get in there and they didn't really give a shit because there wasn't anything we could do. We'd get blamed for misfiling stuff, and it's not like maybe we didn't do it sometimes, but it's pretty basic to file stuff, and we're college students and we're pretty intelligent even though we're football players. It got to a point sometimes that we didn't want to file because we'd get blamed for shit if it happened, so it was basically like, let the secretaries do it. They were really cool.

"So we get in there and we'd make long-distance phone calls to our girlfriends and stuff because they had an 800 line. I thought WATS was you paid one bill. That's what we all talked about. We thought, McDermott's not gonna get billed for this; he pays one fee and you can call all over the U.S. We were wrong about that shit, because it came back and it was thousands of dollars. We're talking like over three summers."

Did McDermott ask you for the money back?

"No. We also used to get paid twenty-five dollars a trip because it was a legal office and they're always sending shit out. Anyway, I remember when it was twenty-five dollars a trip and that was like for every trip, and technically they gave me four packages to deliver. I had to go up to L.A. one time and drive around for like fifteen or thirty minutes or whatever, drop these packages off, and come back. That's technically one trip because I dropped four things off. We logged four trips . . . so McDermott got hit for a hundred dollars. I remember one time I made $985 in a week. Mark Green made a little bit less than me. We would fight for these trips. It was blood and guts. It was like, 'No, no, I was here first. I get this trip.'

"So finally John called us in. He was like, 'Guys, we've got to tone this down because this is getting ridiculous.' So he cut it back to, I'm not sure what he did, to like fifteen dollars locally, twenty-five dollars for one time up to L.A. and stuff. We were still making good money but . . .

"He told me that if I kept my nose clean that these guys [that we worked with] are twenty-six years old and they're making $200,000, $250,000, $400,000 a year, driving 450SLs and stuff, and he goes that I could be one of those guys."

Bond underwriters?

"Yeah. I didn't even know what underwriting was."

Marty Lippincott said something about going to Laker games and that was one of the good things?

"Oh, yeah. Limousines."

What do you remember about it?

"We'd get limousines, actually two limousines because there was a point when it was Mark Green, myself, Marty was up there for a while . . . there was a point where there was like several players working for John at one time. Timmy Brown came out and worked for a while, and Brandy Wells was working there."

When McDermott is asked about the limos to the Laker games and "the front-row seats," he says, "Now we, you know, you're getting exaggerations. We did during the period of the eighties have firm-shared tickets. I think two or three times a year we with some other corporations around here would have group tickets to the Laker games. They were not front-row tickets."

How close to the floor were they?

"Probably six or seven rows back . . . and we went out during the whole 1980s probably three or four times."

Did you take players with you?

"Yeah, we took attorneys and players."

Additionally, Quinn says, "We'd invite these guys to come down and play basketball and come to the club. We'd go in and play basketball and go up and eat. Ninety-four thirty-one was the magic number. That was the number of John's account. Ninety-four thirty-one at the UAC club, and boom, that was it. That got you entry. That got you everything, literally."

Joan Quinn: "Including socks."

Dan: "When Marty came to the club, it's not like I hadn't thought about it, but Marty and I raided, before we left, and I'm talking . . . I'm kind of embarrassed to say this, but I was young. We raided that place. We probably got over a thousand dollars' worth of stuff between the two of us. We're talking sweats, sweaters, shoes, you name it. Marty was up there and he wouldn't steal from you personally if he's your friend, but he's a street kid from Philadelphia."

McDermott tries to downplay the University Athletic Club: "It's modest by Newport Beach standards. It's basically just a small workout club with lunch facilities." (Club membership director Tom Hobbs says it costs $250 to join, with monthly fees of $115, an annual fee of $1,380. The exclusive club, including a basketball court, is limited to nine hundred members and guests are charged $12 a day.)

When asked what other kinds of things he did for his player/employees, McDermott said, "Well, you know, it varies. You know, I'm a pretty active guy. I do things with them sometimes on weekends, which I do with other clerks or lawyers in the firm. We try to have a congenial, enjoyable atmosphere in here and we have fun with them, and they are great young men and we have enjoyed being around them. We on occasion, on a weekend, will play basketball."

Go on yacht trips?

"Go to the beach, you know, go on firm parties, whatever, yeah."

Do you all do yacht trips and things like that?

"Well, the firm has been involved in taking boats, sure. We've done that before. We will take staff attorneys and clerks and other people, clients, friends, and go on boats, sure."

McDermott denies that Holtz has ever visited him or the firm, but he admits Holtz has talked to him about his employment of Notre Dame football players. Specifically, McDermott admits Holtz did once inquire about the employment procedures after Quinn was asked in a deposition, according to McDermott, if he was paid for any unworked hours. The player swore then, says McDermott, that he was not.

"First of all, I don't have a close friendship with Lou," says McDermott. "I have met him two, three times. I've talked to him on the phone a couple of times, so I don't have a friendship with him. I've met him very briefly, but he has in the past mentioned that it's important that when we are hiring Notre Dame student-athletes, that we make sure we are following all the rules, and he's stated that on a couple of occasions when I've talked to him."

Of primary concern, McDermott said, is the NCAA requirement that athletes get no extra benefits not available to other students.

Asked why Holtz would be so concerned, McDermott said, "I think probably the fact that we've had a lot of Notre Dame students in here over the years." But, basically, the summer help has been athletes. The only nonathletes McDermott can recall are law students who served as clerks.

Might the athletes be going back to South Bend and talking about the kind of job that the McDermott firm gives people?

"Well, I think that might have been prompted also by some problems we had with one or two of the student-athletes, but you know, I don't know what they would say about their employment over the summer."

Have you ever worried that some of the things you do or some of the arrangements here might be a violation of NCAA rules?

"No, we've been very careful to provide them with summer employment, which, as I understand it, is entirely appropriate."

It's Quinn's opinion that Holtz and McDermott are closer than McDermott lets on. Says Quinn, "Coach Holtz knew about John because I know that John talked with him, and that's when John had to scale things back because it was getting out of hand. I really don't want to get John in trouble.

"Everybody back at school knew about our jobs because maybe there were guys that were more mature and kept their jobs under wraps, but we had basically the best jobs you could have. Because maybe people made more money, I don't know if they did, but they might have had to do something. We didn't do a thing. We got up there, made phone calls, went and played basketball, came back, waited around, talked shit, and left to go home before the traffic hit. We made a base of four hundred and forty dollars in a week and then with trips and stuff . . ."

Joan Quinn went to parties at McDermott's home, which she says "were a lot of fun, unbelievable." But she admits that "I wanted Dan to go to Notre Dame because Notre Dame doesn't cheat, it has got impeccable academic credentials for not cheating, which is why I hated USC. And then my son has this job. What can I say? I can't tell him not to have that job. I was worried as hell. Making two hundred thousand dollars after he graduates just sitting? I guess people do that, but I'm from a blue-collar background and people have to work for what they get."

McDermott and Notre Dame officials are understandably defensive when asked about the allegations. Father Joyce simply dismisses Quinn as a "no-good guy." And McDermott grows increasingly uneasy with the questioning and finally blurts, "You know, I think that to avoid problems for you and for us, I think it's really important that you understand that this firm is a, we range between twenty-five and thirty attorneys. We do very high quality corporate work. We have attorneys from Stanford, University of Chicago, UCLA, some of the better schools. We have an excellent reputation in this area. One of the areas of our practice by happenstance is defamation." McDermott then says, "I'm not trying to threaten you."

But Quinn isn't the only player who confirms McDermott's largesse. Mark Green, who plays for the Bears, was furious the word on McDermott's summer job program had reached the coauthors. "Who told you about the job? It wasn't anything wrong," he fumed. "Don't try to get anyone in trouble. Going to those Laker games had nothing to do with being a football player. There were some of his lawyers who went to those Laker games, too. And we had to leave work early. You know why? Because of the traffic. None of us lived in Newport Beach. Sure, we played basketball at lunch, but so did some of the lawyers. It wasn't like getting the job was part of any deal or anything. It wasn't, 'Come to Notre Dame and you'll get a good summer job.' You're just trying to be negative."

Marty Lippincott, who calls McDermott "a great person," says what Quinn disclosed was true. Lippincott says he worked at the firm for two summers and "did very minimal work." He describes the situation as "great. Great food, they have free beer, pool table, pool, we always played basketball."

The players who had the jobs always bragged about the arrangement. Pernell Taylor heard about the McDermott jobs and he says, "They were supposed to be working and they weren't doing anything." Taylor says he didn't work there because "I wanted to work. I didn't want to get favors. I didn't want to owe anybody. Put it that way."

Did everybody know about those jobs?

"Yeah."

Because it was apparently the joke of the team?

"It was. Everybody knew about it."

Among those who heard about the McDermott jobs was Tom Riley, who didn't get one. "It pissed me off," says Riley. "I wasn't part of the summer vacation crew. That was one of their commitments, to get me a good summer job. Instead, I had to go through some employment agency and was told jobs were like six dollars an hour. It was the value they placed on a player. Starters got more of these little things."

Football players can be a loosely wired lot. For example, before a question could be asked of Frank Stams, he said out of the blue, "The Australian crack kangaroo jumps highest during a full moon."

So, in defense of Holtz, it could well be that living in this asylum with all these inmates has made him a little crazy. If true, it's understandable. But never forget, he handpicked the inmates he wanted to be around him. For split end Steve Alaniz from Edinburg, Texas, it was all real simple: "Everybody knows what's right. There are those few screwups that we had."

It is important to remember that those "screwups" were all judged worthy of a Notre Dame education, worthy to be in South Bend, worthy to play on the Notre Dame football team. And does the fact that one has fouled up mean that his opinions and his accounts of what goes on are less reliable than the statements of a straight-arrow? Who has more to lose by telling the truth? Who has more to gain from lying? Keep the words of the following in mind when Notre Dame launches its inevitable counterattack at this book:

Chet Lacheta: "When the players first get there, they start teaching you what to say and what to not to say. You've got to be careful who you talk to and how you phrase things. . . . They teach you how not to tell the truth."

Jason Cegielski: "I think the players from Notre Dame carry [the desire to cover up problems] on. They come out with this attitude. I guess they'd rather play along with it than let anybody in on it."

Gerry Faust: "If there is any place that tries to hide things, it's Notre Dame, because of its image. Above all else, it worries about its image."

George Marshall: "Everybody still wants Notre Dame to be America's dream team. They're the good guys that are winning, and a lot of people love 'em because of that. . . . It may not be the truth, but everybody's idea of it is that it's on top of the world. So you kind of just shut your mouth and say, 'Yeah, it is.' "

What about on-field behavior? Hang on.

As predictably as dawn follows dark and day follows dawn, the Irish started matching their off-field behavior on the field. And that started bringing the ugliness into public view.

In the wake of the 1987 season, when Holtz's Irish lost their last three games to Penn State, Miami (by an unhappy 24–0), and Texas A&M in the Cotton Bowl, a new attitude sprouted. The team was determined to remove the notion of "gentleman" from the image of the Notre Dame man; "sportsman" and "class" went out the window with it.

It was time for winning at all costs. Tim Prister wrote in *Blue & Gold Illustrated,* "Yes, people change, and it's time the Fighting Irish do the changing. It's time to stop crying about all the nasty things other teams are saying. It's time to stop whining about four-letter words and pouting about what was said—after the game, when it's too late to do anything about it."

Indeed, this was the moment that Notre Dame—in particular Lou Holtz—decided no more Mr. Nice Guy. This was the moment Notre Dame—in particular Lou Holtz—decided to get down in the mud with everyone else. As Mike Brennan, a lineman from Severna Park, Maryland, said, "We always run around everyone else. Why should we always be the nice guys?"

In the 1988 season, in the narrow tunnel in Notre Dame Stadium that leads from the locker rooms to the field, there were fights before the games with both Michigan and Miami (said Andy Heck, a captain, "Who threw the first punch? I think we probably did") and again in 1989 with Southern Cal, the latter chronicled in the pages of *Sports Illustrated.* It was that celebrated USC brawl—clearly precipitated by the Irish—that prompted Holtz to say that if any such fights occurred in the future, he'd resign. After Notre Dame started the fight, Holtz said he was "deeply disturbed." Mike Downey later wrote in a column in *The Sporting News*, "He [Holtz] accepted, on behalf of Notre Dame, all the responsibility and blame for the October 21 rhubarb." He did. That was proper. That was right. Father Hesburgh subsequently wrote in his book, "I have no doubt that he meant exactly what he said. . . . I am equally sure that there won't be any more incidents like that, because the players have so much respect for Lou." We'll see.

Although Holtz has publicly always said he was against fighting at games—of course, name one coach who will say he's for it—before the 1988 game with then No. 1–ranked Miami, which the Irish ultimately won 31–30, he endorsed the Irish's fighting spirit in his comments to them after the fight but before the game. Kurt Zackrison recalls he was sitting next to Kevin McShane and "I said, 'Uh-oh, we're gonna get reamed.' " Instead, Holtz told his team that "I don't condone fighting," but then he said, "After the game, after we've won, you can start it up."

What has grown up around the Holtz-led program is the view that pregame fights help win games. Admits Ted FitzGerald of the Miami dustup, "If we don't get in a fight before that game, we don't win that game. We were scared in our own stadium. I can tell you right now, if we don't get in a fight before that game, we're getting blown out. We were pissed off in the locker room and came out and we won the game. They were probably better than us that year, but . . ."

"Coach Holtz didn't want us to walk away and lose our self-respect," said John Foley. "He said, 'If Jimmy Johnson gets involved, I'll get involved.' Everyone went nuts. The whole team went crazy. That's exactly what he said." Tim Grunhard agrees, although he remembers Holtz saying, " 'Save Jimmy Johnson for me.' That was probably the best line that he ever had. That was great. He said, 'I want you to be gentlemen, I want you to play. I want you to play to the best of your ability. No cheap shots. But after the game I don't care what you do, just as long as you don't get Johnson because I want him.' That was kind of a good deal."

In fact, John Foley says the most memorable talk he ever heard Holtz give was prior to this game with No. 2–ranked Miami. Recalls Foley, "Coach says, 'Listen, these guys are trouble. We're in the middle of trouble. Expect trouble. Number one, if I see any of you guys throw a punch or start a fight, you're gone. I don't expect you to take anything, either.' Holtz never said that before. Holtz would sit there and preach you shouldn't do this and you shouldn't do that."

Holtz's message was clear, and his butt was covered, too. After all, he'd told them to be gentlemen, hadn't he? Was it his fault if they only heard the part about not taking any shit?

In spite of Notre Dame's always trying to shift the blame to its opponents for untoward episodes, George Williams says that's so much hooey. "We," says Williams, "didn't give a fuck. We were gonna speak our minds and say and do whatever we wanted to do. I think that carried over onto the field, and that helped us a lot. We would talk shit like those stories you heard about us, starting the fights, we did it all. We started all of them."

Did you?

"Yeah."

Were you in the middle of those?

"Yeah."

Were Notre Dame players talking trash in all these fights?

"We usually talk shit all the time."

On that point, West Virginia, which played Notre Dame in the Fiesta Bowl on January 2, 1989, can speak with authority. The Irish were penalized eight times for personal fouls in a lights-out demonstration of simply awful behavior. Wrote Austin Murphy in *Sports Illustrated*: "University officials click their tongues at such behavior and coaches mouth condemnations of it, and meanwhile everyone is secretly tickled that the boys aren't taking guff anymore."

Afterward, Malcolm Moran quoted Holtz in *The New York Times*: "Our football players got frustrated. They made some comments to the officials completely out of line. They were completely wrong. But they were out of frustration, they were not used in profanity, nor was it because they were talking to West Virginia." Not in profanity? Not talking to West Virginia? That does not square with what players from both teams later said.

In fact, Rick Telander wrote in *SI* of the game, "Notre Dame came out running and smoking and talking more trash than the cast of that old Gipper movie." Said West Virginia center Kevin Koken of the Irish, "They're good, but they need to learn class. That was probably the worst bad-mouth team I've ever played."

. . .

On one of his videos, Holtz says, "You must have the trust of the public, because without it, you don't have a chance."

John Foley is one player who buys the Notre Dame line. "They have more to offer," says Foley, "than just an athletic program. The thing is,

Notre Dame could have the best team in the country, but a lot of kids are looking for other things, cars, what can you do for me. I know there are schools out there giving things out because I ran into it. Notre Dame is straight up. If Notre Dame has to lose every game but have a good program, they'll do it. They won't break the rules."

If Notre Dame was willing to tolerate losing, would Lou Holtz have ever gotten the job in the first place?

CHAPTER
15

The Almighty Dollar

It is impossible to fathom any greater exhibition of greed or arrogance than what the University of Notre Dame perpetrated on the college football world in February 1990 when it announced, in effect, "We're Notre Dame and you're not, so screw you."

That's when Notre Dame's five-year television deal with NBC was agreed to. NBC got the rights to televise all Notre Dame home games through 1995 for about $37.5 million. That part is acceptable; it's free enterprise and it worked gloriously for Notre Dame. You have to hand it to those people in South Bend; they know about money and how to get their hands on it.

To make the deal, however, Notre Dame reneged on its promises to be part of a sixty-four-member coalition of major football schools, called the College Football Association, which had made a television agreement less than three weeks earlier. The Notre Dame hierarchy participated at the highest levels in the CFA discussions with the networks and was privy to all discussions over television deals. It was the classic fox in the classic henhouse.

Incredibly, as the CFA was negotiating with ABC and ESPN—with

Notre Dame attending every major meeting—the Irish were, unbeknownst to Charles M. Neinas, executive director of the CFA, also meeting secretly across the street with NBC.

After months of tedious and difficult negotiations, Neinas, the extremely able boss of the CFA, announced on January 16, 1990, that the sixty-four members would divide up $210 million from ABC and $140 million from ESPN (this part of the deal had been made public several months earlier) over five years. On February 5, 1990, less than three weeks later, Notre Dame announced it was out of the CFA package and had made its own arrangement with NBC. So long, suckers.

Says Neinas, "We were, to say the least, surprised." Notre Dame's athletic director, Dick Rosenthal, sniffed, "We did not see the CFA deal as in our best interest."

Father Joyce jumps to the defense of Notre Dame: "I certainly am not critical." Among the reasons he is for it is that the ABC plan would have been "terribly bad for Notre Dame" because many of the games would have been regional, which limits audience size. Plus, he says, the NBC arrangement allows for the start of all home games to be fixed well in advance, and that helps Irish fans to make travel arrangements.

As we all learned in the cradle, when people say it's not the money but the principle, it's the money. However, in this case, it was both money and principle.

What bothers Neinas most is the underhandedness and double-dealing of Notre Dame. Asked if the Irish were secretive, Neinas answers immediately, and curtly, "Yes."

The hurt runs deep because Neinas has a long, comfortable, and cozy relationship with the Irish. In fact, Joyce was one of the founders of the College Football Association in 1977, and Neinas calls him the "moral conscience" of the organization. Routinely, because of the esteem in which both Joyce and Notre Dame were held, Neinas says Joyce was asked to present the organization's views to others. When various schools around the country would begin having doubts about the CFA, it was usually Joyce or somebody else from Notre Dame who was dispatched to keep them in the fold. Basically, the Notre Dame message was, "We've all got to hang together or we'll hang separately."

The CFA and Notre Dame spoke with one voice. And they were, make no mistake, real chummy. When veteran AD Moose Krause was retiring from Notre Dame, Neinas says that "I recommended Gene Corrigan as the next athletic director to Father Ned, and at his request, I got the two of them together." As the CFA moved toward TV contracts, Neinas says that "both Father Ned and Corrigan stated, on more than one occasion, that what is good for college football will be good for Notre Dame." Ironically, when the Southeastern Conference was considering not going along with a television plan, Joyce was at the meeting as an advocate for the CFA. "He was very effective," says Neinas. The SEC stayed in.

Then came a changing of the guard. In November 1986, Hesburgh and Joyce stepped down, to be replaced by Malloy and Beauchamp. And the very next year, Corrigan resigned, to be replaced by a former banker with no experience in collegiate athletic administration, Dick Rosenthal.

Neinas felt the transition was nearly seamless. Beauchamp joined the CFA board of directors, and later on he became secretary-treasurer, "the best one we ever had," says Neinas. Less than two months after Neinas had made the $140-million strike with ESPN, Neinas received "a nice letter" from Beauchamp, saying that Notre Dame was "very pleased with the cable contract and it was certain it would be with the network deal." Meanwhile, Beauchamp was on the CFA negotiating committee and participated in all discussions.

Suddenly, chaos. Neinas got a call in early February 1990 from Beauchamp, saying he and Rosenthal would like to visit with him at the Denver airport on Saturday morning, February 3. Neinas had no indication of impending disaster. Since he had skied in the past with Beauchamp and Rosenthal (although Rosenthal was a beginner) and had stayed at Rosenthal's home at Single Tree, near the ski area of Beaver Creek, Neinas said, "Look, if you're coming out to ski, let's meet at Beaver Creek." No, he was told, there would not be any skiing this time. So Neinas went to the airport, met the two, and was immediately told by Beauchamp, "We're negotiating with NBC. We won't be involved with the CFA package."

Neinas was blindsided. "My first reaction was anger," he says. "They didn't have any difficulty interpreting my reaction."

What understandably infuriated Neinas was the duplicity of the Irish. They were strong leaders in the CFA, its moral guardians. They had all the advantages of being involved in TV talks on behalf of the CFA, while going to school for themselves. By being insiders, they knew the prices and the terms, which in turn put the Irish in the best possible negotiating position with NBC. A basic in football: any defense can play brilliantly if it knows in advance what play the offense is going to run.

Both ESPN and ABC were less than charmed by Notre Dame's going AWOL, but in a dizzying whirlwind, both networks renegotiated with the understanding that if Neinas could get the remaining sixty-three members of the CFA to sign up, the deal was still on. Neinas told the television people he could, and he did, but the ABC deal had plummeted from a value of $210 million to $175 million, and the ESPN contract was reduced from $140 million to $125 million—a total of $50 million in givebacks.

As all the smoke and harsh words subside, it is true that Notre Dame doesn't bank all of NBC's $37.5 mil. For openers, it will pay visiting teams about $18 million. But don't feel sorry for the Irish, because every time one of their road games is televised on ABC or ESPN, they, too, will be paid by the network.

But the larger point is that Notre Dame, with NBC, gets to have all six of its home games on national TV. That's thirty games, nationally, during the life of the contract. In 1992, ABC also televised Notre Dame at Northwestern, Michigan State, and the University of Southern California. ESPN showed them at Pitt. This put an estimated $2 million more into Notre Dame's checking account. The Irish will end up being on national TV at least forty-five times by the end of the 1995 season.

No other college football team will come even remotely close to that number. No wonder Dan Hampton, now a TV analyst, calls Notre Dame "the twenty-ninth pro team."

Under the CFA agreement, there would have been about 27 appearances. But some of those games would have been regional as opposed to national, which cuts down audience size.

Greed and lust can be laid unequivocally at the Irish doorstep—greed for money, lust for attention—as the motivating forces. That's because Notre Dame is an independent, so it does not have to share its TV revenues with anyone. A school in the Big Eight conference, say, that earns a number of CFA appearances—in the early nineties, that meant Oklahoma, Nebraska, and Colorado—has to share its national TV money with its conference brethren, so at best it could earn around $2.25 to $2.5 million in a year. (The entire Big Eight conference received about $9.5 million in 1992.) We hear a lot about parity in football. This is where it breaks down. Notre Dame ends up with more money than it can say grace over and the competitive advantage is incalculable. Still, it wants more.

For example, take the 1993 Cotton Bowl, Notre Dame vs. Texas A&M.

Each side received $3 million. The Irish put $3 million in their pocket and scurried back to South Bend; Texas A&M got $1,107,839 and each of the other seven Southwest Conference members split the rest.

There is no question that Notre Dame, ethically and morally, owed it to the CFA not to jump out of the Good Ship TV. Especially—especially—the Irish were absolutely out of line to pretend they were in when they were plotting to be out. Then the ultimate slap in the face to its brothers was to drop out after the CFA deal, which included them, was signed. Still, Neinas keeps a stiff upper lip. Asked if what the Irish did was detrimental to college football, he says, "No, it's still a good product. Notre Dame would have enhanced our package. But they may come back. Who knows? I feel like it hurt them more than it hurt us. Notre Dame had the moral leadership role, and they abdicated." That's not a bad summation of the last seven years at Notre Dame.

The heart of the problem is that Notre Dame is the only school in the land that could command such a network television deal. Penn State couldn't ever swing it, nor Miami nor Southern Cal nor Alabama. Only Notre Dame. And even at that, Neinas says NBC had a hard time in 1992 selling the program to advertisers. Further, if the Irish hit the skids and start playing like mere mortals—say 8-3, or, please God, no, 7-4—ratings will drop dramatically and NBC will rethink its investment. The natural question is, how many rules will Notre Dame bend—how many substandard student-athletes will they admit and how many barroom brawls will they tolerate in the future—to keep from going 8-3? These pages are strewn with comments from those willing to forgive Holtz his transgressions because of the pressure he's under. What will happen to Notre Dame's old ideals as that pressure increases?

In this brouhaha, Notre Dame came off looking very bad, not like a team player, and above all, arrogant. Even some extremely wealthy and influential alumni voiced discontent, according to Neinas. *The Chronicle of Higher Education,* in its March 7, 1990 issue, pointed out correctly that the contract seemed, unfortunately, "to endorse and strengthen the ties between big money and winning teams."

John Houck, management professor and cochairman of Notre Dame's Center for Ethics and Religious Values in Business, is worried. Quoted in the *National Catholic Register,* he said, "One of the things Notre Dame has to ask before it touches the money on the table is, 'Will intercollegiate athletics be better off?' " The school took the money, so the answer was either *yes* or *who cares.* Trying to defend the indefensible, Notre Dame's sports information director, John Heisler, asked *NCR*, "Are we obligated to sixty-three other football budgets or are we more obligated to the students at our university?"

In the comments that follow, it's hard to miss the "greed is good" undercurrent that infected the 1980s. It is hard to imagine the good fathers of Notre Dame being at all comfortable with the views expressed here.

Kurt Zackrison does at least struggle with the backstabbing, sleight-of-hand element of the TV deal. "You expect [Notre Dame] to be above and beyond," admits Zackrison. "But it happens every day in the business world. Are colleges businesses? If they weren't making money, they wouldn't be there. They couldn't afford to be there."

John Foley says, "You've got twenty-two positions, you get twenty-two first-team all-Americans and if they all play together, you've got a national-championship team. You sell tickets, you sell T-shirts, you sell hot dogs. You sell television rights for thirty-seven million dollars. Life is a business. I think the five-year plan [NBC deal] was great." Foley says he never liked the idea that the CFA controlled who was going to be on television and who wasn't—never minding, of course, that the well-based theory was to spread the exposure and the money around among all the members for the greatest good of the greatest number. "If Notre Dame is playing, how am I going to see them?" He pauses, thinks it over, then concludes, "I guess I'm being selfish."

Former player David Rosenberg is even more certain that Notre Dame did the right thing. "I thought," says Rosenberg, "it was great for them. You ask anybody in the country about Notre Dame and nobody will say, 'They're okay.' They'll say, 'I love them,' or 'I hate them.' So if you hate them, you'll want to see them lose and you'll watch them on TV. If you love them, you'll want to see them win and you'll watch them on TV."

Is it your attitude that Notre Dame football is just another big business?

"Yeah. The thing about that is, I think Tim Brown summed it up well after he won the Heisman Trophy. He said he'll never apologize for going to Notre Dame. Neither will I. It's whether you hate Notre Dame or whether you love it. That's why Notre Dame said, 'We're gonna make a lot of money,' and NBC said, 'We're gonna make a lot of money,' and they both said, 'Let's do it.' It's like, if you want to be the best, you step on a lot of little ants to become the best." Those stepped on weren't amused. *Sports Illustrated* quoted Penn State's Joe Paterno as saying, "We got to see Notre Dame go from an academic institute to a banking institute." And Georgia AD Vince Dooley groused, "I wasn't surprised by this, I was shocked."

Says Mike Crounse, "Good business decision. They're very money-oriented at Notre Dame, a lot of money. I just feel anything they do as far as money is gonna be something that's gonna get them the most. I think it was just a business decision." John Carney says that "Holtz makes you realize this is serious business. He is not coaching intramurals. He is coaching Notre Dame football and it is pretty popular around the world. If you are not taking it seriously, he makes you aware that you better be."

It hasn't been easy for some of the players to put up with the snide comments others have been making about the University of Notre Dame being located in Greed, Indiana. "A lot of other guys got on me," says Mike Golic, "when Notre Dame signed that contract, but I told them, 'What if your school was in the same position? You know damn well they would have taken the money.' The money was out there, somebody was gonna give it to you, somebody was gonna take it, and Notre Dame happened to be the team that was offered it. There's hard feelings all the time because Notre Dame won't join a conference. Why should they join a conference? There's no need to join a conference because then they've got to split the money. Why do they want to split the money? It's pure business, pure money, pure dollars."

Did you know how serious the business side of Notre Dame football was before you went there?

"Oh, yeah," says Golic. "I saw it when my brother [Bob] was there. I've seen it for ten years. The players can separate it because after a game in college, you go to party, you go hang out together, and you don't care if it's a business. You went out and had your fun on Saturday afternoon and you didn't care how much Notre Dame was making because you weren't making any [of it]. Whereas out in the business world now, you're concerned about how much owners are making because that has a direct correlation on how much you can make. It's different now, but in college I didn't care if they made one hundred million dollars, I wasn't getting any of it. I was having a ball playing on the field and hanging out with my teammates."

There is an ironic—and for loyal Golden Domers, dangerous—twist to the fallout from the television deal. The more Notre Dame defends its actions on a business basis, the less special the university and its teams appear to be. Like a pact with the devil, it is a deal that contains the seeds of its own destruction: the more Notre Dame acts like everybody else, the less reason there is to view it differently—and so the less attractive it will be to a television network. If all Notre Dame is about is dollars and wins, where will the next generation of Subway Alumni come from? Why will even a good Catholic kid want to invest his affections in a team that's no different from a dozen other football factories?

What does Notre Dame stand for? For a public institution such as Oklahoma University or Florida State University, the question would be meaningless; for a major Catholic institution, the most prominent in the nation, it is an extremely important one. In hiring Lou Holtz, Notre Dame declared that what it *won't* stand for is a losing football team. But the other end of that bargain—the reduced academic standards for athletes, the unfeeling treatment of injured players, the on-field incidents, the off-field arrests, the accelerating use of illegal drugs including steroids—makes those who love Notre Dame wonder if the football team is still a fit representative of the university, regardless of its level of excellence. How many national championships are worth the price of one's soul?

Even more than the TV contract, the athletic decision at Notre Dame that disclosed in boldest relief what a business sports—which is to say football—is at Notre Dame is the one by AD Rosenthal to eliminate intercollegiate wrestling. The wrestling program was costing pennies—somewhere, according to a Notre Dame official who knows, between $300,000 and $400,000 a year. Why was it dropped? "We weren't very successful," says the source, shrugging. In fact, the Irish finished thirty-sixth in the NCAA tournament in 1992, which is not terrible. Rather, the decision was made by Rosenthal that the sport was not cost-effective and so it's gone. So much for Heisler's question about benefits to the students.

Kurt Zackrison says he realizes that Notre Dame has its faults and he understands that football is "a business now instead of an extracurricular activity. Maybe I'm talking out of both sides of my mouth here because I am a Notre Dame man. [The TV] money's [supposed to be] going to help other teams in the school. But then I see where they cut the wrestling program, and that angers me. You can't have every team in the black. Not every team is gonna be a big revenue builder. I was angry about that. I said right there, 'That was a businessman's decision.' You don't need to cut the wrestling team. That's part of college athletics, having wrestling."

Tom McHugh says that "knowing what I know now from being at Notre Dame, I think that's really a travesty to cut the wrestling program. I was under the impression that football and a little bit of basketball basically supported our school's athletics, and since we could afford the wrestling program when we were there with the losing record, then I think they could scrounge the money together now. It's kind of like the squeaky wheel gets the oil, and the people that give the money don't really care about the wrestling program." McHugh says he doesn't understand how wrestling could be cut "with a straight face. That to me is hypocrisy."

Mike Golic sees it the same way. The decision to eliminate wrestling, he says, "really disappointed me in Notre Dame. There was no need for that. I, obviously, love wrestling. I wrestled there. I actually love the sport and I was shocked. My brother wrestled there. I didn't like the move at all. It was very bad. That was definitely a business decision and a bad business decision. You can't tell me they're losing so much money on a wrestling program that it's gonna affect the school. They had a pretty good team. They had a good coach. They were wrestling ranked teams and they could have built up and I think it was a very, very bad move. I'm very disappointed. That was definitely a banker business decision."

No question. In fact, it's significant how the role of athletic director has been diminished at Notre Dame. For years, the late Moose Krause was a strong and significant figure. He was followed by the extremely capable Gene Corrigan, now the commissioner of the Atlantic Coast Conference. To the surprise of the college football establishment, Notre Dame brought Dick Rosenthal aboard in 1987. Nobody had ever heard of him. He was a former Notre Dame basketball player who, for much of his career, had been a South Bend banker. To this day, nobody has heard much of him. He was the first appointment made by the new executive veep, Bill Beauchamp. Beauchamp even admitted publicly that Rosenthal didn't know zip about athletic administration, but "I knew he could learn easily."

Rosenthal is not a sports guy, he's a money guy. Rosenthal likes to point out that as chairman and CEO of St. Joseph Bank and Trust Co. between 1962 and 1987, assets rose from $22 million to $550 million.

Above all else, however, is the fact that the hiring of Rosenthal signaled to everyone that Holtz would be in charge. Rosenthal declined to be interviewed about his tenure as AD, but nobody who was interviewed for this book can give an example of a single instance when he has stood up to Holtz.

Former center Tom McHugh from Philadelphia sees the Corrigan-to-Rosenthal transition clearly. He talks of Corrigan's reputation and athletics administrative ability, "but that's maybe not what they wanted. They wanted somebody to come in there and run it like a business. Let's face it, it is a business." In one of his for-sale videos, Holtz points out that he thinks of himself as running a $15-to-$20-million-a-year business with two hundred employees. The whirring sound you hear is Knute Rockne spinning in his grave.

Jim Dadiotis, who transferred from Notre Dame to Colorado, admits that football at Notre Dame "wasn't fun. You weren't doing it for your community, your family, yourself. You were doing it for the alumni and for the money the school could earn." Lost in the mix is that cornerstone value of football: little boys start playing the game because they think it's fun, and the idea is for it to keep being fun as they become big boys.

Jeff Kunz says of the football experience, "It wasn't really fun. It was . . . more like a business. You're taking in millions of dollars or whatever." Nor is he thrilled with the path the Irish have put themselves on subsequently: "Money talks. They're making a lot of money. They're going to big bowls. They've got that contract with NBC. If you look at it from the money aspect, yeah, it's great. If you get back into graduating and what Notre Dame really means, I'd probably say no. It's probably been bad. That's my opinion."

Former team captain Mike Kovaleski concedes that "one thing that I've found a little fault with their program is being a little bit too business oriented, a little bit too money oriented. It's like the NBC contract. It's almost like we're being sold out to guys who give money." For example, in a cold-blooded business decision, Kovaleski says that football lettermen are no longer allowed to automatically buy two season tickets to Notre Dame football games for life. Does it make short-term sense to make those seats available instead to big financial contributors? You bet. Does it break faith with the people who've made the financial gains possible? You bet. Does it erode a player's attachment to the school in the long run? Keep watching.

CHAPTER 16

Is Holtz
Losing It?

Lou Holtz is fond of saying, "You can't win without talent, but you can sure lose with it." He's proving that.

He's also fond of saying, "You're never on easy street." He's proving that.

What's so incongruous is that it has heretofore been unthinkable to put the name Lou Holtz in the same sentence with the words *coaching failure*. His coaching ability is unchallenged and fully documented, as we have seen.

Lately, however, there have been obvious chinks in Holtz's coaching armor. The question is whether they are blips or a pattern. Examples:

—Against Stanford in 1990, the Irish lost 36–31 after leading by 24 points.

—Against Tennessee in 1991, the Irish lost 35–34 after leading by 24 points.

—Against Michigan in 1992, the Irish were tied 17–17 and Holtz opted to run out the clock instead of going for the win, then suffered a meltdown when questioned about it.

—Against Stanford again in 1992, the Irish lost 33–16 after leading 16–0, *at home.*

These tactical gliches give rise to barroom chatter that Holtz just might be losing it, that the pressures of coaching under the Golden Dome are undermining his thought processes. Even Holtz admits it. Not long ago, he was quoted in *Sports Illustrated:* "Sometimes I feel like I'm losing my mind. It's been very, very difficult here. I wish I could explain what it is like to coach at Notre Dame. It's very difficult, and once you win, it becomes really difficult."

If a poll had been taken in the late eighties to determine the best sideline coach, it's a gimme that Holtz would have won. Take the poll now and the result would not be so obvious. It's because Holtz, who has walked the coaching high wire so many times over so many years without benefit of net, seems to be losing his balance. The most popular theories among football insiders are that (a) his arrogance is leading him into making outrageous calls that have no real promise of working, but Holtz convinces himself they will because he is Lou Holtz and the opposing coach isn't; or (b) his increasingly fiery temper has headed him down too many wrong roads.

"Holtz knows how to put together a team," says John Askin, "a group of individuals who can win at any cost. You know how a general in the army does it? Those type of guys. Do the extreme. Coach Holtz would be ideal for that."

While the ability to coach—in spite of a reputation for being very poor at making halftime adjustments—has always been his strong suit, even this aspect of Holtz is now being questioned. It is the 1992 Michigan game that brought the question into sharp focus, which in turn caused people to look back at other suspect coaching performances by Holtz and to look forward with concern.

The 1992 season began with controversy, thanks to the Demetrius DuBose incident. It was alleged that DuBose, a senior captain from Seattle, was given loans and gifts by the president of the Western Washington Notre Dame Alumni Club, Grant E. Courtney—who is also a graduate of the Notre Dame Law School—and his wife, Rose. It was so blatant that Athletic Director Dick Rosenthal was forced to announce immediately that "the university has, in fact, acknowledged that a violation has occurred." It was the first time in its history that Notre Dame had faced NCAA disciplinary action.

Eventually, the NCAA decreed that DuBose, a star linebacker headed for the NFL, would have to sit out only the first two games of the '92 season. Although the NCAA should be commended for its first "investigation" of a Notre Dame athlete, this was a ridiculous example of the favoritism and leniency that the Irish get from the collegiate football governing association. Among the things DuBose had gotten from the Courtneys were assorted birthday and Christmas gifts, a $600 loan, occasional meals, money for school supplies, $300 for a spring-break trip, collect phone calls, and so on. A bank also gave DuBose a $25,000 loan, but bank officials told the NCAA that the loan approval was not based on DuBose's pro football potential, but on his potential as a Notre Dame graduate. The former would be an NCAA violation because it would give a benefit to an athlete not available to a regular student. The bank was saying it would offer the same loan to anyone about to come out of Notre Dame. The NCAA apparently decided the Courtneys were just being friendly, and that all of it had little to do with DuBose's deciding to go to Notre Dame or playing there, and that the bank loan was in no way related to DuBose's football ability—and the NCAA wonders why large segments of the sports-watching public thinks it's a joke. One Notre Dame insider laughed and said, "Can you imagine what would have happened if this had involved Oklahoma?" Sure. Everyone can. The NCAA would have ordered the campus burned to ashes, instructed the school to start over, and gotten a court injunction banning football ever again in Norman.

One of the tenets of NCAA rules is that member schools must exercise institutional control over their athletic programs, and that most definitely includes keeping boosters in line. It's difficult but it's required. That's why Notre Dame, knowing full well it had failed in its responsibilities, immediately announced that DuBose would be ineligible for the first two games of '92. It was a laughably light self-imposed penalty, but the hope was that maybe NCAA investigators could be bamboozled too. They were. Just a week before the February 1993 signing date for new recruits, the timid NCAA ordered that Notre Dame be penalized two football scholarships. This meant that instead of being allowed to give 25 scholarships to incoming players, the Irish could only give 23. To a program as deep in talent as the Irish, this meant nothing; it's the equivalent of fining Madonna $25 for jay-walking. Significantly, the NCAA did not take away income from Notre Dame by curtailing revenue from TV contracts.

When Scott Kowalkowski, a buddy of DuBose's, is asked about that situation, he says, "It's all true. I think Demetrius made a grave mistake. I thought they were gonna suspend him for the whole year." The reason Kowalkowski thought that is because that's what should have happened. That's what made sense. That's what was fair. But Kowalkowski forgot to crank two words into the equation: Notre Dame.

The Irish were already reeling from that black eye when Holtz lost his sense in the Michigan game. With 1:05 remaining against Michigan and the Irish with the ball on their own 11, Holtz called a running play, a draw to fullback Jerome Bettis. It did nothing; Holtz later alibied he wanted to use a play to look at the Wolverine defense. Then, with only thirty-five seconds left, he tried another running play; Holtz later said he wanted to look at the defense again. Inexplicably, Holtz was watching while time was burning.

For openers, he should simply have admitted he played for the tie. That's okay. It was early in the year, only the second game. Notre Dame could win the national championship with a tie to a talented and respected Michigan team, but it could not so easily win it with a loss. In the fabled Michigan State–Notre Dame game in 1966, Ara Parseghian was nineteen yards closer to pay dirt with nineteen more seconds to play, and his settling for the tie resulted in a national championship. That sort of wimpy decision is weak, but it's defensible. But when NBC's John Dockery—remember, this was on The Notre Dame Network— asked him about the play-calling and decision-making in the waning seconds, Holtz turned surly and snide. At one point, he said, "Read my lips," then followed up, "If you want to second-guess me, that's your prerogative." His tone was vicious and ugly. On the other hand, Dockery came off as a calm voice of reason and got high marks for hanging in with dignity in the face of Holtz's sarcasm.

Then Holtz tried other excuses. He said he forgot the rule change that calls for the clock to restart immediately after a penalty is assessed rather than waiting for the ball snap. Holtz doesn't forget rules. He's far too good a coach to use that crutch. Then he said he was worried about punting because his top punt snapper, Lance Johnson, had injured his hand, and his backup, Mark Zataveski, had already bounced two snaps back to the punter.

Great. Instead of telling the simple truth—that Holtz had decided he preferred a tie to trying to win and risking losing—Holtz decided to point a public finger at a second-stringer.

Later, reluctantly—and only when all other alibis had crashed and exploded—Holtz apologized. "I am going to have a difficult time facing our team," he finally confessed while taping his TV show.

Even worse, albeit less celebrated, was the loss three weeks later to Stanford. In that one, the Irish jumped on the Cardinal 16–0 in the first twenty minutes and the rout was seemingly on; Notre Dame lost to the brilliantly coached Bill Walsh–led team, 33–16—a whopping 33-point turnaround. Searching again for an alibi that might fly, Holtz blamed classroom examinations, saying, "We're a tired football team."

Former Arkansas player Micheal Forrest says, "I was sitting at home the other day watching ESPN, and for some reason they had Holtz on and he was talking about that loss to Stanford. His comment was that his open date fell wrong and he had some players hurt. If you know Holtz, you know he never, never says it's his fault."

Blue & Gold Illustrated set the record straight concerning the Stanford loss. Editor Prister, furious, started his column: "Out-played, out-hustled, out-coached." Prister's colleague, Lou Somogyi, was uncharacteristically uncharitable: "It's downright poor when you can't win a single category on your home field." After each game, Somogyi evaluates which team had the upper hand in the running game, passing game, defense, special teams, coaching, intangibles. Somogyi also pointed out that the Stanford loss marked the fourth time in two and one-half years that the Irish had lost a big lead, failing to put an opponent away.

Later on in Holtz's erratic '92 season, he went crazy because holding wasn't called against BYU. The incident occurred with four minutes to go and Notre Dame completely in control, 42–16. Holtz charged referee Thomas Thamert and put a headlock on him. In a recent speech, this one in Denver, Holtz again denied that's what he did; he said he was simply demonstrating to Thamert how a BYU player had held one of his players. Holtz claims he told Thamert, "You're gonna be shocked when you get your paycheck. It's only gonna be half what you think because you're only watching half the players."

Put simply, Holtz went nuts. He should have been ejected, should have been fined, should have been suspended, should have been made to make nice, and should have been put on probation. Instead, he still denies doing what everybody saw him doing. He was penalized nothing for strangling the official—which may give us an idea of the worth of an official's neck—and only fifteen yards for coming onto the field. But the NCAA did nothing, proving that not only is the Notre Dame administration afraid of Holtz, so, too, is the NCAA. The result is that justice wasn't served.

Even Tim Prister wrote that the action was "not what most would call normal coaching behavior." Holtz again tried to finesse his way out of it. First, he claimed that "I really did not know I was out on the field." In fact, he was some ten yards onto the playing surface. Then he said that he didn't even touch the official and that he had sort of "looped" his arm around his neck without touching him. Later, reluctantly, Holtz apologized, "It was my fault and it was completely out of line with what I normally do." It was his fault; it was not out of line with what he normally does—as any player who's practiced under him could attest.

As if the 1992 season wasn't eventful enough, Holtz added a new chapter to the annals of bad sportsmanship when, with the Irish ahead of Boston College by 37 points in the third quarter, Holtz called a fake punt. Play-by-play announcer Tom Hammond was stunned: "Is that rubbing it in? I don't understand that." Analyst Cris Collinsworth promptly agreed, "I don't think you can call it a mercy fake. That, oh, boy, I tell you, that's like stealing a base in the bottom of the ninth inning when you're leading fifteen to nothing [sic]. Boy, I tell you, that's adding insult to injury."

Later, Hammond went on to observe, "You thought, cruising thirty-seven to nothing, with an absolutely brilliant, brilliant game plan on both sides of the football, that this would be a game where Holtz would not be the focus, and suddenly, the fake punt, and you have to wonder again." Said Collinsworth, "Don't think that [BC coach] Tom Coughlin won't remember what happened." Then Holtz proceeded to rub it in one more time afterward: "We're allowed to run it. There wasn't anything illegal about it." Later he moped, "Anytime I turn around, I'm answering a negative."

Even those closest to the school are dismayed over some of the screwy turns the football program is taking. A story in *Blue & Gold Illustrated* on November 30, 1992, by editor Prister—a 1982 English grad of Notre Dame—starts, "Tunnel fights. Accusations of improprieties at Minnesota and rampant steroid use at Notre Dame. Illegal loans to players. Playing for a tie against Michigan. Referee headlocks . . . Lou Holtz has a brimming crisis as part of his weekly game plan." Whatever all this adds up to, it decidedly is not the sum of what Notre Dame has been. It is, however, what the Irish have become.

In a recent speech, Holtz admitted that he "sometimes embarrasses" Notre Dame.

But Holtz is at the point where sorry isn't good enough. During the '92 season, he seemed on the brink of destruction after his own poor performance took the Irish out of the national championship picture —the Irish started off 3-1-1—even before the leaves had fallen and substantially before any frost was on the pumpkins.

Holtz knows his temper is foul and he admits he identifies, he says, with the vulture sitting on a tree limb who is saying, "Patience my ass, I'm gonna kill something."

Says Linc Coleman, "I've never been around a coach with his type of temper. I mean, for a guy that small to come and really grab you and try to jerk you around, he's got a temper."

Joe Allen says the time he saw Holtz go perfectly bonkers was after the 1991 Orange Bowl loss, 10–9, to Colorado. It looked as if the Irish had won the game when Rocket Ismail received a Colorado punt on his own 9 with just forty-three seconds left in the game and returned it for a TD. But Irish strong safety Greg Davis from Hollywood, Florida, was called for clipping. Says Allen, "Greg's just a great guy, really quiet and always busted his ass, and after the game Holtz just was tearing his ass, asking, 'What the hell were you doing? What were you thinking? Rocket would have beat that guy.' I mean, I felt for the guy. It was the last play of the game and you don't know what's going to happen. So he was just trying to make a play, and Holtz tore him a new asshole." The only one who hated the clip more than Holtz was Davis. What Greg Davis was guilty of was going all out to do the right thing, which turned out to be exactly the wrong thing. Greg Davis will be remembered forevermore for this error. Especially in the omega of Davis's life, a smile and a pat on the back from Holtz would have gone a long way. But compassion is not Holtz's way, not when there's blame to be assigned.

Holtz does routinely admit that his temper leads him to, "Ready, aim, fire," often going after a mouse with an elephant gun. Conversely, he says that wife Beth's philosophy is, "Ready, aim, aim, aim, aim, aim . . ." He knows he should learn from her restraint, but he doesn't.

Says Dan Devine of Holtz's temper, "He has one, that's for sure. I guess the concern would be that as the years go by, a Woody Hayes situation would erupt." Hayes ended his storied career at Ohio State in disgrace, losing all control, hitting a Clemson player with his fist during a game. Hayes was summarily fired.

This doesn't matter to Holtz, who says, "I loved Woody Hayes. I don't think you can possibly be around Woody Hayes without having an awful lot of him in you." Holtz, who served as an assistant coach in 1968 under Hayes, says the boss once grabbed him by the throat to "make sure he had my full attention." That, says Holtz, was when Hayes had warned Holtz that USC's O. J. Simpson had better not score a touchdown against the Buckeyes. Unfortunately, Simpson ran eighty yards in the first half for a touchdown. At halftime, Hayes seized Holtz and asked him, "How come O. J. ran eighty yards?" Responded Holtz, "Because that's all the farther he had to go."

If we are all products of our environment, the adoration of such a violent coach may speak volumes concerning Holtz's willingness to let his temper flare at his players and others. It may also provide a crystal-ball look at Holtz's future.

At each coaching stop, there seems to be a watershed event involving Holtz's temper. Once, in a blind fury, he told his William and Mary players that he would probably move on to a school where the players would have "more to give." At North Carolina State, he accused one of the school's professors, Robert T. Ramsay, who was jogging around the football practice field, of being a spy for an opponent. It was a laughable accusation and Ramsay analyzed the situation: "Holtz takes himself much too seriously." Then Faculty Senate chairman Samuel Love said, "Holtz made a fool of himself."

During a turbulent time in 1990, the *Denver Post* quoted Holtz as saying, "I can't say what the future holds for me. I really can't. I don't want to mislead anybody."

Holtz denies any interest in leaving Notre Dame, but incredibly, late in 1992, a few people at Arkansas—probably very few, but still— wondered if Holtz might be interested in returning to Fayetteville for a reprise after Frank Broyles had fired Jack Crowe. That's pretty funny: leave the premier coaching job in America to return to a second-tier job at best, where people were sick of you and you had already been fired, and where you have no real chance of ever winning big?

Lou Holtz was very much interested.

"I'll tell you the whole story," Arkansas booster Pat Wilson said when asked about the rumor. "The assistant athletic director, Terry Don Phillips, called me one night and said, 'Frank asked me to call you and see if Lou would be interested in coming back to Arkansas.' I said, 'Terry, let's not pull my string. Are you serious about this?' He said, 'I'm serious and Frank is serious.'

"I said, 'You think about it a little bit and you call me back. I want to be damn sure that you are serious before I mention anything to Lou Holtz.' After about a half hour he called me back and said he'd had a meeting with Frank and they were serious about Lou coming back. So I thought it in my best interest to call Lou and explain to him exactly what had happened, which I did.

"I called him and said that Terry Don Phillips had called me and wanted me to call you to see if you had any interest in coming back to

Arkansas. I said the first thing I asked them was were they serious. They told me they were. Lou said, 'I'd be willing to talk to anybody about a job. I'll think about it and I'll call you back in a couple of days.' I said that's fine, so I hadn't much more than hung up from Lou than Frank Broyles called and he said, 'Pat, do you think that I could talk to Lou?' I said, 'Frank, that's not my judgment. That's your judgment.' He said, 'I'd like to talk to him. Have you got his home phone?' I said, 'Yeah, and I got his office number, too.' I gave both of them to Broyles and he said, 'I'm gonna call him.' So he called him and had from what I'm told was a fairly decent conversation.

"The bottom line was that Lou told him he was trying to get ready for the Southern Cal game and he'd have to talk to his family to see if there was any interest in it and he would call him back. I guess time was a big factor for Frank at this point. A lot of people were pushing him to act, Orville Henry being one of them.

"But anyhow, Lou told me in sort of a backhanded way that Frank offered him the job and Frank told me that he offered it. But Lou wanted to find out who his bosses were going to be and what the setup was going to be, and they weren't prepared to give him that information in a form that Lou thought would enable him to make an intelligent judgment about it. I think they ended the conversation with Lou saying, 'If you want to discuss this further, we'll have to do it after the Southern Cal game. I'm leaving in the morning for that, and I've got to have my focus on that game.' In the meantime, [Arkansas] hired Danny Ford."

No question, Irish alums care and create pressure. Still, Holtz told *Blue & Gold Illustrated* one time, "I'm not going to let the job devour me." That may be the last and most crucial area of failure for Holtz. His erratic behavior is certainly evidence that the job is getting the upper hand over the man. In turn, Holtz acts increasingly sour, which prompted Lou Somogyi—remember, Somogyi is a big Holtz supporter —to write in *Blue & Gold* on November 2, 1992, "I believe Holtz is currently at his lowest point of popularity among many Irish fans."

CHAPTER 17

Can the Echoes Be Awakened?

Notre Dame's problem, in a perverse way, is that Knute Rockne was ever the coach in the first place.

He was so excellent—he lost just twelve games in thirteen seasons from 1918 to 1930 en route to his record of 105-12-5—that he became too legendary. In Rock's thirteen years, the Irish won six national championships. Ever since, Notre Dame has been waiting for the next Rockne, who was neither Irish nor Catholic, to show up. Notre Dame can't help wishing. There's nothing wrong with that. We've all wished for impossible dreams.

But since Notre Dame can't seem to wish Rockne back to South Bend, then it wishes for the return of Frank Leahy. Leahy coached from 1941 to 1943, was away for two seasons during World War II—a respite Lou Holtz says must have been a relief—and returned 1946–53. In his eleven seasons, he was 87-11-9, had six undefeated seasons, five national championship teams, and put together an unbeaten streak of thirty-nine in the late forties. He was only the second-best coach in the history of college football. At age forty-seven, Leahy resigned because, as the late Moose Krause once said, "He was cracking up."

That same pressure may be getting to Holtz.

If the position of the moon in the sky is favorable, Holtz will say of his critics, "I still have my detractors, but I really don't care, just as long as my wife isn't one of them." *The Chicago Tribune* once observed,

"His critics have cracked that if he wasn't a football coach, he'd probably be working in a carnival."

But while comments such as these are more banter than substance, there is no question that the criticism gets to Holtz. His overriding problem is that the criticism doesn't just appear for no reason like summer clouds. Holtz does something and then people make their judgments on it. Sometimes the judgments are critical. In November 1992, *USA Today* carried a story quoting former pro player and TV commentator Cris Collinsworth: "They don't want to be criticized at Notre Dame. It's Camelot. When we talk about Notre Dame sitting on the ball, running up the score, or Lou choking that [referee], they view us as the outside evil empire."

But Holtz can be deceptive in trying to handle his critics. In a *Blue & Gold Illustrated* story, Holtz says, "There have been some articles written about me that were so negative, yet nobody bothered to talk to me or check out the authenticity." Truth may again help us here. First, like all high-flying celebrities, Holtz can be absolutely inaccessible when he wants to be. He can not return phone calls with the best of them. Second, this book is the perfect example: Holtz refused to be interviewed for it. We tried. Remember that when he makes a statement like the one above about this book's contents. Notre Dame has recently hired a public relations firm to help him cope with "a wide variety of topics," including, some say, this book.

In another interview with *Blue & Gold,* Holtz said, "I just believe that nobody can do as good a job at Notre Dame as I do." The time may be at hand when that theory will have to be tested.

Could Pat Wilson down in Arkansas, one of Holtz's best friends and confidants, ever really see Lou Holtz leaving Notre Dame?

"Yeah, I think he'll leave."

Why?

"Well, there are a lot of reasons. The hierarchy at Notre Dame is damn near dictatorship."

Might Ohio State be in his future? It might. He has talked for years about the school, once telling a *Sports Illustrated* writer, "I've always wanted to coach at Ohio State. I think Ohio State's a great job, a great school, a great state. I went to school there, grew up there, I'm from Ohio. My wife's from Ohio. . . . I think you can't possibly have the background I have without having strong feelings for Ohio State. It's the first score I look for in the newspapers." If Holtz ever starts talking about his grandfather who listened to Buckeyes games in the thirties and forties, watch out.

Gene Corrigan also thinks Holtz might leave, but he blames pressure, not dictatorship. "The job," says Corrigan, "has taken its toll on Lou. I saw him not long ago, and he looked like he was twenty years older that when he got there."

When Notre Dame took on Lou Holtz, it got wins, but at what price? Did the Irish get a great coach and a lousy human being? Is Notre Dame proud of what it has become under Holtz? Will Notre Dame do something about it? Can it? The Irish must win football games, and so if they dump Holtz, might the result be losing games?

Our best guess: Either Holtz will have one more fully inappropriate act on the football field in front of a national audience—such as punching an opposing player—and he will finally be executed by the Notre Dame hierarchy, which will at last get over its fear of him; or Holtz, in a fit of pique, will walk the plank on his own, without benefit of blindfold.

Even *Blue & Gold* published an article in 1992 headlined, "When the Time Comes, Who Will (Can) Replace Lou Holtz?" The fantasy is, and has been for some time, former 49er and now Stanford coach Bill Walsh. That's a good idea, but Walsh's time has passed. He'll coach the Cardinal for a few years, then retire.

Oblivious to all, AD Dick Rosenthal wrote in a forward to Lou Holtz's book: "He [Holtz] is a man of principle and has lived his life in complete harmony with his values. Never have a person's ideals meshed so completely with an institution's philosophy than have Holtz's and Notre Dame's. He is the consummate Notre Dame man." Rosenthal also writes, "Lou is a very humble man."

Holtz loves to remind people that "losing tells you something, mostly that you are not good enough." Notre Dame simply will not stand for such a reminder. It will not because it cannot. Notre Dame is football. Without it, Notre Dame is simply a small Catholic institution with a great chemistry department in a small northern Indiana town with lousy weather.

Tom Riley says he's not surprised Notre Dame puts up with Holtz and his various and varied shortcomings "because he's winning. You have no idea how much that means at Notre Dame. I remember students who were making calls on capital campaigns telling stories around the dorms of alums who said, 'I'll send money when you start winning football games.' For this particular coach, the administration has turned away and let him run wild."

Back in some of Notre Dame's dog days, the much-beleaguered Joe Kuharich—the worst coach in Notre Dame's history—grumped, "This insatiable appetite to win has become so strong it is ludicrous."

Still, Holtz wrote in his own book, "A loss is absolutely disastrous. You cannot give me one reason in the world why we should ever lose a game at Notre Dame—not a one. There is no reason. . . . Less than perfection is a personal embarrassment to me. . . . For us to ever represent the University of Notre Dame with less than perfection is totally inconsistent with our goals, our objectives, and our beliefs."

Holtz always gets wound up telling one story that illustrates—in an apocryphal way but with an underpinning of truth—Notre Dame's thinking on football. Many times, including at an Orange Bowl luncheon in 1990 before a game with Colorado, Holtz has related how he was told before arriving in South Bend that he should have a competitive team. He said he felt he had met that requirement when five of his six losses that first year were by a total of fourteen points. He continued, "They said, 'You don't understand. What we meant by competitive is win.'" Then Holtz went on to say that when he went to the Cotton Bowl the next year and ended up 8-3, he was told, "You still don't understand. When we said win, we meant win 'em all." Then the third year, Holtz recounted, the Irish did win them all, but he was told, "You don't understand. We meant win 'em all by a big score."

Give Holtz his due, though. He has proved his ability to overcome adversity. This book will fall into that category for him. First Holtz will deny all the critical parts of this book (he will not, however, deny any of the complimentary aspects), he will say it's all lies, he will make up reasons why the authors and their many sources might have done such a dastardly thing to him, he will talk about how disruptive it is to the team, then he will send the Irish onto the field. Along the way, he will point out that he hasn't read the book but he has heard about it. If they win, Holtz will take credit for having banded the Irish together and made them achieve against all odds; if they lose, Holtz will point to the impossibility of overcoming a book such as this.

So concerned has Holtz been over this book that he had defensive coordinator Rick Minter send out a questionnaire to a number of

Holtz's former assistants. Basically, says one coach who got the questionnaire, it "amounted to a character reference. It asked if we knew of any cheating he had done that the NCAA might investigate, if he had done anything wrong recruiting, if he was a racist, how his ethics are, things like that." Holtz wants to have these documents in hand so he can make an effort to counter this book.

This particular coach who received the questionnaire says that "for my self-protection, you better not use my name."

Former player Jim Baugus knows that much of what has become Notre Dame football is nonsense. "I think," says Baugus, "that a lot of Notre Dame's alums are hypocrites. They think you've gotta be the best and you can never lose a game. But then they say you've gotta make sure you're squeaky-clean getting there. It's a great goal, but it doesn't happen. The whole thing is, there's gonna be some push and give somewhere and you're not gonna be the best every year. I would love it if from August to December, alums weren't allowed on campus or to call or anything." Baugus says what he has in mind is absolutely no contact for alums with anything having to do with the school during football season. That's an idea that may be slightly ahead of its time.

Mike Golic is one of many who frets about some of the forks in the road that Notre Dame is choosing. Says Golic, "It seems like the alumni feel like, 'It's not exactly the way we want it, but we're winning again so we're gonna kind of let it slide.'"

How long do you think they'll let it slide?

"Notre Dame is back in the title chase every year, and I think that's what's keeping the alumni happy. But if they keep seeing these things pop up, the Prop 48s, redshirting, the steroids, and the Demetrius DuBose thing . . . I think they still want Notre Dame to be the pure thing, and eventually I think people are gonna start voicing that. I think it's still in a transition period where, 'Hey, we're winning, so maybe we'll look the other way for a little bit.' After all, it went from such a bottom during my years at Notre Dame—my years under Coach Faust have been blocked out—back to prominence. It may take a little while for people to say, 'We shouldn't be getting into trouble like this for the expense of a good team. We have standards that we want to keep.'

"I don't know what that time frame is, but hopefully it will come."